THE CRETAN GLANCE

THE WORLD AND ART
OF NIKOS KAZANTZAKIS

THE

CRETAN

GLANCE

Morton P. Levitt

OHIO STATE UNIVERSITY PRESS: COLUMBUS

Grateful acknowledgment is made to Simon & Schuster, Inc., New York, N.Y., for permission to reprint excerpts from the following works by Nikos Kazantzakis and copyright © by Simon & Schuster, Inc.: *The Fratricides*, trans. Amy Mims, 1964; *Freedom or Death*, trans. Jonathan Griffin, 1955; *The Greek Passion*, trans. Jonathan Griffin, 1953; *The Last Temptation of Christ*, trans. Peter A. Bien, 1960; *The Odyssey: A Modern Sequel*, trans. Kimon Friar, 1958; *Report to Greco*, trans. Peter A. Bien, 1965; *Saint Francis*, trans. Peter A. Bien, 1962; *Spain*, trans. Amy Mims, 1963; *Zorba the Greek*, trans. Carl Wildman, 1952; and from Helen Kazantzakis, *Nikos Kazantzakis: A Biography Based on His Letters*, trans. Amy Mims, 1968.

Excerpt from Dante's *The Inferno*, trans. John Ciardi, copyright © 1954 by John Ciardi, is reprinted by arrangement with The New American Library, Inc., New York, N.Y.

Excerpts from Dante's *Paradiso*, trans. Dorothy L. Sayers and Barbara Reynolds, published by Penguin Books Ltd, are reprinted by permission of David Higham Associates Ltd, London, England.

Excerpts from Kimon Friar, trans. and ed., *Modern Greek Poetry* (Simon & Schuster 1973), copyright © 1973 by Kimon Friar, are reprinted by permission of the author.

Excerpt from Michael Llewellyn Smith, *The Great Island* (Longman 1965, Allen Lane 1973), copyright © 1961, 1965 by Michael Llewellyn Smith, is reprinted by permission of Penguin Books Ltd.

Chapter 4 originally appeared in somewhat different form as "The Modernist Kazantzakis and *The Last Temptation of Christ*" in *MOSAIC: A Journal for the Comparative Study of Literature and Ideas*, Vol. 6, No. 2 (Winter 1973), 103–24, published by the University of Manitoba Press, to whom acknowledgment is herewith made.

Other chapters that originally appeared in different form and are copyright by the Ohio State University Press are: chapter 1, under the title "The Cretan Glance: The World and Art of Nikos Kazantzanis," in the *Journal of Modern Literature*, Vol. 2, No. 2 (1971–72), 163–88; chapter 3, "A Modern Byzantine Mosaic: *The Greek Passion* of Nikos Kazantzakis," in *Neo-Hellenika*, Vol. 3 (1978), 7–36; chapter 5, under its present title, in *Comparative Literature Studies*, Vol. 14, No. 4 (December 1977), 360–80; chapter 6, under its present title, in the *Journal of the Hellenic Diaspora*, Vol. 5, No. 2 (Summer 1978), 19–45.

Library of Congress Cataloging in Publication Data
Levitt, Morton P.
The Cretan glance
Includes index
1. Kazantzakis, Nikos, 1883–1957—Criticism and
interpretation. I. Title
PA5610.K39Z777   889'.3'32   79-23990
ISBN 0-8142-0304-3

For Gussie, in loving memory
of what she was
For Polly and Ioulios, who represent in life
what is best in these fictions
And for Annette

CONTENTS

FOREWORD ix

PREFACE xiii

CHAPTER ONE 3
The Cretan Glance: Local History
Become Metaphor for Man

CHAPTER TWO 20
Freedom or Death and Rebellion on Crete

CHAPTER THREE 34
The Greek Passion: Persecution and
Politics in Asia Minor

CHAPTER FOUR 60
The Last Temptation of Christ: A Modernist
Myth in the Holy Land

CHAPTER FIVE 88
The Companions of Kazantzakis:
Nietzsche, Bergson, and Zorba the Greek

CHAPTER SIX 110
Kazantzakis' *Odyssey:* A Modern Rival to Homer

CHAPTER SEVEN 143
Saint Francis, or Asceticism

CHAPTER EIGHT   160

The Fratricides: Symbol, Act, and Civil War in Greece

CHAPTER NINE   176

Kazantzakis and the Modernist View of
Literature and Life

INDEX   185

FOREWORD

On reading Professor Levitt's book as he sent it to me, chapter by chapter to Greece, I was, of course, deeply gratified to see that his interpretation was, on the whole, consistent with what I consider to be Kazantzakis' own views as I had discussed them with him when we were collaborating on his works. I do not mean to say that I approve of what Professor Levitt has written solely because it agrees with my own point of view, but it is important for me to believe that he does correctly delineate and expound the basic principles of Kazantzakis' thought and art. I am also in agreement with the relative evaluation he gives to the works. There are always areas where a reader or a critic may interpret Kazantzakis in many different ways, and in these areas I find that Professor Levitt is not only creative, plausible, and valid but that he also brings new insights to perplexing problems and extends the range of possibility and intention. In my opinion, Professor Levitt is sound and correct in his basic assumptions, interpretations, and conclusions, and brings creative refreshment to areas where a true critic may extend the range of an author's work into social, religious, and perhaps philosophical implications.

In *The Saviors of God: Spiritual Exercises*, Kazantzakis has set down, once and for all, the basic principles of his vision of life; it is the key to all his work, and Professor Levitt was wise to appraise this and use it as a touchstone for further exegesis. Since *The Odyssey: A Modern Sequel* is the chief embodiment of *Saviors* (specifically condensed in Books XIV and XVI of that epic), it was perceptive of Professor Levitt to include *The Odyssey* in a study of the novels, for although it is written in metrical form, it has, like Homer's two epics, attributes of plot, characterization, structure, motivation, and psychological, political, and ideological contents which are all attributes of the novel.

Indeed, this epic is as much a "novel" as Joyce's *Ulysses* and *Finnegans Wake* are "epics," and among Professor Levitt's most penetrating expositions is the comparison he makes between these two great writers.

Professor Levitt has given further coherence to his interpretations by utilizing the Cretan Glance with which Kazantzakis viewed all endeavor, using it as metaphor for man and history in the stream of the modernist movement in fiction. He has wisely penetrated beyond the superficial resemblance of Kazantzakis' works to the nineteenth century novel to find the existentialist agony that places Kazantzakis side by side with such figures as Camus, and which makes him a true representative of our modern and transitional era. The Cretan Glance confronts the annihilating abyss into which life terminates, not only with the terror and hopelessness of the modern man, but also with courage and affirmative ecstasy. The Glance is neither Greek nor European, but specifically Cretan, and Professor Levitt is right in emphasizing throughout Kazantzakis' deep Cretan roots. Kazantzakis would happily have embraced such an emphasis. This is not the only valid approach to his works, but it is a sound and penetrating one, and has given Professor Levitt a point of reference from which to expand his interpretation into many areas.

Some modern Greek scholars may question the validity of a work written by an author who does not himself know Greek well enough to make extensive use of sources in the original, but many superb studies of foreign authors have been written by American critics who have dealt with an author's work in translation only by concentrating not on linguistic problems but on structure, motivation, characterization, vision, motifs, and other elements which are not distorted by translation. Besides—and this is of utmost importance—Kazantzakis, like Goethe (and unlike Shakespeare), was a man cut in a monolithic mold, a man of one all-impelling vision which he has, fortunately, delineated for us in his *The Saviors of God*. Because all his works, as he himself has insisted, are only various aspects of one unique though complex vision, a knowing reading of his works in translation is now sufficient for a scholar such as Professor Levitt, who has himself a penetrating glance. Again, fortunately, all the major works of Kazantzakis (with the exception of his play *Buddha*) are already available in English in the novel, travel, epic, philosophy, and drama. Further research into Greek texts would simply have made available to Professor Levitt more material to support his main thesis and his insights. There is always a small group in Greece, of course, and a small coterie of modern Greek scholars, who would resent work by an "outsider," but the majority of Greeks and scholars would wel-

xi

come, I believe, the freshness of vision and the originality of approach which one can bring to foreign works exactly because he is not native to the field.

I should like to stress that Professor Levitt has had the advantage of talking and corresponding with Mrs. Helen Kazantzakis, who has also supported him in his interpretation. It remains for me to say that Professor Levitt writes with grace and clarity, that he has organized his material well, and that there is as yet no other book to rival it in its field, neither in Greek, in English, or in any other language, so far as I am aware. I know of many doctorate and masters theses being written every year on various aspects of Kazantzakis' thought—primarily on his philosophical attitudes—but no other person has written any sustained study of the novels, by which Kazantzakis is best known in almost forty languages. By considering *The Odyssey: A Modern Sequel* and *The Saviors of God* also in his study, and by making extensive use of Kazantzakis' last book, his spiritual "fictive" autobiography, *Report to Greco*, Professor Levitt has dealt not only with the fictional material per se but also with the other three great books in the Kazantzakian corpus. The serious reader will find in this book an excellent analysis of the novels and an insightful exposition of Kazantzakis' basic vision of life.

KIMON FRIAR
Athens, Greece

This study began in the summer of 1966 with a journey to Crete, that fabled island. It was impossible at that time to do much serious research on Crete: scholarly facilities were not readily available for the study of literature, and I, quite frankly, did not always know at that time what resources I sought. But I was able to test out, initially at least, the hypothesis that had brought me there in the first place. It seemed to me then—it seems to me even more certain today, more than a dozen years and many resources afterwards—that it is his Cretan background which distinguishes Kazantzakis, his life and his art, from his Modernist contemporaries in the West. Only this heritage, I believed, could account for the distinctions in subject matter, in tone, in their conceptions of man's role in a changing universe, between Kazantzakis and such a writer as D. H. Lawrence, whom he otherwise so closely resembles. This discovery in 1966 promised a potentially exciting approach into his fiction: developed successfully, it could help make accessible to readers beyond Greece the one Modernist master who had yet to acquire critical repute worthy of his accomplishment. (Perhaps also it would help to reintroduce Kazantzakis to those Greek readers who had been distracted away from his work by the extraliterary controversies that seemed always to surround him.) It appears to me today, however, to offer in addition a unique perspective on Modernism itself, a new means of assessing the central literary phenomenon of this century. For it seems to me increasingly clear that Kazantzakis and Crete, in certain ways on the periphery of the literary history of our time, provide an insight central to that history—a bright, focusing lens that helps to illuminate not just our literature but our age as well. The book thus begins as Kazantzakis does, with the metaphor of Crete—he himself called it the Cretan Glance—and it ends with an investigation of his status as Modernist artist, as the one major writer of his time who continued to believe that the old values of humanism, and the old forms as well, remained relevant in an inhumane age.

The structure of the book is quite simple, if not entirely straightforward: its development is not chronological but metaphoric, and it deals primarily with the works of the last two phases of the author's long and varied career—with his great epic poem, *The Odyssey: A Modern Sequel*, over which he labored for thirteen years, and with the novels to which he turned with renewed vigor and force during the final two decades of his life. Much of Kazantzakis' huge canon has not yet been translated, but it is already clear that it is on these works of fiction, in both verse and prose, that his reputation must finally rest. The book thus follows the metaphor of Crete as it develops and expands through Kazantzakis' fictional canon. It begins with *Freedom or Death*, the most explicitly Cretan of his novels—one of his few works set entirely on Crete, it derives from a famous event of local history, the unsuccessful revolution of 1886 against Turkish rule, and serves to demonstrate the historical and mythic forces that make up the metaphor. Thereafter, in successive chapters, it emphasizes the various aspects of the complex metaphor: from the political claims of *The Greek Passion*, which transfers the action to Asia Minor, where the ancient communities of Greeks are being persecuted anew—as if they were Cretans—both by their Turkish masters and by the established forces among their compatriots; to the development of religion and myth in *The Last Temptation of Christ*, which finds in the lifetime of Jesus of Galilee an experience analogous to that of Crete and which offers in its turn one more way of transcending such an experience; to the philosophical base of *Zorba the Greek*, at once the most popular of the novels and the most metaphysical, again set on Crete but informed by the thought of the Westerners Nietzsche and Bergson.

The sixth chapter returns to the *Odyssey*, the most monumental of modern epics and the synthesis of Kazantzakis' thought, the text which he considered his *Obra*. It includes in its reach all the world known to the ancient Hellenes—including Minoan Crete—and descends as well through a spiritual realm into the Southern Hemisphere. It is the most compelling and knowing of all the Modernist endeavors to recreate myth in our time.

The following two chapters to a degree are anticlimactic; their concern is with the minor novels, and their claims are more indirect. *Saint Francis*, for example, is the one work by Kazantzakis that can be called a failure: its value is as negative example. For it is the voice of the ascetic that speaks in this narrative. Implicit throughout the canon, here it dominates, overwhelming the vital, humanistic impulses of the other novels, ignoring the metaphor of Crete. Its lesson is that the author dare not stray so far from his native sources, that his creativity and strength are dependent on the imaginative use that he has made of his ancestral inheritance. *The Fratricides*, finally, is the most contemporary of Kazantzakis' works, a conscious effort to return to those sources: its setting is the Greek Civil War of 1946–49. Because it was left unfinished on the death of the author, however, it is impossible to judge this book definitively, but it does demonstrate clearly the consistency of his entire career: the strengths and weaknesses of his narrative technique, the autobiographical impulse present in all of his work, the vigor and force of the Cretan Glance even beyond the boundaries of Crete—its universal potential as metaphor. *The Fratricides* serves also, in the end, to relate Kazantzakis to the other Modernists, not only to those, like D. H. Lawrence, who seem so close to him on the surface, but even to Joyce, who at first seems so different. It is the comparison of their odysseys that demonstrates finally the worth of Kazantzakis.

A note on spelling and pronunciation and on terminology. On the advice of Kimon Friar and following in part the system advocated by Kazantzakis, I have attempted to resolve some of the difficulties that Americans have in pronouncing Greek terms by adding acute accent marks to them to indicate emphasis and by spelling them phonetically. Thus, Michales and Mavrudes in Jonathan Griffin's translation of *Freedom or Death* here become Mihális and Mavroudhís (the "dh" representing a vocalized "th" sound). Father Ladas, Priest Grigoris, and Archon Patrearcheas, in Griffin's translation of *The Greek Passion*, are similarly turned into Ladhás, Grighóris, and Patriarhéas. For the sake of consistency, I have also altered certain spellings over which translators have differed, e.g., I have chosen Carl Wildman's phonetic Sifakas, in *Zorba the Greek,* over Griffin's alphabetic Sefakas, but I have preferred the latter's Nikoliós (in the nominative case) to Wildman's Nikolio (in the vocative). However, I have left untouched such Italianate names as Vincenzo Cornaro and such familiar ones as Eleuthérios Venizélos and Domenicos Theotocopulos. As for terminology, there are certain repeated images, within the context of the Cretan metaphor, that possess for Kazantzakis connotations far more intense than their literal meanings would appear to justify. Thus, a "colossus" is likely to have Nietzschean significance beyond mere physical size and a *pallikár* to be more noble than the definition "warrior" can suggest. The antithesis of the terms "Western" and "Cretan" derives similarly from local usage. Minoan Crete may have been the first great Western civilization, but centuries of isolation—

especially under Turkish rule—led the Cretans to see themselves as aliens to both East and West, hostile to the former and cut off from the latter.

My obligations are obviously many. This is almost inevitable in a study that has covered so many years, but it is perhaps even more so where the author began with only a hypothesis and with no direct knowledge at all of the culture about which he would write. For my introduction into the literature and culture of Greece, I am indebted to many people, some of them dear friends, all of them uniquely valuable sources: Eleanora Marovitz, Kostas Myrsiades, Ioulios Iossifides, and Polly Iossifides. None of them, of course, is in any way responsible for the barbarisms that I may have committed. I must also thank some of my colleagues at Temple University who at various points in this study aided me with their encouragement and expertise; most notable among them are J. Mitchell Morse, Maurice Beebe, Maxwell Luria, Charles Dyke, and, above all, Annette Shandler Levitt, who remains my best and most patient critic. I am indebted also to Dean George W. Johnson, formerly of Temple University, who helped to support both the initial research and the completion of this long project.

My greatest obligations, however, are to two people whose qualifications are unique: to Helen Kazantzakis, who spoke patiently and lovingly with me about her late husband, and whose own sense of life is a clear reflection of his; and to Kimon Friar, who from the first encouraged me to undertake this work, who has carefully read each of its chapters over the past several years, and whose criticism has been invaluable. English and American readers are in his debt for making modern Greek poetry available to us; my particular debt is greater still—without him this would have been a much lesser work.

THE CRETAN GLANCE

There is a kind of flame in Crete—let us call it "soul"—
something more powerful than either life or death.
There is pride, obstinacy, valor, and together with these
something else inexpressible and imponderable,
something which makes you rejoice that you are a human being,
and at the same time tremble.

Nikos Kazantzakis, *Report to Greco*

CHAPTER ONE

The Cretan Glance:
Local History Become Metaphor for Man

It is impossible to think of Nikos Kazantzakis without thinking also of Crete. The most important Greek writer of modern times and one of the major figures in what is perhaps the outstanding literary generation of all times, Kazantzakis can be approached either as part of the Greek cultural renaissance of the twentieth century (and thus discussed alongside Caváfis, Seféris, Sikelianós, Rítsos, Elýtis, and others) or as a representative Modernist figure (along with Joyce, Mann, Kafka, and Proust, among others). But inevitably we return to his Cretan heritage: it must be both starting point and end of any study of his fiction, the metaphor around which all of his art and his life developed.

Home of the first great civilization of the West, possessor of a proud and magnificent tradition, Crete in Kazantzakis' time was a cultural backwater, the most insular of islands; those Cretans who for five centuries after the fall of Constantinople played so vital a role in Mediterranean history first had to leave their homeland. Kazantzakis, for one, lived nearly all his adult life in the West. Yet he returns incessantly to Crete in his art: it provides subject matter for much of his fiction and serves as metaphor for his view of man. In leaving his homeland in his youth and returning to it only in his fiction and verse, in fusing its culture with the broader European civilization and thus creating a new and strange and sometimes terrifyingly beautiful hybrid, Kazantzakis was playing out what had become the traditional role of the Cretan artist. Like the great Renaissance painters from the island who spread their own version of Byzantine art to the Continent after the fall of Constantinople—the name adopted by one of them, El Greco, suggests the continuing strength of the native influence—Kazantzakis, the self-exile, never denied the force of his heritage but endeavored always to transcend it. "Crete for me," he once wrote, "is the synthesis which I always pursue, the synthesis of Greece and the Orient. I neither feel Europe in me nor a clear and distilled classical Greece; nor do I at all feel the anarchic chaos and the will-less perseverance of the Orient. I feel something else, a synthesis, a being that not only gazes on the abyss without disintegrating, but which, on the contrary, is filled with coherence, pride, and manliness by such a vision. This glance which confronts life and death so bravely, I call Cretan." And, he went on, borrowing an image from the bull dancers depicted on the frescoes of Minoan Knossos, "The heroic and playful eyes, without hope yet without fear, which so confont the Bull, the Abyss, I call the Cretan Glance."[1]

To the Modernist writers of the West, the experience of the past hundred years is unmistakable proof of the degeneration of our civilization. Thus, Joyce in *Ulysses* inverts the traditional pattern of myth and creates as his hero a man who seemingly fails in all his endeavors, an outsider in the land in which he has lived for all of his life, ironic contrast to the mythic Odysseus; the hero of Mann's *Magic Mountain* attempts for his part to withdraw from this world but returns, ironically, to the holocaust of the First World War; it is only through his art that Proust's Marcel can find order and meaning in his life—and then he finds it late in his life, too late perhaps to complete the work of art that will justify his life; in such a milieu it seems quite natural for Kafka's nameless protagonist to metamorphose into an insect. With what remained of the humanist instinct, the best the Modernists could seemingly do was to suggest that a few individual lives at least could retain some dignity in this diminishing world—small consolation at best. But the experience of Crete led Kazantzakis, so close to his European contemporaries in so many ways, to a far different conclusion, to a view of life in which man retained not just the possibility of dignity but a certain nobility as well, in which the very fact of his likely defeat made his continued struggle heroic, a means by which all men might be redeemed even in an age without grandeur or grace.

There is an apocryphal story about Kazantzakis' death that sums up perfectly the spirit of his life and of his homeland. Refused permission to lie in state by the Greek Orthodox Archbishop of Athens, the body of the poet was returned to Iráklion, the major city of Crete, the Meghálo Kástro of his childhood and of his fiction. The story goes that as the coffin was being lowered into the grave on the Martinengo rampart overlooking the city, a huge man came down from the hills, a colossus out of one of Kazantzakis' books, and performed the task by himself. A photograph in the Historical Museum at Iráklion shows the coffin being handled by four men wearing traditional costumes—strong men to be sure, typical Cretan villagers, but not colossi. Yet eyewitnesses insist that they saw the colossus.[2] The legend persists because it so precisely sums up the spirit of both Kazantzakis and his island homeland. It is this spirit that informs all of his books, those which take place on Crete as well as those set elsewhere, from *Freedom or Death*, the most particularly Cretan of his novels, to *The Odyssey: A Modern Sequel*, which covers all the eastern Mediterranean and Africa, as well as Antarctica, and which demonstrates a profound mastery of Western thought—very nearly the ultimate Modernist fiction. No matter how representatively Modernist his work may appear, however, we are convinced in the end that it is something unique, a vision that is outside our immediate experience. "The human beings in this book," the author wrote to a Scandinavian friend about *Freedom or Death*, "the episodes, and the speech are all true, even if they appear incredible to people who were born in the light or half-light of Western civilization."[3]

The history of Crete is unlike that of any other Western nation, a long and virtually unbroken succession of foreign domination and unsuccessful revolts. It is said that from the early thirteenth century, when the island became part of Venice's commercial empire, to the end of the nineteenth, when her Turkish successors were finally driven out, each generation of Cretan men married, raised a son to continue the line, and went off to the mountains to fight the invaders. The first uprising broke out in 1212, the year the Venetians came to power; during their occupation, which lasted until 1669, the population of the island declined from five hundred thousand to two hundred thousand inhabitants. Venetian power on Crete ended with the twenty-four-year siege of Candia (still another name for Iráklion), which Byron called "Troy's rival." Resentment against the Venetians was by then so strong that even the Cretan militia refused to resist the Turkish invaders. But the Turks proved as despotic as their predecessors; in the period between 1770 and 1897 alone, there were ten rebellions against their rule. Western travelers to Crete during this period reported finding villages whose entire adult population consisted of widows; such a village appears in *Freedom or Death*. Still, the Turks allowed a substantial measure of religious freedom to the Cretans and, in the mountainous interior, a certain political independence as well; but they added no public works of their own and allowed most of the Venetian projects to fall into disrepair. On the whole, Crete was the most poorly governed province in the Turkish empire, as well as the most harshly ruled; aside from the pasha and the local garrison, the entire Moslem population of the island was made up of Cretan converts, who generally could not be controlled by the authorities and whose treatment of their Christian neighbors was often quite savage. Venetian colonists had been so drawn to the island that they had invariably adopted its customs—and often its religion as well—and had even led the natives in some of their bloodiest revolts against Venice; their descendants today are among the most illustrious of Cretan families. But the Cretan Turks—converts more for economic than for religious reasons—have left behind no descendants; they were driven from the island after the Smyrna disaster of 1922. For all their cruelty and poor administration, however, the Turks never equalled the harshness of the Venetians in putting down the rebellion of 1362. As the historian William Miller writes, "The whole plateau of Lasithi was converted into a desert, the peasants were carried off and their cottages pulled down, and the loss of a foot and the confiscation of his cattle were pronounced to be the penalty of any farmer or herdsman who should dare to sow corn there or to use the spot for pasture. This cruel and ridiculous order was obeyed to the letter; for nearly a century, one of the most fertile districts of Crete was allowed to remain in a state of nature."[4]

Énosís, union with the fatherland, finally came to Crete in 1913, seventy-five years after the mainland of Greece had achieved independence and fifteen years after the Turks had been driven out. The final delay was caused by interference from the Great Powers, who could not decide quite what to do with the persistent Cretans. Madame Hortense, the old French prostitute of *Zorba the Greek*—Kazantzakis knew of the original Madame Hortense as the proprietor of a small hotel in Ierápetra—speaks yearningly of the glorious days when she passed from admiral to admiral in the great international fleet that occupied the island.

The most recent foreign conquest of Crete took place in April 1941, when the Seventh German Parachute Corps landed on the island. The elite troops suffered fearful losses—Germany's worst in the war to that date—many of them to untrained natives, including women and children, armed only with their traditional knives and with ancient guns preserved from earlier battles. Some historians believe that the invasion would have failed if the Fifth Cretan Division had not been stranded on the mainland after the Allied evacuation from Greece. The resistance movement that developed during the occupation was among the most effective in Europe; the Germans retaliated by destroying dozens of villages, some of them burned down earlier by the Venetians and Turks. In modern times, portraits of the king and queen, once ubiquitous throughout the rest of Greece—at least until 1967—have often been replaced on Crete by pictures of folk heroes, leaders of rebellions against the Turks. Yet it was reportedly only on Crete that the military coup of the colonels was resisted with armed force; although the resistance was undoubtedly minor, it signifies the continuation of a hallowed tradition: it was not for the monarchy that the islanders fought, but for the principles of freedom that underlay their entire history. The new military government responded by preventing the planned celebration of the tenth anniversary of the death of Nikos Kazantzakis: the dictatorship recognized its enemy even in death.

Many of Greece's most vital men, in Renaissance times as well as our own, have been Cretans: statesmen as well as artists, among them Venizélos, the first president of the modern Republic of Greece, as well as El Greco and Kazantzakis. Nearly all have been exiles, nearly all nourished by an ancient tradition of hardship and persecution, of an unrelenting if unsuccessful striving for freedom, a tradition that set them apart from other people and in which they gloried. As Kazantzakis put it, "Love of liberty, the refusal to accept your soul's enslavement, not even in exchange for paradise; stalwart games over and above love and pain, over and above death; smashing even the most sacrosanct of the old molds when they are unable to contain you any longer—these are the three great cries of Crete."[5]

II

To most Westerners, Crete is the land of Minos, that glorious civilization whose greatness and fall are celebrated in the myths of Daedalus and Theseus. Many Cretans, however, know of Knossos only as an attraction to foreign tourists; ancient Cretan civilization seems to have had no enduring influence on modern Crete. And yet one is surprised at times to find a huge storage jar in some mountain village exactly like a Minoan *píthos,* or to meet a young Cretan girl who looks like the daughter of one of the court ladies in Sir Arthur Evans' restored frescoes. To Kazantzakis, there was a special glory in the ancient Minoans, a glory different from and perhaps greater than that of their mainland cousins, the Myceneans and their successors. "Crete served as the first bridge between Europe, Asia, and Africa," he wrote. "Crete was the first place in a then totally dark Europe to become enlightened. And it was here too that the Greek soul accomplished its destined mission: it reduced God to the scale of man. Here in Greece the monstrous immovable statues of Egypt or Assyria became small and graceful, with bodies that moved, mouths that smiled; the features and stature of God took on the features and stature of man. A new, original humanity full of agility, grace, and oriental luxury lived and played on the Cretan soil, a humanity which differed from the subsequent Greeks."[6] This difference was somehow symbolized in the distinction between Knossos and the palaces on the mainland: in Knossos, "one does not see the balanced geometric architecture of Greece. Reigning here are imagination, grace, and the free play of man's creative power. This palace grew and proliferated in the course of time, slowly, like a living organism, a tree. It was not built once and for all with a fixed, premeditated plan; it grew by additions, playing and harmonizing with the ever-renewed necessities of the times. . . . The intellect was useful, but as a servant, not a master."[7] The master here was God, the spirit, the flame; this, too, is part of the Cretan Glance, that sense of history turned into metaphor.

At the beginning of the Second World War, Kazantzakis returned for a time to Crete, viewed the flying fish on the restored fresco in the queen's apartment at Knossos and thought of Christ, the *ichthys* who sought the same goal as he: "to transcend man's destiny and unite with God . . . with absolute freedom. . . . What good fortune, I reflected, that Crete should have been perhaps the first place on earth to see the birth of this symbol of the soul fighting and dying for freedom! The flying fish—behold the soul of struggling, indomitable man! . . . Shaken and disturbed, I reflected that it is here in this terrible moment of confrontation between the Cretan and the abyss that Crete's secret lies concealed."[8] It was this secret that Kazantzakis' life and work were dedicated to uncovering. He found the solution, as well as other forms of the mystery, not only in union with the Minoans or with the great, anonymous rebels of his father's and grandfather's generations; he found it also in the artists of the Cretan Renaissance of the sixteenth and seventeenth centuries: it is no accident that his spiritual autobiography is a *Report to Greco*, to the man he called "grandfather," the greatest of his precursors.[9]

As autobiography, *Report to Greco* is not very reliable; it is as novelistic in its structure and in its handling of details as any of Kazantzakis' fictions.[10] Its value lies elsewhere, in its sense of life turned into art and of art turned into life, in that mythic confrontation between art and life—between metaphor and history—that characterizes the experience of Crete as Kazantzakis perceives it and as it appears in his fiction. The El Greco to whom he dedicates this work is more than the historical painter, more than a convenient ancestor whom he might claim for a guide. El Greco is important to Kazantzakis because centuries earlier he grew to manhood in the same town and because wherever he went thereafter he bore proudly the heritage of Crete. Thus he too becomes part of the metaphor that his descendant labels the Cretan Glance.

III

After the fall of Constantinople in 1453, the center of Byzantine culture shifted to Crete, one of the few Western outposts remaining in the Levant. For the next two centuries, until the Turkish conquest, it was through Crete that this culture was transmitted to Italy and the West. "In the revival of classical scholarship in the West," writes Deno John Geanakoplos, "Cretan men of letters occupy a noteworthy position. Beginning in the early fifteenth century . . . a surprisingly large number of Cretan intellectuals spread over the Mediterranean area, from Syria in the East to as far as Spain in the West. As emigrés to Western Europe, Cretans filled teaching positions in leading universities, copied manuscripts for patrons of virtually every Latin country, and were closely associated with the development of the Greek press in Venice and elsewhere."[11] But it was not only as transmitter of an inherited culture that Crete happened to flourish; by the time Byzantine culture had passed through the island, it had been transformed into patterns uniquely Cretan. This is immediately apparent in Cretan religious art, which incorporates into the stylized Byzantine tradition certain naturalistic innovations of Western art and thus creates some strikingly new and original forms. There were in the sixteenth century more than eight hundred frescoed churches and monasteries on the island, and Cretan painters worked throughout the mainland—on Mount Athos and the Meteora as well as in other major centers. Little of their work has survived: the harshness of Cretan life has always been conducive to the creation of art, but rarely to its preservation. Perhaps this is one reason that so many Cretan artists have gone into exile. El Greco, the greatest of them, is said to have studied under Mihális Dhamaskinós, the master of the Cretan school, and there is evidence that he did not leave for Venice until he had mastered its technique. Certainly we can find in even his mature work this same strange combination of naturalism and stylization, of traditional patterns inspired by the insight of the creator.[12]

In literature, too, the most outstanding Cretan works represent a fusion of the two traditions, Western and Greek. The masterpiece of the Cretan Renaissance, the *Erotókritos* of Vincenzo Cornaro, takes a stereotypic Italian romance and transforms it into a work of both charm and originality. The action of the epic is set in Athens, but the Cretan nationalism of the poet is apparent throughout, and his language is the wonderfully inventive and easily recognizable Cretan dialect, which "deviates from Athenian Greek about as much as the speech of County Galway from the B.B.C."[13] The *Erotókritos* has remained the most popular work of Greek literature even in modern times; there are supposedly still Cretan shepherds who can recite from memory its more than ten thousand verses.[14] Indeed, its dialect might well have become the national language of Greece were it not for the Turkish conquest of Crete. Cornaro's national epic has had a profound and continuing effect on the local folk idiom, for the vast and ever-growing body of Cretan folk song often refers to it directly or uses it as a model. The subject matter of most of these songs, however, comes not from the Italian romance tradition but from rebellions against first the Venetians and thereafter the Turks; there is even a substantial body of songs that grew out of the Second World War resistance movement, and one suspects that an anti-junta group was formed during the past decade.[15]

The sophisticated freedom of Kazantzakis' language clearly derives from the inventiveness and flexibility of the Cretan dialect as it is seen in the *Erotókritos* and related works. His scholarly detractors claim that he uses so many Cretan idioms that his work cannot really be read by an Athenian, or, alternately, that he invents new words and new forms to fit his immediate needs—that he writes, that is, in the most extreme form of the demotic, the so-called *Maliarí*.[16] Vigorously, the author denied both accusations. As he wrote to the young Greek-American poet and scholar who would soon become his translator and friend:

> It would give me great pleasure to have you come that we may work together, because it would be impossible for you to begin the translation by yourself. Not because my work contains many Cretan words, but because its language is our rich modern Greek tongue which few among our intellectuals know. . . . The scholars in Athens have a superficial language of extreme poverty, and whatever word they do not know they call Cretan. Yet when I translated Dante's *Divine Comedy*, I publicly announced and wagered anyone that in 14,000 verses not only were there not 33, but not even 13 words exclusively Cretan! Of course no one took me up on the wager.

His actual practice was something else—not to use the immediate insular term but to seek for the one most widely in use throughout Greece. "Whenever a better, that is to say, a more panhellenic word exists," he wrote, "I always prefer it."[17] Thus he was doing no more than to follow his native traditions.

Nor was he a *maliarós*, he would insist. Unlike Psihéris, with whom his name is frequently linked, he did not need to resort to slang or to invent new words for lack of an old one, for he was never out of touch with Greece during the years that he lived in the West. And one of the major activities on his journeys to Greece was the collecting of words for his glossary of the demotic.[18] This monumental work—

complete only to the letter kappa—has never been published, but the need for it may still exist: when the Greek Academy published the first volume of its demotic dictionary, on just part of the letter alpha, Kazantzakis found about two hundred words that were in his compilation but not in the official one.[19] For Kazantzakis, as for many Greeks of his generation, the battle for the demotic was not simply a philological issue but one that touched on virtually every aspect of modern Greek life, from the lowest levels of education (hence the primary school textbooks that he developed in the demotic) to the most basic issues of social status and economic and political rights. "The demotic language is our homeland," Kazantzakis contended, the only sure way to effect the modernization of Greece without sacrificing its most valued traditions.[20] The battle for the demotic is not limited to Crete, of course, but the two are inextricably linked in the career of the noblest of modern Cretan masters, joining, as in the *Erotókritos* and the other works of the Cretan Renaissance, a people's language to a literature that emerges from, and is based upon, the life of the people.

We find in the fiction and verse of Kazantzakis this same indigenous combination of Western forms and ideas with the nationalistic spirit of Crete, of modern views of the nature of man and the universe with the Cretan dialect and with local legend. We can find echoes of the *Erotókritos* in Kazantzakis' *Odyssey;* and the famous folk piece "The Song of Dhaskaloyánnis," which celebrates an eighteenth-century revolt against the Turks, provides character and incident for his *Freedom or Death*. The mythopoeic quality of Cretan folk art resounds throughout Kazantzakis' art: his view of man is at once heroic and naturalistic: his heroes are many-faceted, capable of great cruelty and injustice as well as great flights of the spirit; but there are no relatives and neighbors to betray them, no blood feuds or jealousies to divide their followers, no Cretan converts to Islam to outdo their Turkish oppressors. In the mythmaking of Kazantzakis, a process that almost totally ignores the baser aspects of his country's history, only noble *pallikária* are called "captain"—there are no pretenders to the island's most honored title; old sea captains, pirates most of them but patriots as well, abound in his books—although the last Cretan pirates died out with the start of Turkish rule; and the most noble acts of Cretan history somehow accrue to his heroes—it is the brother of Captain Mihális in *Freedom or Death* who blows up the monastery of Arkádi to save it from the Turks and not, as legend has it, the abbot. And yet, in the strange land that is Crete, a land as close to Asia and Africa as it is to Europe, these are not distortions at all, but amplifications that perfectly reflect the spirit of the people. It is this spirit that distinguishes the art of Kazantzakis from that of all his contemporaries. Even his most derivative work, the philosophical essay *The Saviors of God*, is somehow transformed by this spirit into a unique and challenging statement of faith. In it can be found the major themes and symbols of Kazantzakis' life and art.

IV

The alternate title of *The Saviors of God*, the *Spiritual Exercises*[21]— reflecting Loyola—further suggests its metaphysical emphasis. Kimon Friar, who so ably translated Kazantzakis' *Odyssey*, agreed to work on this text too not only because it is the philosophical core of the canon but also because it is wonderful poetry. Its poetry is apparent in its language of personal and spiritual confession; in the vivid dream imagery that permeates the work; above all, in the author's strikingly original conception of the relationship between man and God, a conception that recalls the man-size deities of Minoan art. For God to Kazantzakis is neither the Christian nor the Hebrew divinity, not some ultimate force beyond man's reach, not even the final goal of his achievement. God, like man, is a process in being, a natural force of great creative potential, most akin to Bergson's *élan vital*. He is, as Friar has put it, "that creating evolutionary surge in nature that is ceaselessly striving to purify material into spirit."[22] It is under the intellectual influence of Nietzsche and Bergson, those precursors of the Modernists, that the poem is composed; the final vision, however, comes from Crete. This is one more aspect of Kazantzakis' synthesis.

The form and function of *The Saviors of God* are the same: the ascent to God—to this great creative power—and then beyond. Just as the reader moves through a series of steps—The Preparation, The March, The Vision, and The Action—up to the peak of The Silence, so the soul of man must climb to perilous heights, must lean out over the Abyss and confront terrifying truths: God is as dependent upon man as man is upon Him; to save himself, man first must save God; the fight is unequal, the results seemingly ordained—neither man nor God nor the two fighting together can save themselves. Knowing this but continuing to struggle, man discovers his dignity, becomes himself a kind of God.

In the first step, The Preparation, there are three duties: to see boundaries, to reject boundaries, to become free of all hope as well as all fear; only thus can man ready himself for the march up to God. On The March itself, he moves from the ego, to the race, to all mankind, and finally to the earth: from an awareness of self to a recognition that the individual is also one of a race of men, with ancestors and descendants; from a further acknowledgement that both he and his race are but parts of a greater humanity to a final discovery that mankind, too, is united with all the other creatures of the earth in a single entity. This is no proper pantheistic insight, but a "dread vision" (p. 88). The earth is no nourishing mother, but a "beast that eats, begets, moves, remembers. She hungers, she devours her children—plants, animals, men, thoughts—she grinds them in her dark jaws, passes them through her body once more, then casts them again into the soil" (p. 82).

It is at this point that the physical ascent begins, as the visionary perceives Job-like, Christ-like man becoming God, panting, struggling, clawing his way up the mountain to the peak: "Difficult, dreadful, unending ascension!" (p. 93). Rising in a kind of Darwinian process from the plants to the animals to man and beyond, God creates not Adam, but Himself. Then this stubborn, beast-like, blood-splattered God abandons the plants, to "encamp in [the] loins" of the animals and finally to "struggle to escape beyond us [too], to cast us off with the plants and animals, and to leap farther," to reach, in short, the Abyss (pp. 89–90).

Living in a new age, an age created partly by his masters Nietzsche and Bergson, Kazantzakis devises a vision of God different from those of earlier ages, for, as he sees it, they have now lost all meaning and relevance. Man today serves God by going to His aid in His unending struggle for survival. If God falls, man falls with Him; if He is victorious, man is saved. But this new Old Testament deity can be defeated. And so men must band together out of mutual love and responsibility and sacrifice in order to fight God's fight, in order to destroy and purify the old world by fire and to establish the new world that may arise from its ashes. "Set fire! This is our great duty today amid such immoral and hopeless chaos.... Sow fire to purify the earth! Let a more dreadful abyss open up between good and evil, let injustice increase, let Hunger descend to thresh our bowels, for we may not otherwise be saved.... For it is only One who struggles at the far end of earth and sky. And if He goes lost, then we go lost" (pp. 113, 115).

This heretical vision perceives a divinity with dramatic possibilities: it is as if Milton's Satan really could defeat his eternal adversary. The vision is the result of Kazantzakis' life-long effort to reconcile the universals of Christianity with the ideals and rhetoric of Marxism, to combine the clear, unassuming simplicity of Buddha with the Nietzschean views of the *übermensch* and the death of God and with the *élan vital* of Bergson; and its images are those of all of his works: the clawing ascent, the fire of the human soul, the abyss that it confronts and flies over as a bird. "The soul of man is a flame," he writes, "a bird of fire that leaps from bough to bough, from head to head, and that shouts, . . . Where do we come from? Where are we going? What is the meaning of this life? . . . And a fire within me leaps up to answer: 'Fire will surely come one day to purify the earth. Fire will surely come one day to obliterate the earth. This is the Second Coming. . . . Fire is the first and final mask of my God. We dance and weep between two enormous pyres.' . . . This ultimate stage of our spiritual exercise is called Silence." Leaning out over the Abyss, the man who has reached the peak of Silence sings a "profound and magical incantation" of belief in God in all His historical guises, of belief in the man who has climbed to His rescue, of belief in the ultimate unreality of the existence of both man and God:

> BLESSED BE ALL THOSE WHO HEAR AND RUSH TO FREE YOU,
> LORD, AND WHO SAY: "ONLY YOU AND I EXIST."
> BLESSED BE ALL THOSE WHO FREE YOU AND BECOME
> UNITED WITH YOU, LORD, AND WHO SAY: "YOU AND I
> ARE ONE."
> AND THRICE BLESSED BE THOSE WHO BEAR ON THEIR
> SHOULDERS AND DO NOT BUCKLE UNDER THIS GREAT,
> SUBLIME, AND TERRIFYING SECRET: *THAT EVEN THIS
> ONE DOES NOT EXIST!* (pp. 127-29)

Knowing that they cannot win, but still struggling—struggling because they cannot win—the heroes of Kazantzakis, like the generations of Cretan heroes before them, confront themselves at the abyss and affirm the divinity of man and the painful beauty of life.

The Saviors of God demonstrates dramatically the blending of Western and Cretan sources that characterizes Kazantzakis' fiction. The image of the ascent, for example, has roots in the naturalistic novel and in the Marxist theme of the inevitable revolution, as well as in the perpetual Cretan struggle for freedom—and even perhaps in the often inaccessible mountains that cover so much of the island. The suggestion of inevitable failure derives similarly from the philosophical determinism of the late nineteenth century and from the history of Crete. But the continuation of the struggle, the confrontation at the abyss, is uniquely Kazantzakian, the product of his own experience and of that of his homeland. A student of Bergson who discovered Nietzsche with a shock of recognition, a frustrated reformer who initially admired the new Russian regime but who tried to live himself according to Buddhist ideals, a man both pretentious and unassuming who loved both the common man and the masterful figures of history, Kazantzakis in his own life and work displayed the same dualities that characterize his fictional heroes.

Torn between intellect and spirit, like Boss in *Zorba the Greek;* between the demands of patriotism and those of the flesh, like Captain Mihális in *Freedom or Death;* between respect for tradition and recognition of the need for change—even for violent change—like Father Yánaros in *The Fratricides;* between the desire for a normal life and the compulsion to martyrdom, like Saint Francis, like Jesus, like Manoliós in *The Greek Passion,* Kazantzakis' heroes strive for unity and self-knowledge but rarely attain them. Only Odysseus among them achieves oneness, and so he alone becomes a kind of divinity. He is the measure of their small successes and of their ultimate failure—or at least of what appears to be failure. For he too remains a contradictory figure, a mass of dualities: the unity that he appears to achieve is but the sum of their dualities. What seems to be inconsistency is thus no more than a continuous process of reinvestigation and development, a recognition that such problems as these may never be completely resolved: thus, even after he has become an ascetic, just before setting out on his final voyage into the southern mist, Odysseus fondles with joy a young woman's breast. So it is through him that we learn that what Kazantzakis seeks in the end is not some simple harmonious form, not the resolution of tension, but the accretion of tension, not unity but multiplicity. There are no final, well balanced reconciliations in his fictions, no closed and definitive endings. The tensions in his art and his life are ongoing tensions, and it is from them that creativity emerges: this is the final synthesis of Cretan experience.

At one point, under the influence of Nietzsche and Bergson, Kazantzakis composed a series of terza rima cantos on the great men whom he called the "Companions of the Odyssey"—among them Moses, Christ, Don Quixote, Dante, Lenin, and Nietzsche himself. If he admired these figures, it was not simply for the philosophical truths that they represented, or because they were so different from himself—he knew without affectation the heroism of his own literary career—or even because they recalled the image of his father, the original Captain Mihális. Like Odysseus, like El Greco, each of them embodied what the creator labeled the Cretan Glance, that attitude of bravery with which man alone confronts the abyss and prepares to play with life as the Cretan boys and girls once played with the bulls of Minos.

Whatever their ostensible nationalities, Kazantzakis' heroes are ultimately all Cretans, and their adversaries—whether they are called Turks or Pharisees, Dominicans or Royalist Blacks—represent the forces that have been opposed to Crete throughout its history, the same forces that eternally confront God and man at the abyss. Their

16

metaphysical conflict is played out in all the fiction against a backdrop that is at once naturalistic and symbolic, demonstrating both the sources of Kazantzakis' art and its uniqueness. In him the Modernists of the West would have recognized a Companion, and yet he is finally so different from them, so unmistakably Cretan. From him we can learn not simply of Crete but of ourselves, an attitude toward life that his Modernist contemporaries, in their different milieus, could not quite perceive. Crete in our time may be terribly insular, but the Cretan Glance, as Kazantzakis perceived it, remains universal.

1. Cited in Kimon Friar's introduction to *The Odyssey: A Modern Sequel* (New York, 1958), p. xix.

2. Kazantzakis' widow, Helen, has written this author that one of the pallbearers was indeed "almost a giant. As I dared to raise my eyes (in the Cathedral) he was so shocked, so infuriated, that I was afraid—if alone he would at once kill me—a widow not having the right to look at men!" Geneva, August 10, 1972.

3. Letter to Börje Knös, Antibes, May 5, 1950. Cited in Helen Kazantzakis, *Nikos Kazantzakis: A Biography Based on his Letters*, trans. Amy Mims (New York, 1968), p. 487.

4. William Miller, *Essays on the Latin Orient* (Cambridge, 1921), p. 185.

5. *Report to Greco*, trans. Peter A. Bien (New York, 1965), pp. 440–41.

6. *Greco*, p. 151.

7. *Greco*, p. 149.

8. *Greco*, pp. 454–55.

9. Kazantzakis wrote to Börje Knös from Lugano on July 10, 1955: "Here I'm thinking of beginning the new work, *Letters to Greco*. A kind of autobiography—I shall make a confession to my grandfather, El Greco. Yesterday, a wise friend came to see me, von der Steinen, and he told me that Petrarch had written *Letters to Cicero*, whom he loved very much. I was pleased. So my idea is not a personal one, but an ancient need of the creator to converse with a beloved dead person in whom he has confidence and to whom he can tell his grief." Cited in Helen Kazantzakis, p. 534.

10. Pandhelís Prevelákis, Kazantzakis' fellow Cretan and his literary executor, has said of this work that "Kazantzakis has here made a myth of his life.... He has confused the dates, put ideal order into his struggles, given harmony to his life. Imagination has given him whatever life denied him. The *Report* is not an autobiography: it is the chronicle of the fight with the daemon, the mythical preparation for the *Odyssey*. It is an ascent affording a magnificent view, the total conception of the world." *Nikos Kazantzakis and His Odyssey*, trans. Philip Sherrard (New York, 1961), p. 167. Kimon Friar tells me that Kazantzakis was fond of quoting Goethe to the effect that all works of art are forms of confession. In this respect, the "autobiography" is unquestionably true, another of those archetypal patterns that seem to develop so naturally in the author's art and in his life: paying such homage to the grandfather figure is a practice common among preliterate societies.

11. Deno John Geanakoplos, *Greek Scholars in Venice: Studies in the Dissemination of Greek Learning from Byzantium to Western Europe* (Cambridge, Mass., 1962), p. 41.

12. "Dans sa vie, dans son nom, dans les livres, dans sa technique, dans ses oeuvres, on trouve une permanence sublime ou un souvenir stable et actif du monde hellénique, de sa patrie, de sa culture et de son esprit. On dirait qu'il s'agit de la nostalgie persistante de la patrie, telle cette d'Ulysse errant ou celle des grecs de la diaspore qui vivent à l'étranger.... Avec une noble fierté et une admiration de la patrie hellénique il souligne continuellement qu'il est un Crétois de Candie." Sebastien Cirac, "L'Hellénisme de Dominique Theotokopoulos—Crétois ou Grec," *Kritiká Hroniká*, 15–16 (1961–62), Part 2, pp. 215–16. Seeing an El Greco portrait of a saint in the National Gallery in London, George Seferis was convinced "that the model for this picture must have been a Cretan boatman." And two brush strokes on the shoulder, his companion added, are "like Cretan fifteen-syllable lines." Seferis, *On the Greek Style: Selected Essays in Poetry and Hellenism* (Boston, 1966), pp. 95, 166. Prevelakis, whose doctoral thesis was concerned with El Greco, explained in an interview some of the significance that El Greco has held for him as a Cretan artist, suggesting in the process some of his importance for Kazantzakis as well: "El Greco was for several years the basic crystal around which my intellectual concerns solidified.... El Greco, the heir of an ancient cultural tradition jealously guarded as a life-line during the dark ages of foreign occupation, came into contact with the modern civilisation of the West, was temporarily attracted by it, renounced it, and finally combined it with his original culture. This ordeal of the great Cretan was, I may say, an archetype which I have often invoked during my intellectual career." "Pandhelís Prevelákis Talks to Peter Mackridge," *Omphalos*, 1 (March 1972), p. 34. The analogue with his immediate mentor, Kazantzakis, is obvious.

13. Patrick Leigh Fermor, introduction to George Psihoundákis, *The Cretan Runner: His Story of the German Occupation* (London, 1955), p. 22. Earlier travelers to Crete have commented on the uniqueness of the Cretan dialect. In 1837, the Englishman Robert Pashley observed with surprise, "although I thought myself sufficiently acquainted with modern Greek when I landed in Crete, yet I discovered, the very first time I spoke with a Cretan peasant, that I was still at a great distance from a knowledge of *his* language; and so numerous are its peculiarities that, for some weeks, I had to spend much of my time in endeavouring to render myself familiar with them." *Travels in Crete* (London, 1837), p. 11.

14. The *Erotókritos* "has remained the favourite reading of the Greek people for two hundred years.... It is only since the [First World] War with the multiplication of newspapers and the massed entertainments of industrial life that its popularity has begun to wane.... And all the time it has been monotonously insulted by the historians of Greek literature who, quite apart from the question of its uncongenial [i.e., demotic] language, have felt for it something of the jealous contempt which the highbrow reserves for the best-seller." John Mavrogordato, *The Erotókritos* (London, 1929), pp. 1–2. For a discussion of its borrowings from Western literatures, see Gareth Morgan, "French and Italian Elements in the Erotókritos," *Kritiká Hroniká*, 7 (1953), pp. 201–28; and for its ultimate originality, see Alexandre Embiricos, *La Renaissance Crétois* (Paris, 1960), p. 132.

15. "Cretan oral peotry... is rich in illustrative material for Homer. The per-

18

sistence in Crete of the heroic age into the present, the geographic isolation of villages in the mountains of Sphakiá, the recitation of old poems . . . and the creation of new ones . . . at social and religious festivals . . ., the absence in their heroic poems of supernatural or shamanistic elements and the presence in them of a humanistic epic mentality, all make the Cretan poems an interesting laboratory." James A. Notopoulos, "Homer and Cretan Heroic Poetry: A Study in Comparative Oral Poetry," *American Journal of Philology*, 73 (1952), pp. 228–29.

16. The argot of the *maliarós*, "the hairy ones," i.e., the lowest classes of society. Kimon Friar suggests that it is more appropriate to characterize Kazantzakis' language as *Laïkí*, a similarly inventive but less colloquial idiom. In a letter to this author, Athens, November 25, 1971. For a most useful account of the war between the various forms of *Dhemotikí* and those of the more formal and stilted *Katharévousa*, see Peter A. Bien, *Kazantzakis and the Linguistic Revolution in Modern Greek Literature* (Princeton, 1973).

17. Letter to Kimon Friar, Antibes, May 2, 1954. Cited in Friar, "A Unique Collaboration: Translating *The Odyssey: A Modern Sequel*," *Journal of Modern Literature*, 2 (1971–72), p. 221. There are some marvelous stories in this account of Kazantzakis' popularity today among the people of Crete.

18. For the *Odyssey*, Kazantzakis told Friar, he had invented only five words. In a letter to this author, Athens, October 13, 1971. As for his collector's zeal for new words, one moving incident can serve to illustrate Kazantzakis' methods and goals. Traveling near Sparta with his friend Sikelianós, Kazantzakis came across a strange flower whose name no one knew. But an old woman of the town would know the name, a young boy told them, and as he ran off to ask her, "we waited, holding the flower. We admired it, sniffed it, but were impatient, we longed for the word. And then, in a short while, the boy returned. 'Auntie Lenió,' he said, 'died day before yesterday.' Our hearts constricted. We sensed that a word had perished; perished, and now no one could place it in a verse and render it immortal. We were terrified. Never had death seemed to us so irrevocable. And we left the flower spread out on the fence, like a corpse." Nikos Kazantzakis, *Journey to the Morea*, trans. F. A. Reed (New York, 1965), p. 90.

19. Interview with Helen Kazantzakis, Geneva, July 28 and 30, 1971.

20. In a letter to Prevelákis, cited in *Omphalos*, p. 38. For all of his creative life, Kazantzakis was an active warrior on behalf of the demotic in this complex and emotional issue, and he recognized how central it was to his art. "Our demotic tongue is analytic," he wrote in an early letter to Friar; "it does not have many participles and connects its phrases usually with an 'and.' It loves adjectives inordinately (demotic songs and Cretan love songs). I personally need adjectives for reasons which you well understand. For this reason you are right in saying that these two devices characterize our demotic tongue, and in particular my personal style. A translation, therefore, should retain the chief characteristics of the prototype even though these may startle strangers to the tongue. We orientals love adjectives, repetition, and every sort of comparison in narrative (a most habitual characteristic in Homer, our grandfather)." Rogaška Slatina, July 22, 1956, cited in Friar, "A Unique Collaboration," pp. 241–42. As he explained to Ghalátea, his first wife, concerning his *Odyssey*, "My art is not clean, pure, great. The colors smother the spirituality of the line, the images come in crowds and are expressed through exagg-

eration.... I couldn't find simplicity, I couldn't overcome the loud and showy ornamentation." Cited in M. Byron Raizis, "Kazantzakis' Ur-Odysseus, Homer, and Gerhart Hauptmann," *Journal of Modern Literature*, 2 (1971–72), p. 214n.

21. The title of the original edition, in 1927, was *Salvatores Dei* and the subtitle *Askitíki*, or "Asceticism." The order of the titles was reversed in the revised edition of 1945, and then again—by Friar, but with the author's approval—for the first American edition. All page references are to this edition, *The Saviors of God: Spiritual Exercises*, trans. Kimon Friar (New York, 1960).

22. In a letter to this author, Athens, November 25, 1971.

CHAPTER TWO

FREEDOM OR DEATH
and Rebellion on Crete

In 1889, when Nikos Kazantzakis was not yet seven, the Christians in a village near Meghálo Kástro killed an important agha: the signal for another massacre. Barricaded in their home, surrounded by hostile neighbors and the local garrison, with the four gates to the walled city closed and guarded, he and his family watched through the night. "My mother, my sister, and I sat glued to one another, barricaded within our house. We heard the frenzied Turks in the street outside, cursing, threatening, breaking down doors, and slaughtering Christians. We heard dogs barking, the cries and death rales of the wounded, and a droning in the air as though an earthquake were in progress. My father stood in wait behind the door, his musket loaded. In his hand, I remember, he held an oblong stone which he called a whetstone. He was sharpening a long black-handled knife on it. We waited. 'If the Turks break down the door and enter,' he had told us, 'I plan to slaughter you myself before you fall into their hands.' My mother, sister, and I had all agreed. Now we were waiting."[1] In the morning, before other Christians had dared leave their homes, his father took him to pay obeisance to the bodies of the men hanged from the plane tree on the edge of the town square. In *Freedom or Death*, it is Captain Mihális and his son Thrasákis who await the marauding Turks, and the lifting of the siege is a sign for them not of eternal martyrdom of Crete, but of the necessity to rebel anew. And so they go to war in the mountains, where, months later and now fighting almost alone, Mihális dies the futile heroic death that Kazantzakis' father may always have desired for himself. And Thrasákis will certainly become, perhaps unwittingly, a *pallikári* like his father and not, as Kazantzakis would put it, a detested scribbler. So much did the writer alter his personal history, and yet many of the episodes and characters of *Freedom or Death* are unmistakably drawn from his own life.

The character of Kosmás, for example—the Europeanized nephew of Mihális, a man of letters and a socialist, who returns to his homeland with a Russian-Jewish bride—is based loosely on Kazantzakis himself: on his politics and exile, on his most intimate friendships. When Kosmás is confronted by an image of his dead father demanding that he fulfill his heritage and fight for Crete's freedom, he is merely duplicating the experience of Kazantzakis' own father. The memory of this grandparent, who dwarfed his titanlike son, is also recalled by old Sífakas, father of Captain Mihális, a patriarchal figure who leaps unaided onto his horse even after his hundredth birthday. And Títyros, the ineffectual schoolmaster, youngest brother of Mihális, is drawn from the author's first teacher and perhaps as well from himself. When Kosmás and his schoolmaster uncle shed their veneers of education and culture and become *pallikária*, they seem to represent some sort of wish fulfillment for Kazantzakis, who felt as inferior to his father as the older man had felt to his. "The new novel on Crete will soon be ready," the novelist wrote to a friend. "I am trying my utmost to resurrect my father. To pay back my debt in this way: by giving birth to him who gave me birth."[2] The old man had died quietly in his bed. "The man-beast whom Kazantzakis had feared all his life and had regarded as deathless had collapsed. He had symbolized, while he lived, the roots, the original beast: the mud of which the son was destined to make spirit."[3]

Freedom or Death demonstrates its Cretan roots in other ways as well, for its central plot appears to be derived from the most famous of Cretan folk songs, the eighteenth-century "Song of Dhaskaloyánnis." Dhaskaloyánnis—literally "John the Teacher," a title of respect and not of vocation—was the foremost citizen in the independent and warlike province of Sphakiá, a descendant of the famed Kallérgis family of Venetian times. Lured by a promise of Russian aid—Catherine the Great had just declared war against Turkey and professed to be anxious to open a new front—he led his entire province into rebellion. This was in 1770, and the revolt failed when the promised Russian fleet failed to appear—although the eight hundred Sphakians held off twenty-five thousand Turkish regulars for several weeks; in *Freedom or Death*, Russian assistance is again promised and again disappoints. Dhaskaloyánnis continues to resist in the mountains despite demands from the Pasha that he surrender and a letter from his own brother seemingly endorsing the peace terms; Mihális too fights on despite repeated requests from both Turks and Cretans—in the novel, the Cretan resignation is again expressed in a letter, this time from the Metropolitan, which is carried to Mihális by his nephew Kosmás. It is at this point that Dhaskaloyánnis suddenly walks into the Turkish camp and surrenders, still refusing to sign a truce and stoically accepting his torture and death; Mihális, however, does not surrender—although, like his predecessor, he refuses to escape—and instead dies charging the enemy. In the folk epic, a priest who originally opposed the revolt voluntarily submits with the rebel leader; in the novel, Kosmás, convinced of the need for capitulation until some more propitious time, nevertheless dies fighting alongside his uncle. " 'Don't flinch, nephew,' said Captain Mihális to Kosmás. 'There's no hope. Long live Crete.' 'You're right,' " answered the younger man. " 'There's no hope. Long live Crete!' " (p. 432).[4]

The events in both folk song and novel are epic, growing out of history and somehow surpassing it. Just as the song is an elaboration of several oral versions composed immediately after the revolt—in the earlier versions, Dhaskaloyánnis is a businessman frustrated by Turkish trade regulations and not a patriot at all—so Kazantzakis' rendition intensifies further the epic possibilities. Dhaskaloyánnis is defeated only when one of the Sphakians betrays a secret mountain pass to the Turks; but it is safe for Kosmás to follow the hidden passage to Mihális' stronghold minutes before the final battle: the act of betrayal, so common to the history of Crete, has no place in the fiction. Mihális, moreover, is far more heroic than his original, for Dhaskaloyánnis is something of a prideful fool as well as a brave warrior—he surrenders in order to get better peace terms and then stubbornly refuses to bargain; but Kazantzakis' hero knows that his continued resistance belies the Turkish claim to the world that the Cretans have willingly stopped fighting. At the end, "a wild light haloed his face, which was filled with an inhuman joy. Was it pride, godlike defiance, or contempt of death? Or limitless love for Crete?" (p. 433). The making of myths, it is clear, did not die out in the eighteenth century.

II

The mythos of *Freedom or Death* provides a unique sense of historical continuity, a picture of traditional Cretan life that remains valid to this day. For the resistance of the Cretans to foreign domination assumed cultural as well as political forms; the people fought as much to retain intact their ancient traditions as they did to regain their freedom. There are few reminders in Crete today of seven centuries of alien rule; those that do survive—like the neglected Morosini fountain in the main square of Iráklion, or the occasional mosque that now serves as a warehouse or barn—merely remind us with a shock of the failure of their builders to alter the ancient rhythms of Cretan life. Outlasting both Venetians and Turks is the insular, often primitive culture of Crete, a sense of life that has exerted a powerful attraction on its conquerors and has itself remained largely unchanged despite new emigration from the mainland: it took only one generation for the many Caucasus Greeks who arrived after the disastrous war of 1919–22 to become indistinguishable, even in dialect and local pride, from the native-born Cretans. Only today, under the influence of tourism, is this way of life beginning to change, and then only in the cities. The young people of Iráklion wear Western clothes, but theirs is still a male-dominated, parent-centered society, and even here one can sometimes see retiring women dressed entirely in shapeless black and proud men wearing the national costume—the high black boots, black headband, fierce black mustache, and long, ornamental knife. In the mountain villages, the old ways go on as before; it is this ancient society that Kazantzakis brings to life in *Freedom or Death*. The view of life underlying these customs informs each of his works.

In Captain Mihális' Meghálo Kástro—a town recalled today by the old quarter of neighboring Réthymnon—women are totally subservient to their husbands and fathers. Even Katerína, whom Mihális has married because of her independence and strength, has finally "bowed her head" to him (p. 32), and Renió, his daughter, has been forbidden from puberty to appear before him. "The girl could scent his footsteps far off, and would hide at once. The cat too would scent him, and she too made off, even sooner, with her tail between her legs. It had to be so. Her father was right. Renió could not unravel the 'why.' But she was sure her father was right" (p. 35). Her instinct may help to explain why the facts of Cretan life have for so long remained unchanged.

Bridal abduction is an old Cretan custom, even when the marriage has been agreed upon by both families—"did meat which one had not stolen taste good?" (p. 326)—and Sífakas had acquired his bride by threatening to burn down her entire village (pp. 375–76); as recently as 1950, a similar incident nearly led to civil war in Crete. As shepherd for his father, young Thodorés has often stolen from neighboring flocks on Mount Seléna (p. 218); sheep stealing is still practiced, although on a much reduced scale, in the mountains of Sphakiá. And blood feuds may last for generations, not only between Greek and Turk, as in the novel, but among the Greeks themselves; the family of George Psihoundhákis, who has written the only native memoir of the resistance movement, was involved in such a feud soon after the war. More pervasive still is the deeply rooted hostility of the villagers to intellectual concerns; when Mihális shows his scorn for his educated nephew and brother, he is demonstrating not a personal idiosyncracy, but the general Cretan rejection of any values that might detract from the fight for freedom: in *Freedom or Death*, monastery libraries are willingly sacrificed to make cartridge cases (pp. 33, 279). Only today are efforts being made to preserve the surviving church manuscripts and frescoes, but the visitor detects even among educated Cretans the lingering feeling that literature and art are somehow unmanly. Certainly Kazantzakis himself never quite overcame this attitude.

Only the folk culture has been able to thrive continuously in this atmosphere. The persistence of a vital folk literature—Pátasmos, the old lyre player, is respected like some great *pallikári* (p. 190)—and of a large body of superstitious lore—the usurer Harílaos is feared "as though he were not a human being, but something between human and demon" (p. 108)—also connect Mihális' Crete to the extant culture of the island. The most basic continuity, however, one which goes back at least to Homer's *Odyssey*, is the custom of hospitality which governs the social life of all Cretans; in the poorest home, the guest is honored above all men and his welcome placed above all considerations, even above mourning. A recent visitor to the White Mountains of Sphakiá records the death song of a young man wounded in battle, "perhaps by the Turks," perhaps by the Germans:

> Mother, should my friends come, should my brothers come,
> Do not tell them I am dead, for they will weep.
> But spread the table, give them food and wine.
> Spread the table, let my brothers sing,
> And in the morning, when the sun comes up,
> Tell them I died.[5]

In *Freedom or Death*, one of Mihális' followers sleeps at the home of his godfather and discovers only the next day that the family is in mourning for a dead son (p. 294); during the resistance, George Psihoundhákis tells us, he too slept unknowingly in a house of mourning, in the bedroom of the dead son of his godfather. If art and life appear to imitate one another in Crete—if past and present, fiction and fact, seem virtually interchangable—it is merely a reflection of the continuity of Cretan tradition, of a living heritage which itself seems almost a work of art.

Kazantzakis' account almost inevitably seems exaggerated to Western readers: even its admirers are uneasy before its "excessive richness of incident and personnel,"[6] while its critics complain of the "overwhelming intensity" of the narrative, because "in Kazantzakis' fiction, everything is larger than life-size . . . inflated and unreal." The

Crete of *Freedom or Death*, however, is no "quasi-mythological world,"[7] but a real one; a creation not of the artist's imagination alone but of ancestral memories and everyday life, a modern successor to the folk tradition in which Kazantzakis was raised. His accomplishment is to make of this heritage not hyperbole or mere local color, but a narrative as consistent as the life itself, to draw from it the metaphor that distinguishes his art from that of all his Modernist contemporaries.

III

On a deeper level, the mythos of *Freedom or Death* reflects also Kazantzakis' sophisticated, Westernized view of the interrelationship among man, God, and nature, a view that retains still the primitive force and immediacy of Cretan life. This is apparent both in the basic image patterns of the work and in its philosophical premises. In its simplest form, animal imagery is associated with all the characters, especially with Mihális, the naturalistic protagonist, who is described variously as a wild boar, a dragon, a lion, a bull, and a minotaur, the descendant of "hairy ancestors out of the caves of Psilorítis" (p. 94). Various women emit a scent like animals in heat, and the men react to it as stallions surrounding a mare—the Circassian Eminé moved half-naked to her window and "ardently stretched out her arms toward the Greek quarter. She saw in the dark the eyebrows, beard and strong hands of Captain Mihális, and whinnied like a mare" (p. 44). It is Nuri Bey's mare, coquetting with Captain Mihális in a kind of love play, that lures the Greek to the home of his Turkish friend, where he first sees the woman (p. 10). When Nuri dies, emasculated by the knife of Mihális' brother Manóusakas—Eminé now calls him a mule (p. 204)—he asks only that the mare be killed over his grave, but the surviving Turks are unable to slaughter the beautiful animal. Later, Mihális, distracted from his duty to Crete by the persistent vision of the Circassian woman, cuts her throat while she sleeps, thus fulfilling symbolically his blood brother's final desire. As an old Turkish landlord advises the Pasha, " 'This Crete is a great savage beast. Let's not wake it up—it devours men!' " (p. 142).

All of nature, in fact, is anthropomorphic: the first spring air came to Crete in the night, "leaped over the fortress walls and, through the chinks of doors and windows, fell upon the women like a man and upon the men like a woman, allowing them no sleep. Malignant April came to Crete like a thief in the night" (p. 40). Man, too, is a force of nature—Mihális, "like an earthquake" (p. 114), a "hard, knotty bough on the tree" (p. 421); old Sífakas, his father, "like a great oak tree" which has "breathed storms, suffered, triumphed, struggled, labored for a hundred years" and is still thirsty (p. 323); and Kosmás, in the rain, "like a rock, a Cretan rock. To the marrow of his spine he felt the joy of the rocks and the earth as they drank their fill" (p. 404). The very island itself seems to Mihális to be "a living, warm creature with a speaking mouth and weeping eyes; a Crete that consisted not of rocks and clods and roots, but of thousands of forefathers who never died and who gathered, every Sunday, in the churches," bearing the banner on which "the undying Mother, bowed over it for years, had embroidered with their black and gray and snow-white hair the three undying words: FREEDOM OR DEATH" (p. 224).

The relationship of the Cretans with their God—a God of nature—is similarly anthropomorphic, suggesting the dealings between the Children of Israel and the God of the Torah. The nature and animal images are thus more than mere naturalistic description, more even than a kind of Homeric simile; they become a part of the religious symbolism of the novel, offering a view not of man degraded by his naturalistic surroundings, but of man rising above them, ascending perhaps because of them, because there is no hope in the natural order of things.

Like the representative hero of naturalistic fiction, Captain Mihális ends up not only dead, but dead in the gutter—shot through the mouth and head, his brains splattering the stones—and his fate seems as preordained as that of Hurstwood or McTeague. " 'Don't you know,' " says the Pasha, " 'that a true Mussulman is never disturbed? For he knows that everything that happens in the world has already been written, and no one can strike it out' " (p. 156). He adds, responding to a choice offered him by the Metropolitan, " 'No, not as I will, but as it is written by God!' " (p. 157). But Kosmás rejects this Turkish view: " 'There's no such thing as fate,' " he cries. It was he who " 'grasped [his wife] by the hand that evening, nobody else' " (p. 358). His uncle seems to agree, for he fights on in the mountains so that the oppressor cannot claim that Crete had "gone back under the yoke of her own free will" (p. 425). In the conflict between Turkish fatalism and Cretan free will, between a naturalistic and a heroic view of man, it is the latter that somehow wins out, so that man is ennobled by his apparent defeat and not degraded. This surprising victory, built on naturalistic foundations, arises out of the union within the narrative of the all-pervasive religious metaphor with the Marxist view of the nature of man, the Freudian interpretation of dreams, and the Jungian collective unconscious: a modern, highly sophisticated, highly personal, Cretan form of a primitive Christianity.

IV

"There are peoples and individuals who call to God with prayers and tears or a disciplined, reasonable self-control—or even curse Him. The Cretans called to Him with guns. They stood before God's door and fired rifle shots to make Him hear" (pp. 58–59). The Metropolitan believes that he has failed in his religious duties because he has not been a good patriot: how many of his predecessors, he asks, "'will take their places before the Incorruptible Judge, bearing in their hands the gear of martyrdom—knives, axes, whips and stakes. And I shall stand there with empty hands. O God, grant me to die for Thy honor and for the honor of Thy poor daughter [Crete]'" (p. 147). Mihális calls out to God in anger over the state of his people (p. 134); old Sífakas complains to God about the mortality of great heroes who should have been made immortal (pp. 325–26); Bertodhóulos, the guitar teacher from the mainland, speaks of "'the great Maestro, whom the unmusical call God'" (p. 119); and Efendina, the saintly Turkish madman, carries about in his brain the flames of God, "with their heat, thirst, dirt and God-filled delirium" (p. 89). It is Efendina who saves his Christian neighbors during the massacre by evoking a vision of Saint Minás on horseback, the patron saint and protector of the city riding out to save his children (pp. 261–62). God is thus no distant abstraction to the people of Crete; He is immediate, a force to be encountered in the daily life of each man. He speaks through the voice of the Prophet to Efendina and through dreams to his neighbors; He appears to them as the Old Testament deity appeared to Abraham and to Moses, both concretely and as a symbol. And He is joined by His New Testament counterpart; for Christ, crucified and yet to be resurrected, is the perfect symbol of martyred Crete.

At the Mass honoring Saint Minás, the Metropolitan preaches of the oncoming Easter season: "'My children,' the old man said, 'now comes a great time of fasting, the sufferings of Christ are approaching; fear must dominate Man, and he ought to direct his thoughts only to the blood which was shed upon the Cross. And yet, God forgive me! I speak of the sufferings of Christ, and I am thinking of Crete'" (p. 97). In his drawer, wrapped in white linen, the priest keeps a painting of the Crucifixion, which he shows to a visitor. "'But,' said old Mavroudhís, 'that's not Christ on the cross. I am a sinner, my God, it's a woman, wearing cartridges and silver pistols.' 'It is Crete, it is Crete,' said the Metropolitan in a voice stifled by emotion. . . . 'Crete is nailed to the cross in the form of a tortured mother in black, whose blood runs down on the remains of her children'" (p. 150). Martyred like Christ, some day to be resurrected like

Him, Crete lives through the years in a kind of perpetual Passion Week: "In the whole of Christendom there was no people that shared so deeply, so bloodily, in so special a way, in the sufferings of Christ as the Cretans during these decades. In their hearts Christ and Crete were mingled, the sufferings of both were the same: the Jews crucified Christ and the Turks Crete. . . . The Jews [of Meghálo Kástro] always bolted themselves in early during the sacred and dangerous time of Passion Week" (p. 162). The central events of *Freedom or Death* take place in springtime, before Lent or at Easter: in the first scene of the novel, Mihális reads a letter and decides, "He won't come . . . this Easter either" (p. 3); the letter is from Kosmás, who for the first time is connected with Christ, the image of Cretan freedom. Later, Mr. Idoménéas, who writes frequent letters to European monarchs imploring aid for his fallen nation, envisions the arrival of a savior in a Crete free of Turks: " 'Suddenly Saint Minás' Easter bells will start ringing loudly, and the Christians will run madly into the streets strewed with myrtle and laurel. Men and women will stream to the harbor, to greet the Greek king's son. As he steps from the ship, they will kiss one another and shout: "Crete is risen! Really risen again!" ' " (p. 211). Prince George of Greece received just such a welcome when he arrived in Crete, in 1898, to become high commissioner.

There is even a sense in which Crete need not wait for freedom in order to be reborn, in which she is resurrected anew with each new generation. Looking at the grandsons gathered around him, Sífakas, a patriarch out of the Old Testament, smiles. "Everything's in order, he thought, I have confidence. The old go under the earth and come again out of the earth. Made new. Crete is immortal" (p. 278). Later, just before his own death, he sends an order to the pregnant wife of his eldest grandson: "Call him Sífakas, d'you hear? That's how the dead rise again!' " (p. 387). But there will be no easy rebirth for him, for Noëmi miscarries—seemingly struck in the stomach by the specter of her husband's dead father—at almost the same instant that Kosmás himself is killed, his severed head thrown at the face of Mihális, who raises it like a banner and rushes to his own death (p. 433). The symbolic union that might have come about through their son—the grandchild of a Russian rabbi and of the hero of Arkádhi—is aborted; in this fertility cycle, death is as prevalent as life. And so the body of Sífakas is carried around the village, and at each crossroads "the girls threw basil and marjoram onto the corpse, as if it were a picture of the Crucified One" (p. 401). And Mihális calls out to his remaining men before the final Turkish attack, " 'We who are dying are doing better than they who will live. For Crete doesn't need householders, she needs madmen like us. Such madmen make Crete immortal'" (p. 428). Most mad of all is Kosmás, whose death accomplishes no practical end but whose continued life would have served Noëmi, his wife, his unborn son and Crete, his homeland. But perhaps his death is not so surprising, for he is much more than a Westernized Cretan: his coming after so many years has been an "annunciation" of his grandfather's death (p. 364); he is a Christ figure who must die in the autumn so that Crete can be reborn in the spring.

This rebirth, of course, will be in large part political, and it will presumably reflect in some way the Marxist view of the regeneration of man through revolution. For Kosmás, like Kazantzakis, is a follower of Bergson and Nietzsche, a Marxist sympathizer who has been educated in Germany and has traveled through Russia. The Metropolitan has faith in the continued Orthodoxy of the Russian Church and its people; Kosmás, however, believes in "a new godhead, a cruel, great-power one," that is, in science and the revolution of the masses (p. 357). But the Cretan revolution in truth has few social or economic roots, or even—except in the broadest sense of the word—political ones. Its concept of freedom is in no way theoretical, but a vital force to be experienced sensuously, one of the essential forces of life. And so, when Kosmás dies alongside his uncle, it is not because of any dialectical belief; his death is an inevitable and necessary act of his life. Marxism for him is not a cause of Cretan revolution, but a manifestation of it; he has found in this seemingly alien theology not an excuse for dreaming of freedom, but an intellectualized, Western version of this ancient Cretan dream. As Kazantzakis wrote Victor Serge, "I am not a Marxist... because... I cannot content myself with hypersimplified affirmations and negations [and]... because I am not a man of action. If I were..., Marxism would be very suitable for me and for our own time, a most rigorous and seminal rule of action. The only one."[8] When he accepted the International Peace Prize for 1956, "it was finally only in the name of Crete.... She alone... having won peace so dearly, deserves a reward like this."[9]

The residents of Meghálo Kástro dream not only symbolically of freedom but also literally of the daily events of their lives: the tavern keeper Vendúsos dreams of the Virgin as a wine goddess (p. 84); Efendina, sanctified by his pilgrimage to Mecca, dreams of sinning on pork and wine (p. 44); young Thrasákis, son of the fiercest hero on the island, dreams of violence (p. 35); the Pasha, frustrated by Mihális' fearlessness, dreams of combat between him and Suleiman the Arab, the Turkish champion (p. 113); and Mihális dreams of Crete's freedom and of Eminé (p. 83). When the Pasha awakes from a nightmare of an olive tree bearing "guns and cartridges and daggers and black headbands" instead of fruit (p. 154), the Metropolitan—like Joseph before Pharoah—interprets politically: "'The olive tree hung with weapons that you saw is Crete. You stood under the lightning-scorched tree, and your face darkened. Here your destiny begins to be troubled. . . . It is in your power to bring love to the island. God sent you the dream at the right moment!'" (pp. 156–57).

But not all dreams are such welcome visitors. To Mihális, sleep is "a Turkish creature, a mad one" (p. 41), and dream a "demon" (p. 120) intent on "dishonoring" him (p. 159). He fights against the demonic intruder and warns his brother Manoúsakas, recently killed by Nuri Bey, not to bedevil him: "'Don't come into my sleep to accuse me and make me wild. I know my duty. Have no anxiety'" (p. 196). But the dead man's image does appear at night to his son Thodorés, to reproach the youth for not seeking vengeance (pp. 213–14). It was a similar reproach from his dead father that had led Nuri to lie in wait for Manoúsakas: "His father now visited him in his sleep regularly. He did not speak and no longer even remained standing over him. He did not turn to look at him, but went past him with bare feet and long, dragging steps, in his rags. He went and yet was never out of sight; all night he was there with averted face, inexorably present" (p. 175). On the night after Nuri has decided on his revenge, "he fell into sweet, unbroken sleep. That night his father did not visit him" (p. 176).

But it is Kosmás, absent from his homeland for so many years, who is most haunted by the image of his long-dead father. As his ship reaches the harbor of Meghálo Kástro, he feels "that his father had struck roots within him that would not be destroyed. Abroad, he had often thought of him, and a trembling would come over him at these times. But never had he felt the dead man so near as at this moment—or so menacing" (p. 352). He walks through the narrow streets to his home "as in a dream" (p. 352), and that night, the first in many years in his parental home, he comes downstairs to sit in his father's place: "He wanted to challenge the dead man, to drive him from the house and courtyard to which he clung, and to bolt the door behind him so that he might never come back and harm his wife. Ancient dreads had awakened in him. It was in vain that in the land of the Franks he had tried to free his mind from them. His heart was still a dark cave full of specters" (p. 362). He hears the tread of the dead man climbing the stairs and stopping before Noëmi's door at the same moment that she wakes from a nightmare (p. 363). For it is she who will have to live alone in this alien room, she who will hesitate to shut her eyes for fear that she might dream, but who will nonetheless be found lying on the floor in a pool of blood, her child stillborn. "Did sleep overcome her?" Did she dream? "She did not know" (p. 420).

There is a dreamlike quality to much of this harshly realistic land-scape, and there is a sensitive core within each Cretan that responds profoundly to each dream. It may not be the footsteps of his dead father that Kosmás hears, or his blow that Noëmi suffers, but some force within each of them makes the dead man seem very much alive. It may be an Oedipal impulse that is reawakened in Kosmás by his return to his father's home, or a memory of the pogrom in which her father died that recurs to Noëmi—or simply a crude objectification of a profound psychological force—but this all is irrelevant. For it is of Crete that these characters dream ultimately, and not of themselves, and this dream is really the same for them all, the source of the dream imagery of the *Spiritual Exercises,* the dream of all Cretans through the centuries: Freedom or Death.

V

The persistence of their ancient customs into modern times, the long history of their suffering land that is part of each Cretan, the sameness of their dreams—all these suggest a continuity of Cretan experience that, in turn, is suggestive of Jung's concept of the collective unconscious. It is not only that this experience has become archetypal; the same ancient specters that fill "the dark cave" of Kosmás' heart are active within his uncle: "These demons were savage voices; most of them were not human voices, but bestial ones, bellowing inside him as soon as the portcullises below opened, letting ancient images spring forth: a tiger, a wolf, a wild boar, and after them the hairy ancestors out of the caves of Psiloritis" (p. 94). Mihális—"Captain Wildboar" to those who fear him—a figure out of the pre-human past of his people, is a creation both of his father and of his father's father—Mad-Mihális, who continually watched the coast for the Muscovite fleet and who carried on his shoulder the bow and arrows of his own grandfather (p. 5). Kosmás, too, despite his European culture and sophistication, is a creature of his father, of the *pallikári* who blew up the monastery of Arkádhi to save it and its defenders from the besieging Turks. He has gone to Mihális' camp to convince his uncle to withdraw, "but Kosmás did not rise. Smeared with powder and blood, he was listening now to his heart, which had gone wild. In his breast his father, the terrible leader in battle, had awakened, and his grandfather, and Crete. This was not his first battle: for a thousand years he had been fighting, a thousand times he had been killed and had risen again" (p. 430).

If all of this seems to suggest a lack of free will, if the continuity of Cretan history into the present seems to deprive the living of the power not to rebel—if the memory of Dhaskaloyánnis and Arkádhi, of the revolts of 1821 and 1866, of generations of martyrs, is as ever-present as the plane tree on the square and the Kule prison—the suggestion is misleading. For Mihális and Kosmás do choose their fates. Just as Sífakas learns the alphabet so that he can write before he dies—and virtually to die as he writes—the ages-old motto of Crete, so his son and grandson write their own slogans. " 'Freedom or death,' [Mihális] muttered, shaking his head fiercely. 'Freedom or death! O poor Cretans! "Freedom *and* death"—that's what I should have written on my banner. That's the true banner of every fighter: Freedom *and* death! Freedom *and* death!' " (p. 426). So he and Kosmás die, not as Nuri does or the Pasha will, because of external forces that control their fates, but as free men, the wielders of their own destinies.

In the end, it is this belief that characterizes the experience of Crete, this insight that most distinguishes Kazantzakis' life and art: in an age whose fictional characters become heroes only in spite of their insignificance—as Joyce's Leopold Bloom does—or because they acknowledge their insignificance in an insane world—as Kafka's K. does, as Mann's Hans Castorp does—his characters are heroic because they refuse to accept the fact of their insignificance: the Western sources are at last overwhelmed by the Cretan. This may seem hyperbolic to a Westerner—Kazantzakis himself "had judged his own art severely and had mistrusted his liking for color and ornamentation"[10] —but it does conform to the realities of Cretan life. Perhaps the history of their martyred nation should have taught them otherwise, but Kazantzakis' Cretans attest to the ultimate nobility of the man who will not be defeated by his surroundings, who will not be ruled by history or fate or even by God. Their lesson, the artist tells us, is universal in its import. Captain Katsirmás, an ancient pirate, has come at his friend's call to be at the deathbed of Sífakas, who asks what he has learned in his long life. " 'I've made voyages,' " he responds. " 'I've seen the whole world. I've slept with women of all kinds, I've pushed far down into Africa, where the bread is toasted by the sun. I've been in great harbors and little ones, I've seen millions of black men, millions of yellow men—my eyes have brimmed over with them! At first I thought they all stank. I said: "Only Cretans smell good; and of the Cretans only the Christians." But slowly, slowly, I got used to their stink. I found—I found that we all smell good and stink in the same way. Curse us all!' " (p. 395).

In the preface to the first Greek edition of *Freedom or Death*, in 1956, Kazantzakis wrote of the Cypriote rebellion against British rule: "Cyprus is not a detail, a simple island at the end of the Mediterranean Sea; today it has been transformed into the destined center where the moral values of contemporary man are at stake."[11] In an earlier day, Crete was the "destined center" of man's moral conflict. In *Freedom or Death*, as in all Kazantzakis' fiction, Crete serves as a metaphor for those human values that somehow survive the trials of history, that must survive if man is to survive. The Cretan experience—the Cretan Glance—is unique, and yet, Kazantzakis contends, it is the experience of all men in the modern world; it is precisely because his vision is so unique that Kazantzakis at his best is so representative: he endeavors to speak not just for Crete, but for mankind.

1. *Report to Greco*, p. 87.
2. Letter to Börje Knös, Antibes, December 12, 1949, cited in Helen Kazantzakis, p. 485.
3. Prevelakis, p. 150. Helen Kazantzakis never met her husband's father, but she is sure that he could not have been such a beast as Captain Mihális. She points for proof to an old picture of Kazantzakis' sister—no Renió at all, but a well-dressed, beautiful, happy girl—and asks if she could be the daughter of a beast. In an interview with this author in Geneva, July 28 and 30, 1971.
4. All page references are to the Simon and Schuster edition (New York, 1955), trans. Jonathan Griffin.
5. Michael Llewellyn Smith, *The Great Island: A Study of Crete* (London, 1965), p. 5.
6. Brendan Connolly, *"Freedom or Death," America*, 94 (March 31, 1956), p. 722.
7. C. J. Rolo, "Cretans and Turks," *Atlantic*, 197 (March, 1956), pp. 88–89.
8. Gottesgab, August 10, 1929, cited in Helen Kazantzakis, pp. 222–23.
9. Cited in Helen Kazantzakis, p. 544.
10. Prevelakis, p. 123. The apparent hyperbole of the phrase "freedom or death," for example, is not that of the author but is derived from his subject: as recently as 1972, under the dictatorship of the colonels, a Western traveler to Crete reported finding this ancient cry painted anew on the mountains of the interior. Alan Linn, "Wild, Lovable Crete," *Reader's Digest* (October, 1972), p. 134.
11. Cited in Theo Stavrou, "Letter from Cyprus," *The Charioteer*, 7 and 8 (1965), p. 188.

CHAPTER THREE

THE GREEK PASSION
Persecution and Politics in Asia Minor

Early in 1919, in a daring attempt to reconquer the captured lands of Asia Minor, the armies of Greece marched into Anatolia, which the Allies had promised to the Venizélos government for its aid in the war against Turkey. (Venizelos had sought originally to annex Thrace, which also had a large Greek population and which adjoined mainland Greece; but this province had already been promised to Bulgaria.) The invasion, initially, was highly successful, extending more than sixteen hundred miles into Turkey—a front longer even than that in Napoleon's Russian campaign—and Smyrna was ceded to Greece by the Treaty of Sèvres in 1920. Everywhere they passed, the Greek armies were greeted as deliverers: the Greeks of Asia Minor had for centuries thought of the Turkish occupation as temporary, had long expected to regain the holy city of Constantinople. In the general election of 1920, however, Venizelos was defeated, and King Constantine was recalled in the controversial plebiscite which followed. The Allies seized the opportunity to withdraw their support, which, after all, had been granted to the pro-Western premier and not to the neutralist monarch. The great powers seem to have acted here with the same cynicism and self-interest as in the Cretan crisis of a generation earlier. By 1922 the revitalized Turks under Kemal Ataturk had driven the invaders from the land; the Greek populations that remained behind suffered terrible retribution. Smyrna—now called Izmir—was again ceded to the Turks by the Treaty of Lausanne in 1923, and a massive exchange of populations was concluded. It was at this time that the Muslims of Crete were exiled from their homeland, to be replaced by Greeks whose Anatolian ancestry predated the Ottoman Empire by many centuries.

In May 1919, Venizélos appointed Kazantzakis, his fellow Cretan, as director general of the Ministry of Public Welfare; it was his task to rescue the Greek minorities of the Caucasus and Transcaucasus from persecution by Bolsheviks and Kurds alike. "It was the first time in my life I had been presented with the opportunity to engage in action, to wrestle with living, flesh-and-blood men instead of having to struggle any longer with theories, ideas, Christs, and Buddhas. I was delighted.... The moment was ripe to test whether action, by slicing its sword through the insoluble knots of speculation, was alone capable of giving an answer."[1] During the course of a year, from Georgia and Armenia—from Batoum, Sukhumi, Tiflis, Kars, and Taigan—he helped save more than one hundred thousand people. Their resettlement on the mainland, however, was less successful, and Kazantzakis resigned his ministry when Venizélos fell; he rarely referred to this period in later life.

This is the milieu of *The Greek Passion:* the personal experience of the writer, his first call to action, provides background and setting for the fiction. The Bolsheviks and Kurds who persecuted the Caucasus Greeks become the Turks of Asia Minor; the suffering Greeks remain unchanged. The place is somewhere in Anatolia, near the Greek village of Lycovríssi, and the time is 1920 or 1921. Life is good, the soil fertile, the passage of events seemingly timeless. But there are signs of contemporaneity: the saddler Panayótaros, "the Plaster-eater," has gained his nickname by eating plaster busts of Venizelos and Ataturk (p. 2);[2] and the people of a neighboring village ask the tradesman Yannakós, their one contact with the great world outside, " 'do you know anything about the Greek troops that came and then vanished again like a flash of lightning? What's happening over there in Greek territory...? What massacres, what burnings and what disasters?' " (p. 114). Their answer is brought by the refugees from the village of Saint George, somewhere to the west: " 'One day voices were heard on the roofs of our village, crying: "The Greek Army! The Greek Army! We can see the kilts upon the hilltops!" I at once gave the order: "Ring the Easter peal! Let the people assemble.... The Greeks are coming, earth and heaven are uniting; men and women, take up arms, and chase the Turks to the gates of Hell!" ... The Hellene battalions were decimated and beat a retreat; we remained. We remained and the Turks returned. The Turks returned: that word says all' " (pp. 36–38). The old, regular pattern of life in Lycovríssi alters with their arrival, takes on a form still more ancient: in *The Greek Passion,* the Cretan experience, the metaphor of man struggling against history to renew himself, is relived on the mainland of Asia.

II

It is Easter Tuesday, after Mass: the Agha of Lycovríssi sits on his balcony celebrating the sensual joys of life, and the village elders gather to select the cast for next year's Passion Play. Archon Patriarhéas, miserly Father Ladhás, Captain Fortoúnas, and Hadji Nikolís, the schoolmaster, hear Priest Grighóris explain the symbolism of the drama: " 'The words become flesh, we see with our eyes, we touch the Passion of Christ. From all the villages around, the pilgrims come flocking; they pitch their tents around the church, groan and smite their breasts all through Holy Week. . . . Many miracles take place during those days . . . ; many sinners shed tears and repent' " (pp. 10–11). Some of their choices are simple: for Mary Magdalene, the widow Katerína, " 'a fine whore with golden hair' "; for Judas, Panayótaros, " 'sturdy, spotted with the smallpox, a real gorilla . .; and what's even more important, he's got the beard and hair for the part: red as the Devil's in person' "; for the Apostles, the innkeeper Kostandís—" 'He's thin, fierce-looking, crabbed, and that's how they represent the Apostle James' "; Yannokós, the traveling merchant—" 'A passable Peter. . .: narrow forehead, gray curly hair, a short chin. He loses his temper and calms down, flares up and goes out as easily as a tinder; but he's a good heart' "; and Mihelís, the archon's son, for John—" 'He has everything required: well-fleshed, black hair, almond eyes, and of good family, just as the well-beloved disciple was' " (pp. 11–13). His father has urged Mihelís for the role of Christ, but he is rejected because he does not look the part: he is too fat, too soft, too dark. For the elders choose their actors according to physical likenesses; the Passion Play for them is purely symbolic, so that the characters seem almost to grow out of traditional icons.

For Christ, they choose the shepherd Manoliós. " 'He is as mild as a lamb, . . . has blue eyes and a short beard as yellow as honey, a real Christ like an icon. And pious into the bargain' " (p. 12). But the young man protests his unworthiness—he is about to be married, is too tied to his senses to be Christ; Grighóris silences him: " 'You have drawn the winning number, Manoliós,' said the priest in solemn tones. 'You are the one whom God has chosen to revive by your gestures, your voice, your tears, the Holy Passion. . . . It is you who will put on the crown of thorns, it is you who will be scourged, it is you who will carry the holy cross, you who will be crucified. From today till Holy Week next year you must think of only one thing, Manoliós, one thing only: how can I become worthy to bear the terrible weight of the cross' " (p. 19). The priest, of course, is speaking metaphorically; Manoliós is not to become Christ, or even Christlike;

he is merely to play at Christ. The Passion Play, to the elders, is a sign of the continuity of tradition, an affirmation before the Turks of their essential identity, a warning to their own people of the sanctity of the social institutions under which they live; the drama for them is a device for conservation. But for Manoliós, their chosen Christ, it is revolutionary; the role for him is real, not symbolic, his sacrifice a matter of life, not of play. "'Aren't you ashamed, Manoliós,' I said to myself, 'you think it's play, the Crucifixion? Do you imagine you're going to take in God and men like that? You love Lenió, you want to sleep with her, and you'd like me to believe that you're Christ? Shame on you, impostor! Make up your mind, hypocrite!' From that moment I resolved: 'I won't marry! I won't touch a woman! I'll remain chaste'" (p. 165). His first gesture in his new role is to reject the sensuality of life in Lycovríssi.

Not only the Agha but the Greeks of Lycovríssi as well lead lives devoted to the senses. Patriarhéas recalls with pleasure the women and banquets of his youth and attempts almost desperately to relive them in old age; Grighóris drinks his favorite wine, fondles his huge paunch, and praises the justice and mercy of God; even miserly old Ladhás—who denies himself food, clothes, and pleasures—acquires new property with sensuous glee. Captain Fortoúnas alone is honest in his self-indulgence. The old sailor and patriot—he had volunteered to smuggle arms into Greece during the war of 1897—derides the hypocrisy of his peers and openly acknowledges his own joy in his senses. Lying on his deathbed, he thinks back over his life. "A thick fog was falling on this world below; from all his life one event alone emerged, bathed in light, through this opaque mist:" in Batoum, in April, many years before, he had sat with three friends in a garden in a fine rain. "How delightful it had been, how gentle! Life had chirruped in the palm of man like a little, warm bird. . . . Captain Fortoúnas racked his brain, but could remember nothing else. . . . That pleasure party and the light rain of Batoum had survived alone" (p. 135). We admire Fortoúnas for his forthrightness, but his life shows indisputably that the joys of the body do not survive. Some time later, on hearing of the sudden death of the archon, the Agha comments, sniffing his coffee, "'He was a fine man, . . . the kind that goes to Paradise: he liked good living, knew how to revel and wench. Pity he wasn't a Moslem, he'd have gone straight to our Paradise where pilaff, boys and women abound. That's where you should have had your place, my poor Patriarhéas; now it's too late!'" (p. 304). But this is a Turkish Paradise, not a Christian one, and even the Agha does not believe in it fully: "'suppose both our religions were fooling us?'" he asks Fortoúnas. "'This world's a dream, life is raki, one drinks and one gets drunk... to tell you the truth, it worries me!'" (p. 136). His boy Youssoufákis sings to the dying captain their favorite *amané*, "'*Dounia tabir, rouya tabir...* World and dream are but one, *aman, aman!*' Never had the captain felt so deeply how world and dream are but one. He must surely have fallen asleep and dreamed that he was a captain and had plied between the ports of the White Sea and the Black Sea, that he had gone to war, that he was Greek and Christian and that now, so it appeared, he was passing away. But no, he wasn't dying, he was waking up, the dream was over, day was breaking" (p. 137).

Manoliós, above all, recognizes the seeming impermanence of sensual experience and the supremacy of spirit over body. But the flesh makes demands even on him. He has easily given up Lenió, his fiancée, but he remains obsessed by the widow Katerína, the town whore; pursued everywhere by Panayótaros, she herself pursues Manoliós. He has decided at last to leave his sheepfold in the night and go down to her in the village. As he imagines her impassioned welcome, "a cold sweat flowed over his whole body; he passed his hand over his face... and gave a cry: it was all bloated, his eyes were no more than two tiny balls, his nose was lost between his ballooning cheeks, his mouth was a mere hole. This was no human face, but a mask of bestial flesh, repulsive. No, it was no longer his face; a foreign face fixed itself over his own" (pp. 105-6). His tragic mask saves Manoliós from his lesser, physical self and enables him to fulfill his spiritual role. He reveals himself to the widow, calls her "sister" and redeems her as well—"delivers" her, as she puts it (p. 150)—turns her from whore to Magdalene. In this new cycle of events, she will give her life to save his, and her loss will turn Panayótaros unalterably against him. The mask itself disappears as Manoliós goes again to the village, this time to offer himself as a sacrifice for the people.

There is something melodramatic about all this, some kind of miraculous circumstance that seems at first to deny the essential reality of the novel and to cheapen its metaphor. Yet it is based upon fact: Kazantzakis himself had worn this mask, many years before the novel was written, as a young man in Vienna. He had made an assignation with a girl he had met casually in a movie theater.

> And then something incredible happened, something which makes me shudder even now when I recall it. Man's soul is truly indestructible, truly august and noble, but pressed to its bosom it carries a body which grows daily more putrescent. While on my way back home, I heard the blood mounting to my head. My soul had become enraged. Sensing that my body was about to fall into sin, it had bounded to its feet, full of scorn and anger, and refused to grant permission. The blood continued to flow upward and mass in my face, until little by little I became aware that my lips, cheeks, and forehead were swelling.... An appalling mask of flesh was glued to my face; ... I was not a man, I was a demon.[3]

This was no simple case of eczema; he had developed the symptoms of leprosy, which had so appalled and frightened him as a child.

Recognizing that the cause was more than physical, Kazantzakis consulted Dr. Wilhelm Stekel, the noted disciple of Freud. His disease, Stekel announced, "is called the ascetics' disease. It is extremely rare in our times, because what body, today, obeys its soul?"[4] It would persist until he left Vienna and the temptations that threatened him. Even then, however, he understood the positive significance of his disease. "Ever since that day I have realized that man's soul is a terrible and dangerous coil spring. Without knowing it, we carry a great explosive force wrapped in our flesh and lard. And what is worse, we do not want to know it, for then villainy, cowardice, and falsehood lose their justification..., [then] we ourselves must bear the blame.... How terrible not to know that we possess this force! If we did know, we would be proud of our souls. In all heaven and earth, nothing so closely resembles God as the soul of man."[5] In the Kazantzakian universe, even the mask of a leper is a sign of God's presence within man. It seems as well the ultimate sign of the victory of soul over body.

Yet the primacy of man's spirit does not entirely negate the body. Kazantzakis personifies the soul in his autobiographical account not merely for literary effect but because body and soul are truly entwined, because all human life is a kind of duality, a product of the tensions coiled within man and ready to spring. Saint and sinner, Virgin and widow, Greek and Turk, life in this world and in heaven, the road of man and that of God—these are only a few of the dualities that help to structure the novel and to form its characters. "What a miracle this world is!" Manoliós thinks. "If I open my eyes I see the mountains, the clouds and the rain falling; if I close my eyes, I see God, Who created the mountains, the clouds and the falling rain" (p. 281). The village of Saint George had once been prosperous, the village, like Lycovríssi, divided into landowners and workers, the rich and the poor. Now, each one starving alike, they can see at last with an inward eye. "'The soul has been freed from full bellies,'" their leader, Priest Fótis, tells them; "'it can fly now'" (p. 155). Driven from the village by the elders, they settle on the mountain above Lycovríssi. There, on the Sarakína, Manoliós learns at last about his dual nature and makes his final choice. Alone on the mountain with his demon mask, he has carved out of boxwood the mask of Christ that he planned to wear in the Passion: "Serene, suffering, full of resignation and kindness" (p. 109). That Christmas, as he leads the refugees in rebellion, he carries instead another mask, Christ the warrior, with a gaping wound painted red from temple to chin. As Priest Fótis tells his flock, "'Christ is not only a sheep, He is also a lion. And it is as a lion that He will come with us today' " (p. 392). It is as a lion then that the shepherd goes to his final sacrifice. He has come a long way during his nine months as Christ-elect: he has come to reject all the traditions—social and religious alike—that the elders chose him to represent, to react against their sensuality, and to glorify his own soul. Yet he instinctively reaffirms this life as he goes to his death; as he walks down the mountain he sees with joy the beauty of the natural world, the foreshadowing of spring in the now barren land (pp. 417–18).

III

From the beginning, even before he is cast as Christ, Manoliós has a feeling for martyrdom. When he is named for the role, "his throat was tight, he could not speak. The thing to which he had aspired from his tenderest childhood . . . behold, now God was granting it to him" (p. 24). He steps into the part with ease, naturally: he gives up Lenió willingly, almost joyfully; he is pleased to think even of his disease as a sign of divine concern; he visualizes scenes from the life of Jesus, with himself present as a disciple. From a lowly shepherd, he becomes God's chosen. When the Agha imprisons the elders as revenge for the death of his boy Youssoufákis, Manoliós exults that he can die for them, that he can take on himself the burden of their guilt. As he goes to his intended sacrifice, he sees the cornfields in the distance. "God be praised, he said to himself. We shall have a good harvest this year, the poor people will get enough to eat" (p. 217). It is as if he is the nature deity whose death will ensure the harvest. But even the Turk will not believe him: " 'Him a murderer?' " he asks himself in confusion, " 'or a madman? or rather, a saint? Devil take me, I can't make it out!' " (p. 202). The confession has unexpected, ironic results: it saves Panayótaros, who rages at life and wants to die; it leads the life-loving widow to offer herself as a sacrifice; it fails even to save the village. (It is hunchbacked Martha, the Agha's slave, who discovers the true culprit and eases her master's wrath.) His "resurrection" is almost a parody of the original: " 'Christ is risen!' " his friends cry as he returns. "Manoliós said nothing, did not smile. Yes, certainly, he was glad to be still alive, to be eating and drinking with his friends, to feel the evening breeze pass over his sweating forehead. Yet he had expected to be elsewhere this evening, and a supraterrestrial sorrow veiled his face" (p. 225).

This early failure at martyrdom predicts his later, more serious effort: the death of the widow makes an enemy of Panayótaros, who will later betray him; the villagers' willingness to be saved by his death—"'Let him die to save us, afterward we'll make an icon to him . . . and discover that he's a saint. For the moment, let him die'" (p. 210)—prepares us for their participation in his murder; his inability to protect the village foreshadows his failure to save the people of the mountain. This second attempt, however, is in no sense parodic: his act now is equally futile, but it has meaning beyond its results. There are superficial similarities between Manoliós and Jesus—the miraculous tales that grow up around them, the cries of the people for their deaths, the physical aspect of their corpses—but he is no more a literal Christ than before. He is still too eager to play the role of the martyr, but his death now points up the problem of human existence: it may seem futile to struggle against natural order and social order alike, but man must continue to do so. It is this struggle that humanizes man, raises him above his own limitations, makes of each man a potential Christ. "'Yes, every man . . . can himself save the whole world. I've often had that thought, . . . and it makes me tremble. Have we then such a great responsibility? What must we do, then, before we die? What way must we follow?'" (p. 296). The way of Manoliós, long inherent within him, is determined by his role as savior.

The lives of those named to act with the shepherd—the Apostles, the town whore, even the Council of Elders—are similarly changed to fit their new roles. Under the influence of his father's servant, Mihelís abandons the luxurious life of a young archon and asserts his manhood—not as his father had, in sensuality, but by abandoning his fortune and following Manoliós. "'It's Christ I am choosing,'" he tells the old man as he leaves his parent's home (p. 273). At the end, with Manoliós dead and the rebels defeated, he alone is left on the Sarakína, "'that lamb of God'" turned into a hermit (p. 55). As he tells Kostandís, "'I'm all right here. . . . I don't want to see men any more, the good no more than the wicked; no one! I'll live and I'll die here!'" (p. 431). More perhaps than the others, he acts out the implications of his new role, for Saint John is the reputed author of *Revelations*, the apocalyptic book that predicts the Messiah's return. It is a visionary work, centered in Anatolia, an attack on the Dionysian cults of the region, a judgment of doom on an unjust world. Alone in his hut on the mountain, Mihelís awaits the savior foreseen by the original John.

As Peter denied Jesus, so Yannakós at first falls in with Ladhás' scheme to bilk the refugees; but he too will be forgiven, Priest Fótis assures him (p. 87). He finds himself offering honest weight to his customers and soon gives all his goods to the new community: "'I don't want any money, you'll pay me in the other world! I trust you!' " (p. 242). He is the first to leave the settled life of the village for the Sarakína; he is the incendiary who fires Ladhás' hoard, symbol of the old way of life in Lycovríssi; he departs in the end with the pilgrims. Like Saint Peter before him, he is left behind to feed the Christian sheep.

Henpecked Kostandís maintains the strongest ties of all to a settled way of life; only he among the Apostles has a business and family. In his timidity, he is appalled at the arson of Yannakós and abandons Manoliós to the Agha's judgment. " 'And what's my way, Father?' " he asks Priest Fótis as the pilgrims go on their way to the east. " 'Go back home, Kostandís . . . ; go back to your wife and children; that is your way' " (p. 431). Of those who have witnessed the transfiguration, he alone remains in the village. " 'I'm frightened,' " he says, " 'I shiver and shake, my heart beats fit to burst, but I'm ashamed. If one day I let everything drop so as to follow Christ, it won't be from goodness, or from bravery, but from self-respect. I shall tremble and be frightened, but I shan't retreat' " (p. 335). Left behind in Jerusalem, Saint James was the first of the disciples to be martyred.

Unlike the Apostles, Panayótaros recognizes from the first the meaning of his new role. " 'Don't ask me to betray Christ,' " he warns the notables. " 'I'll never do it!' " The priest assures him, " 'It isn't you, you idiot, who will be betraying Christ, you'll be *pretending* to be Judas and to betray Christ . . . ; for the world to be saved, Christ has to be crucified. . . . Judas is indispensable, more indispensable than any other Apostle. . . . He's the one that's most necessary, after Christ' " (pp. 17–18). And Mihelís adds, " 'but it's a play, a sacred play but only a play, not real. Is Manoliós Christ once and for all? Am I really John, His beloved disciple? How did you come to get an idea like that into your head? It's a real sin! It was simply that you had a red beard' " (p. 332). Panayótaros knows, however, that it is not play; he can singe off his beard, but he cannot escape; he need not pretend: he is Judas from the start. When Mihelís opens his father's storerooms to the refugees, it is the saddler who informs on him; it is Panayótaros again who sounds the alarm when the refugees descend to claim their inheritance from the new archon; in the end, he betrays Manoliós to the Agha. Cast in his demanding role, he curses rebels and elders alike, refuses to be saved by his enemy's sacrifice, and promises to kill himself once he has killed Manoliós. His only excuse for his hatred is the widow's love for the shepherd; but he has even greater motivation—the dialectic of the Passion Play itself. For he acts throughout with total consistency, fulfilling at each step the demands of the role he alone understands from the start, long before the directing elders, before the other supporting actors, even before the sacrificial lead. He acts, however, without free will, like a Turk; so he abjures his role as he seems to fulfill it. The Passion of Christ can have meaning only if each participant wills it, only if each goes to his fate by choice, as a free man. The shepherd chooses his fate freely; his betrayer is driven to his "like an ox trying to get rid of its yoke" (p. 31)—a bad man perhaps, but an excellent Judas, a perfect traditional counterpoint to Manoliós as Christ.

To Katerína, the whore, there is nothing miraculous about men becoming God. "'All men, even Panayótaros, are God for a minute. A real God, not just in words!'" (p. 72). It is only natural for her to try to seduce Manoliós. But something miraculous does happen, and, like the original Magdalene, she closes her door to the men of the town: the shepherd gives her his trust, calls her his "sister." With no greater motivation than this, she gives her life attempting unnecessarily to save his, her death foreshadowing his own: both meaningless sacrifices, both of value only to those who love this life yet wish to escape it, to themselves alone.

The notables, on the other hand, are too tied to this life to be willing to leave it even as martyrs. In the Agha's prison, frightened at the threat of execution, they fight spitefully among themselves. When they are released, Priest Grighóris crosses himself and proclaims without irony, "'We entered here as simple men, we go out as heroes and martyrs of Christ!'" (p. 222). Their true roles in the Passion are somewhat different. Originally, Patriarhéas is cast as Pilate. "'Don't frown,'" the priest instructs him, "'Pilate, too, was a great nobleman; proud in manner, well stuffed, double-chinned, well groomed, with just your bearing. A good man, too; did what he could to save Christ, and at the end even said: "I wash my hands of this." By that he escaped sin. Accept, archon, and you'll enable us to give grandeur to the Mystery'" (p. 13). With Patriarhéas' death, this honor is left to the Agha, another "good man" who, like Pilate, is moved to act only by the threat to the Empire.

Old Ladhás is cast as Caiaphas, and he is the one who calls out for Manoliós' blood. But the role is really Grighóris'. "'Deliver up to me Manoliós,'" he entreats the Agha, "'that I may judge him; the whole village implores you through my voice!'" (p. 412). Like the High Priest before him, he foregoes the political rights of his people as a whole for the immediate advantage of his own social class. "'In the name of Christ,'" he ordains, "'I take the sin upon me!'" But he seems to reconsider and calls out again, as he sprinkles the blood upon the impassioned crowd, "'May his blood fall upon the heads of us all!'" (p. 427). In this fatal ceremony, the villagers reenact not only the martyrdom of Christ, but also the annual Dionysian rite. Their act makes possible, symbolically, not only eternal salvation, but the continued cycle of the seasons as well. In the life on the plain, in the attempt to create life on the mountain, Mihelís sees the Passion of Christ, the seasonal rhythms of nature.

> Standing there, without stirring, he felt life turning on and on, never stopping. The wheel of the earth was turning. It had now reached the vintage. The turn of the olives would come; then that of the birth of Christ. The almond trees would blossom afresh, the corn would be sown again, the harvest would come around. It all went on as if Mihelís were tied to that wheel and rose and fell with it under the sun, under the rain. Tied to it with him, day and night also rose and fell. Christ new born with them, grew, became a man, went forth resolutely to spread the word of God, was crucified, rose again, came down again from Heaven the next year, was again crucified. (pp. 290–91)

IV

Life in pastoral Lycovríssi is part of the "wheel of the earth," and the new life on the mountain above the village follows closely the movement of the seasons. The refugees arrive in spring; in summer, their hopes of founding a living community flower; hardship and despair set in in autumn; and in winter they rebel. Manoliós' new life also follows the seasonal pattern: in winter he gives his life for the people that they may be reborn in the spring. But he is more than a Christ figure; there is something about him that suggests the pre-Christian fertility cults of the region. Chosen by the people and condemned by them, he crystallizes their guilt, yet absolves them of it; like a pagan fertility god, he is torn to pieces in the church of Lycovríssi, his blood anointing the celebrants. It is the day of the eve of the birth of Christ.

Throughout *The Greek Passion* form and function become one: to relate old myths, Kazantzakis develops new ones; out of problems rooted in, and unique to, his own era, he creates archetypes. Human life in the novel thus reflects and dramatizes both the ancient patterns of myth and the timeless rhythms of nature, both the life of Christ and the still older forms of pagan fertility rites. Nature, myth, and human history coalesce here in a continuous cycle, enriching and enforcing one another, so that it is impossible finally to tell them apart. In this cycle, man's life is an analogue to the life of nature; the present somehow repeats the past; and mythic truths are more immediate and compelling than apparent objective truths: the sun is personified (pp. 81, 112) and man likened to a tree (pp. 80, 156); an old man climbs into a grave with the bones of his ancestors, lies down among them and dies, himself becoming a founding father, one of the ancestral dead to be carried off by another ancient to another site; and characters out of Homer and the Hagiographa come to life in modern times and demonstrate the continuity of human experience. "'We call truth legend,'" explains Priest Fótis. "'I'm going to tell you a legend'" (p. 153).

In this myth-laden atmosphere, every tale, every parable, takes on archetypal overtones. Even the simplest image patterns are transformed and assume at times distinctly philosophical implications. Animal imagery, for example, performs its traditional naturalistic function of defining characters living close to nature, but it offers other possibilities as well; in the end, it becomes part of the myth itself. For man in Lycovríssi is part of the delicate balance of nature, potentially at one with the plants and the animals and the angels of God. In this spiritual ecology, only man can destroy the balance. The wanderers find his mark on the Sarakína:

> Men must have lived there in the past—you can still make out a crumbled wall, some fragments of pottery, some fruit trees... turned wild once more. The paths are obliterated under a raving of grass and rubble; the houses have returned to their original elements;... the wolves, foxes, and hares... have come back in triumph. Earth, trees, and beasts breathed again, recovering their liberty; no longer now would they know the menace of the ephemeral two-legged monster, which had appeared for a moment, altered the law of eternal things, then disappeared. And lo and behold, that perpetually agitated animal was back again. (p. 79)

Nature, of course, wins out again; with the aid of men from the village, the newcomers are driven off, and again the mountain is bare. Only a hermit is left behind—Mihelís, the archon's son, become an ascetic instead of archon. When old Patriarhéas rebukes Manoliós for the fate of his son, the shepherd thinks, "What a wild beast the heart of man is!... Even you, my Christ, could not tame it" (p. 73). To Yannakós, watching in silence as the new settlers trace invisible walls and bless unbuilt gates, the situation is still more complex, the possibilities more awesome: "What are these creatures? he asked himself with dread, men? wild animals? or saints?" (p. 84).

In the midst of nature, untouched by spiritual concerns, man may well become a kind of beast. Nikoliós, the youth who aids Manoliós with the flock, bounds like a kid from rock to rock (p. 91), butts unsuccessfully against the lead ram (p. 97), walks "like a he-goat on its hind legs" (p. 125). Lenió, once so anxious to marry Manoliós in the spring—although "'only donkeys wed in May'" (p. 8)—takes Nikoliós instead. "'That girl! She'd have accepted a goat,'" Yannakós says of her (p. 147). Nikoliós' Pan plays his flute to the sheep, and Lenió responds "as if she heard her name" (p. 131); on the ground, up against the coupling sheep, Nikoliós mounts her like a ram (p. 132); again he wrestles with the bellwether and this time defeats him (p. 289).

It is in Lycovríssi, " 'the Wolf's Fountain' " (p. 154), and especially in Priest Grighóris, its spiritual leader, that the order of nature is most unbalanced. He is no worse than the average village priest—more or less benign, if somewhat venal—so long as the natural order, as he recognizes it, is maintained. To Manoliós the shepherd he offers kindness and the honor of playing Christ; for the would-be shepherd of men, however, he has only rage and the terror of excommunication. But "the anathema he had hurled at him was not enough; he wanted to tear out his eyes and eat them; ancient cannibal atavisms, wild prehuman instincts had awaked within him. . . . A wolf, come from the depths of the ages, had exploded the crust of his soul; it gazed at Manoliós and howled" (p. 409). Manoliós, he contends, is no shepherd but a wolf (p. 280), a wolf in the sheepfold (p. 415), at best " 'a scabby sheep' " (p. 315). But the Agha knows that surrendering Manoliós to the priest is like " 'giving a lamb to the wolves' " (p. 422). To the Turk, however, this is not really unnatural. " 'God has placed the sheep alongside the wolves,' " he instructs his subjects, " 'for the wolves to eat the sheep. This is God's order' " (p. 334). Yet he knows in his heart that the Greek sheep are worse than wolves. "Devil's own race," he thought. "Wolves don't eat one another; Greeks do" (p. 420). When the refugees finally march down the mountain to rebellion, it is "Saint Wolf"—the Prophet Elijah in his most terrible guise—who leads them against their rapacious neighbors (p. 373).

Humane, sophisticated voices are clearly out of place in this atmosphere. In the simplicity of peasant life in Anatolia, intellecutal concerns appear superfluous, even destructive. A learned theologican had lectured one Easter at the Saint Panteleímon Monastery about the mystery of the Resurrection. "He had gone up into the pulpit with a pile of fat tomes under his arm. For two long hours he had spoken. . . . Up till then the monks had thought of the resurrection of Christ as a very natural thing . . . as simple as the rising of the sun every morning." Afterwards, in his cell, saintly Father Manassé admitted to the novice Manoliós, " 'God forgive me, my son; this year, for the first time, I have not felt Christ rise' " (p. 244). In Lycovríssi, the representative of the intellect is Hadji Nikolís, the schoolmaster—younger brother of Priest Grighóris—whose wares are far less relevant to the lives of his people than is the superstitious lore of Mother Mandalénia, the old village coffiner.

Scorned by others—"A schoolmaster! What good can come of that?" thinks Captain Fortoúnas (p. 21)—Hadji Nikolís lives vicariously, "delighted at having to tell a terrible story, which made him, for a few moments, terrible" (p. 57). He comes alive only when he speaks of the history of the Greek people; he is the voice of their past nobility and advocate of their continued glory. In reality, in the present, he is incapable of action: he recognizes the justice of the immigrants' cause but is afraid to oppose his brother; he attempts always to be a mediator, the voice of reason, to effect compromise between opposing factions. In the first battle between the villages, he is beaten by both sides; " 'Serves me right,' he confessed. 'I'm neither sheep nor wolf, I'm a bastard, the wolves bite me and the sheep vomit me. I know very well what's right, my friends, I haven't the force to do it. I know very well where the truth lies, but I keep silent. I'm afraid. . . . Lycovríssi and Sarakiní have thrashed me without mercy. They're right! They're quite right, by my faith, it serves me right!' " (pp. 334–35). He again attempts to mediate in the second battle and this time is killed. The intellect, Kazantzakis tells us, is useful only when it is combined with action. The man of wisdom who cannot act is worse than the fool, self-destroyer of his role in society.

The wolves and sheep in this myth are thus more than a symbol of man's potential bestiality, more than a concrete sign of a disrupted order. They offer implicitly a philosophical standard against which man is to be judged, a kind of Great Chain of Being for primitive societies. There is nothing inherently evil—or even negative—in these associations: Lenió and Nikoliós are not condemned for their animality. As creatures of instinct who cannot develop spiritually, their place in the scheme of things is rightly among the sheep. Manoliós, too, might once have settled for such a place; it is not intellect that saves him, or even his novitiate in the monastery—although he reads the Gospels with natural wisdom. It takes extraordinary events—the casting of the Passion Play and the coming of the strangers—to lead him beyond his senses to a discovery of his spiritual potential, to reach out, in the end, for godhead.

Only those who recognize their possibilities and deny them must be condemned; only they are outside the natural order. Even the starving wolves who stalk the Sarakína are merely fulfilling their natural function. But Hadji Nikolís betrays his own ideals in his inability to act, miserly Ladhás his humanity in his psychotic grasping for wealth, and Priest Grighóris his place among the angels in his connivance for power. This is not a matter of reward in some hoped-for afterlife. This Great Chain covers only the earth; man's spiritual potential must be developed in this life, not only in his dealings with God, but in his relations with other men, in his discovery of himself. So even the Agha can achieve some measure of humanity. As he mourns his dead Youssoufákis, "This was no longer a wild beast let loose; suffering had made it a human being" (p. 210).

V

Paralleling both Christian metaphor and nature myth, central to the novel's theme as well as its structure, is the essential Kazantzakian scheme of *The Saviors of God*. As naturalistic imagery and as metaphysical speculation, it provides a measure of man's true potential in nature and society; it becomes, in a sense, the myth underlying the entire fiction, its roots as much political and psychological as they are literary. The fire that purges both men and societies, the wings that liberate body and soul, the abyss at whose edge man is forced to confront himself—this familiar pattern opens a path to renewal, a means to identity for the individual and his society. To the people of the Sarakína, forced to wander perhaps for all time, it offers salvation; to the stable, complacent life in the village, it holds out no hope: the Lycovríssi folk are doomed to the life they elect to defend. The images of fire and flight, of the perilous climb and the dreadful abyss that threaten the climber, express in the novel—as in the earlier philosophical poem—the challenges that ultimately confront all men in all circumstances of life.

Fire is the rather obvious symbol of all human passion, sexual or creative, religious or political. It touches nearly all the characters, placid Mihelís and fiery Katerína alike, Priest Grighóris as well as Priest Fótis, somehow transforming, even transmuting them. Patriarhéas visualizes the "bolsheviks" besieging his village as "half men, half beasts, flooding down from the north in clogs with iron studs. At their passage the stones spat sparks and the villages caught fire. At their head ran Manoliós. . . . Flames were coming from his mouth, and with outstretched arm he was pointing at Lycovríssi" (pp. 293–94). The shepherd himself seems willing to accept this characterization, and fire becomes for him a sign of his martyrdom, of his progression beyond the normal passions of men: "He could not forget the superhuman joy he had experienced as he went, that day, to give his life. That flame had not gone out, it was still there in him, distant as a Paradise lost. The daily struggle seems to him slow and dull" (p. 347), and he dreams of an incendiary Christ descending the mountain to purge man and redeem him.

For fire is also the symbol of divine punishment, the metaphorical flames of God's justice (p. 86) become literal in the hands of Yannakós. " 'If Christ came down on earth today,' " he asks Mihelís, " 'on an earth like this one, what do you think He'd have on his shoulders?

A cross? No, a can of petrol'" (p. 382). It is Yannakós who performs the miracle of the petrol, turning it into fire in the storerooms of Ladhás. The small tradesman has himself turned revolutionary; the unthinking tool of a repressive and dehumanizing system turns on its chief representative. This revolution, however, is not specifically Marxist: the rebels understand Bolshevism no better than their accusers. They do not attack one mechanism in order to replace it with another; their goal is the regeneration of man—a visionary goal, not a political one—and their guide, metaphorically and literally, is the Prophet Elijah, "Prophet of fire" (p. 387).

Near the crest of the Sarakína stands the almost abandoned Chapel of Elijah, around which each year the villagers celebrate a kind of fertility festival: for fire and fertility are mythically one, death and rebirth part of the same human cycle. The "terrible Prophet" is shown on an icon "on the edge of a precipice, in a chariot of fire drawn by four purple horses. The robe he wore was also purple, and flames issued from his head" (p. 251). To the worshippers, he seems like the sun; a spark from his flame has come down to the rebels: it is this icon that Priest Fótis—who "looked indeed like the Prophet Elijah astride the flames" (p. 252)—bears as he leads them to battle. It is the twenty-second day of December, "'the birthday of light, the birthday of the Prophet Elijah'" (p. 386). At once pagan divinity, biblical seer, and Byzantine emperor, the Prophet Elijah in his fiery chariot suggests the continuity of man's struggle and the hope for his ultimate salvation. In the Passover ritual, immortal Elijah is champion of the oppressed; at the final seder which Jesus celebrated, it was Elijah who was expected to announce the Messiah's advent. "Inflamed with the Word of God," both poet and doer, the Hebrew prophet may have been Kazantzakis' ideal image of himself.[6]

Twenty years before *The Greek Passion*, in the verse drama *Christós*, Kazantzakis envisioned a revolutionary Messiah who descends to earth "like fire to cleanse the heart, the mind and the inner being of man."[7] His hero is no simple, Christian savior, but a destroyer who commands his disciples to set fire to the earth so that a new world may rise from the ashes. "My Apostles, scatter and burn the earth to its root; do not pity it, my brothers. . . . And if the just must burn in the fire let them become ashes if it is God's will."[8] Scattered throughout the world, preaching their revolutionary gospel, the disciples of this new Messiah are quickly killed by the established forces which they threaten—tribal chiefs, lamas, and priests. By undertaking their foredoomed task, however, by transcending their own human limitations, they point the way to Manoliós and his followers: they too save not the world, but themselves.

To express such hypernaturalistic phenomena, Kazantzakis appears at times to rely on worn-out, conventional metaphors: as Lenió races happily to meet her fiance, we are told, "her heart had wings, went up the mountain quicker than she could, reached the sheepfold . . . and lovingly pecked at his nape and throat" (p. 129); in his joy in his new role, as he hastens to save the village from the Agha's wrath, Manoliós too "felt wings under his feet" (p. 195). This is more than a cliché, however, for these are angel's wings that compel his upward progression, that bear him along the rising path. This image too is derived from *The Saviors of God*. And so the shepherd welcomes Mihelís to the mountain. " 'The road is rocky,' " he warns him; " 'the rise is steep, at first one hurts one's feet. . . . But gradually you grow wings, angels take you under the arms and you climb the sheer mountain of God gaily, singing' " (p. 276). This progression is in no way predestined, for man must will the steep ascent. The village beadle has always felt that he should have been bishop, for miraculous signs accompanied his birth. And once, in the village church, he had seen the Archangel Michael, "on the left of the iconostasis, slowly unfolding his wings." The beadle had fainted. "Since then he had wished to see no angel, and miracles frightened him" (p. 249). He had remained fixed to the earth, lured by the beauty spots on the wings of a young girl's nose (p. 250). The archon, too, tied to his senses, sees only the black wings of the Archangel announcing his death (p. 303). He has said of Manoliós in the beginning, before accepting him for the role of Christ, lightly, jokingly, " 'a real little angel, only the wings missing' " (p. 8). By the end, just before his ironic and futile death, the shepherd has grown the missing wings: " 'you're mad,' " the Agha tells him, " 'and a saint all in one; you want to cover all the villainies of the world with your wings, like a broody hen' " (p. 422). His sacrifice cannot save even the Sarakiní; the refugees bury him on the mountain and continue their flight to the east. This Christ figure redeems only himself, and perhaps, on his difficult ascension up the mountain to the peak, something of God as well.

The figurative mountain of *The Saviors of God* becomes in the novel the harsh Sarakína, the mountain of Manoliós the shepherd, Mihelís the hermit, and Fótis the prophet of fire. It is at its peak that hunter and hunted alike look out at themselves and choose their fates. Saved by his disease from the abyss of the widow's flesh (p. 168), Manoliós finds himself instead at the precipice of martyrdom (p. 165). Unafraid now of his fate, anxious to save whom he can, he leaps out over the void, leaps freely and gaily, and thus serves his God. The journey upward is more difficult for Mihelís, for he is not born to the mountain as the shepherd is, and he cannot even hope to save anyone but himself. His choice, moreover, must be renewed each day of his ascetic's life, as he looks down at the lands he once owned, the lives he might have controlled. As for the refugee priest, who has long since been deprived of his worldly position—he is the first to climb the figurative mount. Looking up at the peak, foreseeing the fate of his people, "his eyes plunged into the abyss" (p. 47). That winter, his people beaten and starved, he leads them into rebellion. " 'We have reached the edge of the abyss,' " he tells them all now (p. 392). They defeat the wolves of the village, seize the vineyards willed them by Mihelís, but are forced to flee before the Turkish horde. Now all the people confront themselves, this time at the edge of the shepherd's new grave. " 'In the name of Christ,' [the priest] cried, 'the march begins again; courage, my children!' And again they resumed their interminable march toward the east" (p. 432).

VI

" 'We shall not vanish!' " Priest Fótis calls out as the strangers first enter the village. " 'For thousands of years we have kept alive; we shall keep alive for thousands more' " (p. 35). And, as they leave Lycovríssi for the last time, " 'We are no longer anything but a hand-ful of Greeks on the earth; let us grit our teeth and go forward. No, they shall not get us; our race cannot die!' " (p. 430). As the people of Saint George pass through Lycovríssi, the Cretan experience is re-newed in the East. It is not merely that the fields and the villages, the rocky mountain and the abandoned chapel recall the face of Kazant-zakis' homeland; the whole spirit of the work is derived from Crete. As Mihelís says on the death of his father, " 'Every Greek in this world, down to the humblest and most ignorant, is, without knowing it, a great archon. He has a heavy responsibility. Every Greek who doesn't take, if only once in his life, a heroic decision, betrays his race . . .; before the grave of my father I swore to myself to take the noble precipitous road my race followed, thousands of years ago' " (pp. 306-7). Certainly, he reflects the pride of all Greeks in their heri-tage and the love of the Anatolian Greeks for their land. But there is something more here, more than the nostalgia of Venézis' *Beyond the Aegean* or the fraternal feeling of Clement Lépidis' recent *The Fountain of Skopelos.* In the expulsion of the Eastern Greeks from their home-land, Kazantzakis had found a parallel to the long history of Crete, a reflection of the facts of his own life, a metaphor of man's continuing struggle against invincible forces.

To Fótis the mystic, whose name means "light," the expulsion of his people from their village has been a God-sent blessing. The rich, easy life of Saint George, he declares, " 'was enslaving our soul.' " Once they were blind to the evil around them; now, persecuted themselves by injustice, they are free at last. " 'Misfortune has opened our eyes, we have understood. Hunger has opened our wings, we have escaped from the net of injustice and of the too-easy life. We're free here! Now we can begin a new life, a nobler one, God be praised!' " (p. 154). There will be no injustice here, no rich and no poor, no souls surrendered to bodies. The rich men of Saint George suffer on the Sarakína along with the poor, freed from the lands and the trees they once owned. On the Sarakína they plant the seed of the ideal society that Kazantzakis had long envisioned. Here men and women work together in groups called "brotherhoods" (p. 295); like the earliest Christians, they confess their sins before the community and seek redemption together (p. 163). Each man sows what he can for the common good, and each shares alike in the fruit of the harvest. In the thin, rocky soil of the mountain, the crop which they reap is suffering, that is to say, humanity: " 'We're not complaining. . . . That's what it means to be a *man*: to suffer, undergo injustices and struggle without giving ground!' " (p. 348).

To those on the plain, the classless society above them is an abomination, a threat to their own way of life, the intrusion of light into their blindness. They react to the sight of injustice and suffering with anger, with fear, with renewed persecution. Ladhás, the "oil man," is terrified that debt will be abolished in the new society. But " 'God is just,' " he unctuously reasons. " 'He's a good moneylender like me. He understands business' " (p. 368). "Quick" Grighóris, whose name suggests his elusiveness, his ability to outlive his opponents, also sees God as an instrument of the established order—social as well as religious: " 'God distributes wealth in accordance with hidden laws which are His own. The justice of God is one thing, that of men is another. . . . Woe to him who dares disturb order; he is infringing the will of God!' " (p. 260). And He speaks, this mercantile God, through traditional channels alone: " 'God speaks by my mouth, mine!' " the priest shouts at the rebels. " 'You cannot talk with Him direct! It is through me that His word passes' " (p. 55). It is presumably God then who condemns as bolsheviks those who follow His revolutionary son, whose guide, they claim, is " 'the supreme beggar,' " Christ (p. 359).

The Apostles reject these conclusions; like Job, they question the motives of a God who can allow such inequities, whose sense of justice is so different from man's. Their heresy, like Job's, threatens His order—at least as His interpreters perceive it. Even Priest Fótis rebukes them; like Job's friends, he answers, " 'God is never in a hurry . . .; He works in eternity. Only ephemeral creatures . . . hasten out of fear. Let God work in silence, as He likes to do. Don't raise your head, don't ask questions. Every question is a sin'" (p. 169). But the suffering he sees leads him, too, to revolt. He raises his head, asks questions of God—his questions, like Job's, born of deep faith. At the grave of a child, he preaches acceptance: "'Woe to the man who would measure God by the measure of his heart. . . . He is lost. It can lead him to lose his wits, blaspheme, deny God . . .' He fell silent once more, appalled at the words he still had on his tongue, but he could not hold himself back. 'What is this God Who lets the children die?'" (p. 372). This is not really blaspheming, however, for it is not God that Fótis challenges, but man's use of God to stifle unrest and perpetuate order. Fótis' challenge, like Job's, is an act of faith, an affirmation of belief in a universe in which man can retain his dignity, in a heavenly justice which humans, too, can comprehend. This is a paradox that even Priest Fótis does not quite see: it is when he most doubts that he is most faithful, for how should man presume to know God's ways? If not from questioning God, as Job says to Bildad, "Where then cometh wisdom? and where is the place of understanding?" As God rebukes Job's friends for presuming to know His intentions, so presumably will he honor Fótis for his faithful questioning. But there are no miraculous appearances in this world, no divine confrontations with humans; the only voice from the whirlwind is the voice of rebellion, the note from within which declares that man best serves God by refusing to serve His interpreters, by rejecting that view of justice put forth by Grighóris and Ladhás, by seeking justice in this life according to standards that all men can accept.

This is the path that Manoliós takes almost instinctively. It is the way of Christ, as he sees it, the course for all Christians to follow. He is understandably shocked then when Patriarhéas, his master, accuses him of rebellion. But he learns: as his life follows Christ's ever more closely, he comes increasingly to see the need for complete revolution; he comes in the end to proclaim himself "'bolshevik'" (p. 426). "'This world is unjust and wicked,'" he lectures the Agha; "'the best are hungry and suffer, the worst eat, drink and govern without faith, without shame, without love. Such a world must perish! . . . I should like, Agha, to proclaim revolution over the whole earth. To rouse all men, white, black, yellow; to form an immense all-powerful army and enter into the great rotten towns, into the shameless palaces, into the mosques of Constantinople, and set fire to them!'" (pp. 422–23).

The shepherd calls for a class revolution, but his call is not really Bolshevik: it is mystical and not dialectical, a revolution of the spirit and not one of matter.[9] Surely, he agrees, the system is rotten, a self-perpetuating cause of injustice, divider of men into classes and betrayer of human potential. It cannot be reformed; it must be destroyed. So he calls for a Biblical fire to burn out the roots of the old and make possible a new start for man. But there must be no substitute system, no new collection of orders and values to classify men and restrain their development. Kazantzakis scrupulously avoids positing new frameworks to replace the old, for all systems, he knows from experience—as Manoliós merely intuits—imprison humanity: churchmen as well as parishioners, moneylenders and debtors alike, those holding power and those without. The Marxist call for revolt parallels his, but it is not the same call. Kazantzakis wants not to reform society as we know it, but to abolish it, to give man a new start free of the old encrustations. The rich men of Saint George may mourn their lost pastures and orchards, but they know with Priest Fótis that their souls have finally been saved. And property of the state is as harmful as private possessions; states can be seduced as easily as men. The only solution is joint sharing of the natural world, with each man possessing the fruits of vineyards and fields, the produce of forests and flocks. This is a decidedly agrarian vision, one that seems hardly appropriate to an industrial, urban society. Kazantzakis had seen too much of the world not to realize that his vision was impractical: thus the reformers in his narrative are all defeated, and he holds out no hope for their ultimate victory. That he persisted in offering his vision indicates that its roots are not so much political as they are philosophical, its goals far more humanistic than mechanistic: he seeks not the improvement of man's lot, but his spiritual regeneration.

Kazantzakis would have us return to that primitive religion practiced in the earliest decades of the Christian era—although he knows that even then there were problems of dedication and order. Among the mystical sects of the Jews under Herod—the Essenes especially—as among the earliest followers of Christ, there was a sense of urgency, a recognition of the judgment to come, that led men to seek individual dignity by submerging themselves within the group as a whole. In the primitive communist forms that they devised, we can see not only their need for renewal, but also an idealism as harsh and demanding as the quest of the Cretans for freedom. They failed, in the first place, because the Empire could not let them succeed—what was discipline and self-dedication within the mystical group seemed like anarchy to the Romans—and, more ironically, because they finally did succeed, because the fish of the Christians devoured the eagle of Rome. It is this final failure that leads Kazantzakis to distrust all organized movements: with success, they become as abhorrent as the systems they replace. If they can be kept primitive, however, if man can remain close to his roots in nature and find his dignity there, then there is hope of renewal for all men. The sophisticated, Westernized man of letters, Kazantzakis opts for a return to primitive forms not because they are inherently better than modern developments—certainly not because their practical results will be in any way different—but because in them, at least, individual men can find their own way. His concern, in the end, is not for society, but for the men who compose it. This may seem on the surface reactionary, but it surely is not. It simply reflects the Cretan's glorification of man and his distrust of systems that propose to limit individual impulse. Kazantzakis would certainly approve of the postwar efforts to eliminate sheep-stealing and blood feuds in the mountains of Crete; but he would no doubt regret the accompanying loss of individuality, the sundering of man from the natural world.

Manoliós' sacrifice has no practical effect—it does not save the refugees, and it may even help to defeat them—but it makes possible, nonetheless, his own salvation. He is saved not in the traditional Christian sense of eternal reward, but in the more immediate sense of his personal freedom, because he has achieved at last the awareness of his own identity. In following the path of Christ, the shepherd has for the first time lived truly close to nature; he has learned not to scorn his body but to honor his soul; he has been moved by injustice, and he has moved to correct it. His act may be futile, even egocentric, but it is the act of a free man, asserting his will for the first time in his life. And it leads his Apostles to save themselves, too. They alone in Wolf's Fountain act as free men; the others, Greek as well as Turk, are victims of their own sense of fate.

The Agha's belief in a preordained universe, in which all men's lives have already been written, justifies the world as he knows it—a world of Turkish masters and Greek slaves—and enables him to surrender Manoliós to the villagers. The village rulers, on the other hand, accept the idea of fate not out of religious conviction, but because it suits their position: for them, predestination is a means of repression. As Grighóris angrily explains to the rebels, "'All this nonsense you have talked is against the will of God. He it is who decides, and all that happens in the world happens because He wills it'" (p. 260). In rejecting the social system of the elders, the Apostles also deny their fatalism. The sacrifice of his inheritance, Mihelís tells Priest Grighóris, has made him a free man. "'You are the slave, Father,'" he adds. "'More the pity for the holy habit which you wear!'" (p. 337). Freed from his property, free of the past, Mihelís can will his own fate; in an ironic reversal, the priest is as much the prisoner of his social position as the Agha is of his religion.

VII

There is a small body of Greek critical opinion that argues that Kazantzakis is equally the prisoner of his ascetic philosophy, "that his belief in the transubstantiation of flesh into spirit does not proceed from a free choice on his part. He expressed this view because he could not do otherwise."[10] His first wife, Ghalátea, had said that Kazantzakis was uninterested in sex even as a young man—the result, apparently, of the overpowering presence of his father in his life; Lilí Zográfou reasons from this that his central characters and themes are the product not of his art, but of his neurosis, that he is a mediocre artist because he is unable in his fiction to order the materials of his life. But even if Ghalátea's vengeful account of their unhappy marriage were correct—and there is no convincing evidence that it is—it would be irrelevant to the novel itself: nowhere in *The Greek Passion*—or elsewhere in his fiction—does Kazantzakis advocate the total subordination of body to soul; the critics have confused his characters with their creator. The martyred shepherd and the ascetic young archon, despite their own protestations, are free in the end not because they have learned to deny their physical impulses, but because they choose their fates freely. Certainly Kazantzakis was himself drawn to asceticism—his youthful disease alone will verify this—but his novel succeeds precisely because in it he does subordinate his life to his art, because he exercises in his work an artistic discipline far more complete than his critics have realized.

Even those readers who praise Kazantzakis are defensive at times about the extremes of his style: it is his power they admire, not his control. It is easy, in our sophistication, to condescend to his often inflated plot lines, the seeming obviousness of his symbolic characterizations and the declamatory prose which so many of his characters speak. It would be equally easy—and still more misleading—to ignore the artistic control that exists beneath the hyperbole. Certain of the excesses can be understood in terms of their literary origins—the centuries-old tradition of the Greek prose romance, which is almost totally alien to modern conventions of realism; even such a thoroughly Westernized novelist as Vassílis Vassilikós, who has obviously read and absorbed both Joyce and Proust, follows this fantastic tradition in some of his works. On the surface, there are few indications in the novels of Kazantzakis that he has even heard of the narrative revolution of the twentieth century, especially in point of view and the handling of time: *The Greek Passion* appears to be told from a thoroughly omniscient viewpoint, and its closest approach to simultaneity of time is the frequent appearance of the formula "meanwhile." Yet the shifting narration is perhaps less omniscient than it at first seems, for Kazantzakis remains very close to the objective perceptions of his central characters and rarely intrudes his own observations—hardly an innovative technique, but nonetheless one that is carefully structured.

The whole framework of the novel is similarly ordered, for the first chapter sets out the patterns to follow: the sensuality of life in the village and its closeness to nature, the spiritual conflict developing from within the Passion Play and the theme of individual freedom, the major patterns of imagery, and the metaphor of Christ are all introduced in this opening section. The movement of the action is also foreshadowed here, and we can predict from the start the revolt of the shepherd, his betrayal, and inevitable failure; even our ambiguous attitude toward him is prepared for.

For Manoliós the shepherd, chosen to play at Christ's Passion, whose life follows His ever more closely, is in no sense Christ come again to earth; he is as much nature god as Savior, an idealist who presumes to save mankind through his own sacrifice and who naturally fails to do so. His developing role does not demonstrate simply that man would again crucify Jesus if He came again to earth—the original title, *Christ Recrucified,* is thus somewhat misleading—but that man must first learn to save himself, that we must reorder our lives and our institutions as well if we hope to achieve a new generation. But we are dealing with men and not with divinities, so we both praise and condemn the shepherd's decisions: his first effort at martyrdom is almost satiric in its foolishness; his second attempt—equally futile, equally presumptuous perhaps—is meaningful because it is an act of will and not one of willfulness. *The Greek Passion* is the story of man becoming God, not a literal version of the New Testament Passion, not even a close parallel to it; it is a metaphor of the divine possibilities open to all humans willing to struggle with themselves, with their societies, with their conceptions of God. It gives off as well a sense of Cretan timelessness, a prospect of the ultimate renewal of the Greek people and thus of all mankind. The metaphor of Christ is not the end of the book, but one of its means, one start among many to a new life for man.

In times of great stress, men everywhere have sought instinctively to create myths out of the facts of their lives, to make of their own histories a metaphor like Christ's. Even in Nationalist Spain, in a cause he despised, Kazantzakis saw this process at work. As he spoke with the survivors of the siege of the Alcázar, each one "added something from his own imagination or memory. He was creating history, molding the epic in his own image and likeness. All that was superfluous was discarded. The essential was being discovered.... When the Alcázar died, it became immortal."[11] The process is that of the artist as well. "The great artist"—he is writing now in Greece, but during the same period—"glimpses timeless, changeless symbols beneath the flow of everyday reality. Behind the spasmodic, often incoherent actions of mortal men he views clearly the great currents that sweep souls along. He transposes ephemeral events into immortal air." And so the Classical masters, celebrating victory over the Persians, depicted not the battle of Marathon but a mythical contest. "And beyond the Lapithae and centaurs we discern the two great, timeless adversaries: mind and beast, civilization and barbarism. Thus a historical event... escaped time... and became an immortal commemoration [in which] the victories of the Greeks were elevated to victories for all humanity."[12]

Out of the New Testament vision of Christ and the ancient Orthodox Passion Play, out of Old Testament prophets and pagan fertility gods, out of an abiding feeling for nature and a passionate demand for social reform, Kazantzakis creates a similar myth. Vaguely autobiographical figures—Manoliós, Mihelís, and Fótis all suggest in their various dualities aspects of the author's conception of himself—as well as details drawn from his own life—among them Fótis' fear of his father (p. 265), the young Jewish girl he saves from drowning (p. 266), and the disinterred remains of a pretty young girl that Mihelís sees as a child (p. 144)—are also subordinated in the fiction to the creation of myth. The result is a vision as total and as potentially convincing as the Christian metaphor itself. Kazantzakis' accomplishment in *The Greek Passion*, the proof of his modernity, is the blend of these elements within the Anatolian adventure, his endeavor to make of a footnote in history a myth for our times.

1. *Report to Greco*, p. 424.
2. All references are to the Simon and Schuster edition (New York, 1953), trans. Jonathan Griffin.
3. *Greco*, pp. 353–54.
4. *Greco*, p. 355.
5. *Greco*, pp. 356–57.
6. Kimon Friar, introduction to the *The Saviors of God*, pp. 16–17.
7. Translated from the Greek edition of Kazantzakis' dramatic works

(Athens, 1956) by Michael Anthonakes, in his unpublished doctoral dissertation, "Christ, Freedom, and Kazantzakis" (New York University, 1965), p. 220.

8. Anthonakes, p. 227.

9. "'Well, my friend,'" says one of the characters in Malraux's *The Conquerors*, "'if by Bolshevist you mean revolutionary, then Garine is a Bolshevist. But, if you mean, as I do, a particular type of revolutionary, who, among many other characteristics, is distinguished by a belief in Marxism, then Garine is no Bolshevist. . . .'" Trans. Winifred Stephens Whale (Boston, 1962), p. 8. Manoliós, of course, like his fellow villagers, can make no such distinction, nor evidently could some of Kazantzakis' detractors.

10. Anthonakes, p. 52, citing Ghalátea Kazantzakis, *The Soldier and A Little Heroine*, and Lilí Zográphou, *Nikos Kazantzakis: A Tragic Man*.

11. Nikos Kazantzakis, *Spain*, trans. Amy Mims (New York, 1963), p. 207.

12. Nikos Kazantzakis, *Journey to the Morea*, trans. F. A. Reed (New York, 1965), pp. 67-68.

CHAPTER FOUR

THE LAST TEMPTATION OF CHRIST
A Modernist Myth in the Holy Land

The religious impulse that is undertone throughout *The Greek Passion* becomes theme and substance in the richest of Kazantzakis' novels, *The Last Temptation of Christ*. The Christian story here is not metaphor but actuality, Jesus of Nazareth not an archetypal figure in the background but the protagonist. Manoliós in *The Greek Passion* acts at times as if he were Christ, and Panayótaros blindly betrays him, but they merely play at their roles. In *The Last Temptation*, the central figure is Jesus himself; and his Judas is no oxlike creature who protests helplessly against his involvement, but a colossus who selects his fate freely, the one disciple who remains true to the end. The interplay between peasant lives and the Passion Play creates in the earlier novel a kind of reflexivism in which appearance is more important than reality: it is the ultimate meaning of the shepherd's life about which we care and not its faithfulness to details. But details are vital to *The Last Temptation*, for we are struck from the start by Kazantzakis' imaginative recreation of this familiar story; only gradually do we realize that the meaning too has been altered, that the familiar legend of Christian sacrifice has been recast to its original impulses, given new life by returning it to the old.

"There is no discrepancy between old and new works of art," says George Seferis, "none whatsoever. The great works of the past remain 'aesthetically' distant and emotionally near to us, and all the more so if there are new works constantly arriving to fortify their position."[1] This union of old and new is immediately apparent in the Greek Modernist renderings of Homer—Kazantzakis' *Odyssey* and Seferis' own *Mithistórima*, "The Myth of Our History." It is less readily apparent perhaps but still more significant in the biblical novels of Kazantzakis—*The Greek Passion* and *The Last Temptation of*

Christ—which treat the Old and New Testaments as a storehouse of mythic possibilities and join to them a sensibility typically Hellenic, typically Cretan. In them we find all the major concerns, intellectual and social, of the Modernist era, yet they manifest a quality that no Western artist could have achieved. They are—even more than the *Mithistórima*—the proof of Seferis' statement.

The Last Temptation of Christ marked a new peak of contention in the author's long and controversial career. As a young man he had been an advocate of demoticism at a time when government and critics alike were hostile to the popular tongue, for the language issue in modern Greece has always had political ramifications; his later enthusiasm for Marxism removed him still further from official acceptance. Then the faithful were shocked by the seeming atheism of *The Saviors of God*, and the nationalistic spirit was offended by his ambiguous treatment of Cretan patriots and Anatolian villagers; the controversy over his burial, which is waged even today in Greece, was simply the logical culmination of his entire life. He had lost the Nobel Prize in 1952—by one vote—only because, it is said, the Greek government refused to sponsor his candidacy. But *The Last Temptation* spread the controversy for the first time beyond the borders of Greece.

There were elements in this humanistic portrait of Christ to offend Roman Catholics and Protestants as well as the Orthodox. The German text was placed on the Index of Forbidden Books soon after its appearance in 1954—the Greek edition did not appear until the following year and was not specifically condemned. But Orthodox prelates in America did condemn the work; at least one Midwestern public library banned it after a protest from a local Catholic priest; and an active campaign was organized against it by Protestant clergymen in southern California. Even liberal theologians who had admired Kazantzakis' other novels attacked this one: this "lukewarm cheapness,"[2] this "nonsens[ical] and deliberate perversion of history,"[3] they said, is acceptable only if we read it "not as an image of Christ, but as an image of Kazantzakis' own struggle of spirit with flesh. . . . "[4] Greek critics, predictably, felt no need for even this rationalization: the novel to them was clearly blasphemous, its author akin to such "decadents" as Voltaire, Nietzsche, and Zola.[5]

He expected no more from his countrymen:

> In Greece these books of mine will have no reverberation, because they deal with psychological problems that do not interest the Greeks of the present day. The major and almost the only theme of all my work is the struggle of man with "God": the unyielding, inextinguishable struggle of the naked worm called "man" against the terrifying power and darkness of

the forces within him and around him. . . . The anguished battle to transmute darkness into light, slavery into freedom—all these struggles, alas, are foreign and incomprehensible to the present-day Greek intellectuals. And that is why I am so much of a stranger and so solitary in Greece. . . .[6]

When he wrote this to a Norwegian friend, only one of his novels—*Zorba the Greek*—had appeared in his homeland. He wrote for the West, then, but he can have had few illusions about the likely Western reception of so individual and potentially heretical a work as *The Last Temptation of Christ*, a thoroughly Modernist work in technique and in certain aspects of theme, and yet, in the end, a work that is more Greek than Western. As he wrote in detail to the same friend of his plans for the novel, he revealed his unspoken debt to the traditions of the Greek prose romance, Greek mysticism, and, above all, Greek myth.

> I wanted to renew and supplement the sacred Myth that underlies the great Christian civilization of the West. It isn't a simple "Life of Christ." It's a laborious, sacred, creative endeavor to reincarnate the essence of Christ, setting aside the dross—falsehoods and pettinesses which all the churches and all the cassocked representatives of Christianity have heaped upon His figure, thereby distorting it.
> . . . Parables which Christ could not possibly have left as the Gospels relate them I have supplemented, and I have given them the noble and compassionate ending befitting Christ's heart. Words which we do not know that He said I have put into His mouth, because He would have said them if His disciples had had His spiritual force and purity. And everywhere poetry, love of animals and plant life and men, confidence in the soul, certainty that the light will prevail.[7]

The Last Temptation of Christ is rooted in its times, in both New Testament and Old, in the pagan myths of the eastern Mediterranean and in the history of Roman Galilee. Its characters are Galilean peasants—fishermen, shepherds, farmers, and carpenters—whose lives are a part of the process of nature. In this milieu Jesus of Nazareth is unmistakably a man and only potentially a god; his divinity, in fact, may be no greater than that which all men are capable of attaining. But he perseveres, overcoming the many temptations that confront all mankind, above all, the temptation to live a normal human life, with all its little sorrows and joys. At the end, on the cross, he resists the final temptation to deny the dream of his life—to substitute for it a vision of simple humanity—and attests to the pain of his crucifixion, the pain of all human life. He dies and is not reborn; his resurrection is left to those who come after him, not necessarily to his disciples, but to those, like Manoliós, who can sacrifice themselves for the good of all men.

There is much in Jesus' Galilee that recalls the Crete of Captain

Mihális: the harvests of wine and fish, the windmills and threshing floors, delicacies of lamb's eye and raki, a monastery in the hills and prophetic paintings in a synagogue, joyous hospitality at a village wedding, and peasants with rich black beards, including Jesus himself. Kazantzakis even appears to attribute to the ancient Jews certain customs and beliefs of modern Orthodoxy. But the anachronisms are less great than they seem: it is not merely that windmills exist in Israel as well as in Crete, or that the long suffering of the Jews recalls that of the Cretans, or even—as the introduction points out—that there is a kind of Jungian universality in all men's dealings with God; Kazantzakis had found in pre-Christian Galilee a people and life-style strikingly similar to those of Crete. The Cretan metaphor in the novel thus reinforces the Galilean experience and does not substitute for it.

When Jesus protests to Matthew, his first biographer, that he was born in Nazareth and not in Bethlehem, he is evidencing the national pride of the Galilean, his sense of isolation from more sophisticated Judea. As Hugh J. Schonfield writes, "The Galileans were proud, independent and somewhat puritanical, more resentful of alien domination and infringements of their liberty [than were the Judeans]. They were to be found in the forefront of the resistance movement to the Romans and to the Jewish authorities subservient to them."[8] Even their dialect isolated them from Judea: when Peter is singled out by the servants of Caiaphas because of his speech (e.g., Matt. 27:73), he is closer to this metaphoric Crete—itself separated by dialect from the mainland of Greece—than he is to his neighbors. From that distant time when the land was divided into two rival kingdoms, Galilee in the north, in what had once been Israel, was the home both of strict adherence to the old forms of worship and of new heretical movements. Both tendencies are apparent in the career of the carpenter from Galilean Nazareth.

II

There is virtually nothing in the New Testament about the early life of Jesus: only the improbable story in Luke (2:42–51) of the twelve-year-old boy astounding the elders in the Temple. But there is a good deal of evidence indicating the sources and strategies of the various writers of Gospels. As the needs of the new religion changed, as its potential audience shifted from Jew to Greek, it came to borrow less from the messianic Prophecies of the Jews and more from the mystery religions of the East; the tradition of a flexible and evolving canon was clearly not limited to the Old Testament. *The Last Temptation of Christ* is well within this religious tradition. It also has significant literary forebears: Balzac's "Jesus-Christ en Flandres," Lawrence's *The Man Who Died,* and George Moore's *The Brook Kerith* are similarly based on the notion that Jesus did not die on the cross but came down to live for a time among men; and Goethe, among others, is said to have suggested that Judas may have been following Christ's wishes in betraying his master. But Kazantzakis' narrative alone encompasses a pattern of theology and myth as complex and dense as the Bible itself. In this strange, ironic way, *The Last Temptation* is almost an orthodox statement of faith.

Kazantzakis' Jesus is a young man who has made little of his life; he has never married; his one friend is overbearing and self-righteous toward him; his only trade seems to be making crosses for Roman crucifixions. A visionary, he has had dreams of godhead since childhood. Both the opening and closing scenes of the novel are visions: in the first, he is pursued by agents of the people demanding that he be their savior; in the last, he attempts to escape his martyrdom. The band of pursuing dwarfs and the red-haired colossus who leads them in the opening vision become the broken disciples and the still fiery Judas in the final one. In both, it is Judas the patriot who compels his younger and weaker friend to fulfill his mission, to save ... what? Himself? Israel? Mankind? Neither is sure.[9]

Jesus' life is more or less normal until, at twenty, his apprenticeship presumably over, he goes with his mother to Cana, her village, to select a bride. As he reaches out to his childhood sweetheart, Magdalene his cousin, the only child of the learned Rabbi Simeon, he falls into a fit: "ten claws nailed themselves into his head and two frenzied wings beat above him, tightly covering his temples. He shrieked and fell down on his face, frothing at the mouth" (p. 26).[10] His mother in shame takes him home, and Magdalene—in an act otherwise unexplained—becomes a whore in frustrated revenge. Since that day, "at every opportunity he had to be happy, to taste the simplest human joys—to eat, sleep, to mix with his friends and laugh, to encounter a girl on the street and think, I like her—the ten claws nailed themselves down into him, and his desire vanished" (p. 27). The force behind the claws soon acquires a shape: the head of an eagle, sign of imperial Rome, and a body armored in bronze, recalling the "armor" of Magdalene's jewelry (p. 26). The Curse, as he comes to call it—for he sees it distinctly as woman—suggests both the Furies, the avengers of family honor, and the ascetic's disease. She acts as source and as measure of his affliction, the symbol of his duality; she leaves him only after he sets out on his mission. But she might have appeared in his life even had he not been torn between his yearning for God and his physical desires, for there are other factors in his unhappy family to account for his illness.

Kazantzakis sees Mary as a prototypical Jewish (read Greek) mother: domineering, possessive, embittered by her son's refusal to lead the life she has outlined for him.[11] " 'What good are angels to me . . . ?' " she asks. " 'I want children and grandchildren to be following him, children and grandchildren, not angels!' " (p. 190). When he sits, in his final vision, a simple farmer and carpenter, a patriarch surrounded by his children, he knows that his mother will at last be happy. Mary dominates her family because Joseph, her husband, has long been ill; an old man when he married, paralyzed by lightning before the birth of his son, he lies motionless each day, struggling to speak the one word, "Adonai" (p. 12). A classic Oedipal situation: the dominant mother, the infirm, rarely seen father, the guilt-ridden son. There is also the possibility of sibling rivalry. Although Mary at one point refers to Jesus as her only son (p. 134), this may well be a distraught mother's hyperbole, for it is clear that she has others and that they are their brother's antagonists. Thus lame Simon attempts to prevent Jesus from preaching, and Jacob the Pharisee conspires at his arrest. It is hardly surprising that Jesus should seek surrogate parents—for a father, Rabbi Simeon; for a mother, Magdalene, Martha the sister of Lazarus, and old Salome, mother of the disciples Jacob and John (he even takes to calling the Curse "Mother" [p. 247]); nor is it surprising that a major part of his message is the rejection of all family ties: " 'I shall throw discord into the home, the son shall lift his hand against the father, the daughter against her mother, the daughter-in-law against her mother-in-law—for my sake' " (p. 372).

His statement grows out of the predicament in the novel, but it is also a close paraphrase of Luke (12:53). Kazantzakis' imaginative interpretation of the story of Christ is more deeply rooted in the Gospels than at first seems possible. He has invented Joseph's infirmity, to be sure, as well as Mary's sense of betrayal and martyrdom, but these narrative possibilities were always implicit in the Gospel accounts: Joseph conspicuously disappears from them during his son's childhood—the incident in the Temple is the last in which he is mentioned—and the biblical Jesus never seems to offer his mother much more than respect. There are mythic analogues as well: the lightning bolt that cripples the father recalls Zeus' punishment of Salmoneus, who himself desired to be father of the gods; and the mother who curses her son to the Furies suggests Althaea, whose son Meleager is consumed by the fire of the gods. The novelist has also heightened the relationship among the brothers, for although John

(7:5) speaks of misunderstanding among the "brethren" of Jesus, there is evidence that it was Jacob or James who led the early Christians after the death of his brother; but his tenure was directed largely against the Westernization of the sect, its breaking loose from its roots in Judaism, its deification of Christ. So, in a sense, Jacob was antagonistic, if not to his brother, at least to his brother's new role in the Church.[12]

III

The narrative tension that develops within this familial complex is illustrative of Kazantzakis' technique throughout the novel. Virtually every incident originates in the New Testament, but all are filtered through the screen of comparative myth and enhanced by the author's imaginative vision. Together they form a picture of Jesus that is more compelling—and in many ways more consistent—than the one that emerges from the overlapping tales of the Gospel accounts. For this savior must be judged on human grounds as well as divine.

Some of Kazantzakis' changes are made for the sake of verisimilitude: many of the redundant miracles attributed to Jesus are omitted; others are reported, as it were, from offstage, or explained by realistic analogy; still others are condensed for dramatic effect. We hear nothing about Peter's mother-in-law (this Peter, in fact, is a bachelor), but the fishermen and farmers of Galilee have "already begun to compose the new prophet's legend: what miracles he performed, what words he uttered, which stone he stood on to speak and how the stone was suddenly covered with flowers" (pp. 357–58). The miracle of the loaves is purely figurative (p. 304, but cf. p. 492), the transubstantiation of bread and wine merely symbolic (p. 424). And the miraculous cures of the daughter of Jairus the elder and of the centurion's servant become a single, now more significant, episode. For the child healed by Jesus is the daughter of the centurion Rufus, captor of the Zealot whom some called Messiah, the last of the Maccabees. It is Jesus who makes the cross on which the Zealot will die, but even this desperate act cannot free him from his own sacred mission. And Rufus, we suspect, will be among those who spread the new miracle tale, invented by Paul, of the birth and resurrection of Christ (p. 475).[13]

A similar pattern of narrative condensation and change colors the parables attributed to Jesus. A useful mnemonic in an age of general illiteracy, the parable is the narrative method closest in form to the oral historiography of the time—and to Cretan folk culture as well. Just as the carpenter apparently altered traditional parables to fit his own new designs, so Kazantzakis has structured anew those told by Jesus. " 'Brothers,' " the rabbi explains, " 'forgive me if I speak in parables. I am a simple, illiterate man, poor and despised like yourselves. My heart has much to say, but my mind is unable to relate it. I open my mouth and without any desire on my part, the words come out as a tale' " (p. 183). Later he adds, " 'God speaks to me thus, in parables, and it is in parables that I shall speak now' " (p. 216). He relates almost verbatim parables found first in the Gospels, but his intent is at times almost totally different. For the Synoptic Gospels present the parables as a closed book whose key is available to the initiate only: "Unto you it is given to know the mysteries of the kingdom of God: but to others in parables; that seeing they might not see, and hearing they might not understand" (Luke 8:10; see also Matt. 13:13–16 and Mark 4:11–12). Kazantzakis abhors such exclusivist notions because they are contradictory to the context of Jesus' life, and so he emends those parables "which Christ could not possibly have left as the Gospels relate them." The parable of the maidens is thus given a new ending, and foolish as well as wise virgins are welcome at the wedding celebration (p. 217). The story of the rich man and Lazarus similarly acquires a new, more Christian conclusion. At first Jesus tells it precisely as it is related in Luke (16:19–31), so that the corrupt rich man is doomed to hell, while poor but worthy Lazarus rests in Abraham's bosom. But good-hearted John questions the meaning: " 'How many times have you instructed us to forgive our enemies!... Is God unable to forgive?' " he asks. And Jesus relents, for his God is a force for goodness and not for justice alone. " 'The parable cannot stand as it is,' " he admits; " 'it must have a different ending.' " His Lazarus now pleads with the Lord for the sake of his neighbor, and God too relents. " 'Lazarus, beloved,' he said, 'go down; take the thirster by the hand. My fountains are inexhaustible. Bring him here so that he may drink and refresh himself, and you refresh yourself with him.' ... 'For all eternity?' asked Lazarus. 'Yes, for all eternity,' God replied" (pp. 201–2).

Kazantzakis, like the authors of Ecclesiastes and Job, questions the orthodox concept of punishment and reward, of justice meted out almost by rote, of a God who has no more free will than His people. So Jesus, like Job, rejects the narrow legalism of the Covenant and attempts to free both the Chosen People and their God. His life, like his parables, repudiates established views of man's place in the universe, of his role in society, even of individual worth; but his rebellion, too, grows from biblical roots, is itself an act of tradition. The people await a political Messiah who will free them from bondage to Rome; he offers instead spiritual salvation, the prospect of freedom from all of their chains. So he earns the enmity of each of the factions of Israel: of the intolerant Pharisees, for attacking their narrow conservatism; of the ruling Sadducees, for threatening their comfortable influence; of the Zealots, for refusing to lead them against Rome. With the death of the character known as the Zealot—based most likely on Judas of Galilee, who led the ill-fated revolt of 6 A.D. (see e.g., p. 36)—his followers are forced to look for a new captain, and his red-haired namesake settles hesitantly on Jesus. This Judas is disturbed by his friend's seeming passivity, by the forgiveness which he preaches, above all by his refusal to lead their rebellion. Only the mass of the people, and the religious mystics who correspond to the Essenes, fully approve of his message.

Jesus' closeness to the people is antithetical to the Essene withdrawal from life, but his teaching at times borders closely on theirs. Although there is still no evidence that the historical Jesus lived in the Qumran community, it is certain that he knew of their precepts, for the Gospels themselves attest to their influence. The monastery that the fictional carpenter enters is surely an outgrowth of Qumran, and the newly found prophecy that Simeon cites, "The Testament of Moses" is said to be one of the Dead Sea Scrolls (p. 397; in reality, it is one of the pseudepigrapha, a "presumed writing" that borrows the prophet's name).

The Essenes and Zealots are the two poles of Jewish reaction to Rome, the former withdrawing from society, the latter immersing themselves in it. But both are responding to the same hostile environment, both manifesting their belief that the Last Days have come, that the end of the world as they know it is at hand. And both await the Messiah who will save them from Rome and their own degradation. Although the historical Jesus repudiated politics, he was condemned in the end for political crimes, misunderstood by even his followers, who reacted to his capture and trial as if his rebellion were over, his mission discredited. The Gospels make clear that it was only his escape from the tomb that convinced the disciples that their rabbi's message went beyond social and political concerns. But Jesus, too, may have been naive in believing that the religion of Israel could be divorced from its politics. In the extreme case of the Zealots, it is obvious, as the historian G. A. Williamson comments, that "political objectives could not be disentangled from religious principles";[14] it was their resistance to Roman sovereignty, a cause made sacred by their total allegiance to God, that led to the final, disastrous revolt of 66 A.D. But even the apolitical Essenes eagerly sought the Messiah; "the Messianic hope ... pervaded the nation and distinguished the Jews from every other race. That hope took several forms, but in general it was the hope of a Davidic king who would overcome the nation's enemies by military force."[15] Neither mystic nor nationalist, Kazantzakis' Jesus synthesizes these conflicting reactions and translates them into a new force for change.

In the peaceful and ordered empire of Rome, the provinces of Judea, Samaria, and Galilee were surely governed the worst; their situation resembles that of Crete under the Turks: a foreign oppressor and the native establishment which serves him; an erratic, often destructive system of justice and law; a proud people unsuccessfully striving for freedom. In this atmosphere, it is understandable that the people believed that the Last Days had come. Foretold in various prophecies, but especially in Daniel, the Last Days were the worst and best of times, "a time of trouble, such as never was since there was a nation . . . and at that time thy people shall be delivered" (Dan. 12:1). The date forecast by Daniel had now arrived (by a procedure customary to biblical prophecy, the seventy weeks cited by Daniel had been interpreted as seventy weeks of years and stretched to 490 years; the book itself, written probably in the time of the Maccabees, had been dated back to the reigns of Nebuchadnezzar and Darius, in the sixth century B.C.), and a Messianic passion aroused the whole nation. "By the first century of our era," Schonfield notes, "it had become quite feverish, and had engendered a state of near hysteria among the people."[16] " 'Open the Scriptures. What do they say?'" the rabbi of Nazareth exhorts the faithful. " 'When Israel is hurled from its throne and our holy soil is trodden by barbarian feet, the end of the world will have come!' . . . The prophecies, therefore, have been fulfilled: the end of the world is here! A voice resounded by the Jordan: "He's coming!" A voice resounds within us: "He's coming!" Today I opened the Scriptures and the letters drew together and cried, "He's coming!"' " (p. 306).

And so the people await the Messiah. At weddings, the guests greet bride and groom "expressing the wish that they might give birth to a son who would rescue Israel from its slavery" (p. 218). Rabbi Simeon awakes with the sun and calls out to heaven, "rousing God, reminding him of the promise he had made to Israel. 'God of Israel, God of Israel, how long?' cried the rabbi" (p. 14). His nephew next door begins the new day in fear; he has dreamed again of the dwarfs armed with a crown of thorns and of the redbeard who leads them. They have traveled throughout the land in the night, " 'searched for the most virtuous, the most God-fearing [man]. Every time we found him we cried, "You're the One, why are you hiding? Arise and save Israel!" But as soon as he saw the tools we carried, his blood ran cold . . . and [he] threw himself into a life of wine, gambling and women in order to save himself'" (p. 9); this time they settle on Jesus, who makes crosses to save himself. In the desert, the aged Abbot Joachim listens to the Vision of Daniel, demands that he be allowed to witness the "son of man" during his lifetime; when the son of Mary enters his cell, he blissfully greets him and dies (pp. 101, 138). Even the children play at being Messiah (p. 402), and the Samaritan woman wonders if Jesus is the One (p. 222).

But Jesus is a new kind of prophet, "not a wild one like the prophets of old, but gay and domesticated. He was lowering the kingdom of heaven to earth" (p. 286). The ax that the Baptist leaves him turns in his hand to a branch of flowering almond (p. 254). He is not the same hope that Simeon, Joachim, and Judas have long awaited; even his followers are slow to realize that he might be the Messiah. In his parables, in his travels through Samaria, in accepting the publican Matthew among his disciples, he is rebelling against the formalistic Old Law of the Jews. How different his God is from the "splendid leader of cutthroats" whom Judas admires (p. 246). But he accents his own sense of tradition: "'I have come not to abolish the old commandments but to extend them. . . . The old law instructs you to honor your father and your mother; but I say, Do not imprison your heart within your parents' home. Let it emerge and enter all homes, embrace the whole of Israel . . . and even beyond'" (pp. 345–46). When he returns from the desert, his mind now on fire, he goes beyond his former message of love and simplicity and advocates instead a great leap forward: "'The old Law must be torn down, and it is I who shall tear it down. A new Law must be engraved on the tables of the heart, and it is I who shall engrave it. I shall widen the Law to make it contain friends and enemies, Jews and idolators: the Ten Commandments will burst into bloom!'" (p. 367). All of this, of course, is present within the New Testament, especially in the Gospel of Matthew, written by a Jew to convince his compatriots of the need for change. But this Jesus supersedes Matthew as well, for God, he insists, "'is not an Israelite, he is immortal Spirit!'" (p. 373). And so he opposes the codification of his own new law; if it too becomes canon, it will grow as rigid as the old and lose its universality. As the disciples detail the new scriptures and laws that they will erect after his death, Jesus protests: "'You crucify the spirit. . . . It won't be free any more; it won't be spirit.'" But Jacob responds for his fellows: "'That doesn't matter. It will look like spirit. For our work, Rabbi, that's sufficient'" (p. 427). Their betrayal anticipates the still more structured labors of Paul.

Judas is the one disciple to understand and oppose his master's new teaching: the Savior he seeks carries an ax and not a flowering branch. Ordered by the Zealots to kill the maker of crosses, Judas becomes his follower instead, for he suspects before anyone else that his childhood friend may be the Messiah. In his obsession with immediate political goals, in his insistence on the supremacy of body over soul, he seems antithetical to the man whom he follows. Yet from the first he is closest to Jesus; even uncomplaining John envies their intimacy: " 'When you speak to him,' " he complains to Jesus, " 'why is your voice sweeter than it is when you speak to us?' " (p. 197). And Magdalene, who alone understands the "terrible secret" that binds them (p. 392), wonders why Judas should have been chosen.[17] The only realist in a crowd of self-seekers and dreamers, he is the one disciple able to act, a colossus stronger than the master himself. Thus it is he who must betray Jesus, to enable him to fulfill his mission, perhaps to become the Messiah: " 'It is necessary for me to be killed and for you to betray me. We two must save the world. Help me.' Judas bowed his head. After a moment he asked, 'If you had to betray your master, would you do it?' Jesus reflected for a long time. Finally he said, 'No, I do not think I would be able to. That is why God pitied me and gave me the easier task: to be crucified' " (p. 421). When Jesus dreams on the cross that his crucifixion has never occurred, that he has lived instead a pedestrian life, it is his uncompromising disciple who compels him to return to his mission, to awake on the cross and call out to God.

IV

It is in Bethany, fifteen furlongs from Jerusalem (John 11:18), that the last temptation takes place. Bethany in the Gospels is the place where Jesus prepares for his death, where he rests on his final journey to the capital (Mark 11:11), and where (in the home of Simon the leper, who may well be the father of Judas [John 13:26]) he is anointed for burial (Mark 14:3–9 and Matt. 26:6–13). The Gospel of John identifies Bethany as the "certain village" in which Jesus is welcomed by the sisters Martha and Mary (Luke 10:38–39), Mary as his anointer and Martha as the first to acknowledge him; it is Lazarus their brother whom he will raise from the grave (John 11:1–53). The resurrection of Lazarus is the central event in the ministry of Jesus, "His last and greatest sign,"[18] as R. H. Lightfoot puts it, for it creates the first true believers and inevitably leads to his death. Fearful of his power, the Pharisees resolve to kill both Jesus and Lazarus. Caiaphas, their leader, quoting Isaiah, reasons as Jesus himself might: "It is expedient for us that one man should die for the people.... And not for that nation only, but that also he should gather together in one the children of God that were scattered abroad" (John 11:50–52).

The Evangelist's account of the raising of Lazarus parallels and predicts the resurrection of Christ, who must first die symbolically for his friend to be saved. Even the cave in which Lazarus has lain suggests the sepulchre of Christ, and Jesus' cry to Lazarus to come forth is echoed in his last call to God. "In more ways than one," Lightfoot contends, "St. John closely links the Lord's bestowal of life upon Lazarus with the traditional [Synoptic Gospel] accounts of the Lord's last moments.... According to St. John in the moment at the grave of Lazarus, at least as truly as in ... the moment of the Lord's death, is to be found the lowest depth of the Lord's devotion and self-abasement for man's sake."[19] To Kazantzakis, as to St. John, the role of Lazarus is central to the Passion of Christ. But his evangelism is of a different sort, and with deep sensitivity and insight he makes this seemingly minor figure a key to our understanding of a convincingly human Jesus.

Lazarus in the novel serves as a kind of precursor, as announcer of Jesus' mission, as sign of his power and cause of his martyrdom: before they seek out Jesus in Nazareth, the dwarfs of his vision march through Bethany, " 'where we practically murdered poor Lazarus to no avail'" (p. 9). Jesus learns that his own time has come when the death of the Baptist is reported by Lazarus (p. 274), and the crime from whose punishment Barabbas is freed is the murder of Lazarus reborn (pp. 414, 437). The raising of Lazarus takes place offstage but assumes awesome significance: "The moment had come. This was the sign he had been waiting for. The hopelessly rotted world was a Lazarus. The time had come for him to cry out, 'World arise!' ... It was no longer possible for him to escape by saying, I am unable! He was able, and if the world failed to be saved, the entire sin must fall on him" (p. 372). Lazarus awakes smelling of earth and wonders if he has been dreaming (p. 395); his uncertainty anticipates the last temptation of Jesus, a lifetime so vividly realized that we are uncertain whether its reality is history or dream.

In this final vision, in the instant between the beginning and end of his last call to God, Jesus is saved from death by a green-winged angel and again brought to Bethany. Here he assumes the occupation, the name, even the body of Lazarus and marries both sisters, Mary, the rival of Magdalene—herself killed in this vision by the puritan Saul—and Martha, a substitute mother.[20] With them he lives out the apotheosis of earthly existence, discovering at last that the body is the road to immortality, that it is his work with the land and the children he leaves behind him that alone conquer death. In his old age, his former disciples appear at his home, defeated old men, their lives deprived of meaning by his betrayal. "'I don't believe in anything any more,'" Judas proclaims; "'I don't believe in anyone. You broke my heart!'" (p. 494). They disappear, led off by Judas, and Jesus' home, the trees, the village itself—his dream life as Lazarus—vanish with them. He awakes on the cross and finishes his cry, ELI, ELI... LAMA SABACTHANI. "Suddenly he remembered where he was, who he was and why he felt pain. A wild, indomitable joy took possession of him. No, no, he was not a coward, a deserter, a traitor. No, he was nailed to the cross. He had stood his ground honorably to the very end; he had kept his word" (pp. 495–96). It is not the fruit of man's physical life that survives him, not his yielding to human temptation. The green-winged angel is no symbol of life but a sign of inevitable death and decay, the devil himself, man yielding to his own temptation and moldering like Lazarus. There may be no rebirth for this Jesus—the novel concludes with his "triumphant cry"—but in a sense he has gone beyond his namesake: he has been crucified and still been tested, compelled to choose even to the end. The last temptation is his greatest trial—stronger than those of his dreams, more demanding than those in the desert—his greatest victory over death earned in his final moment of life. What first seems heresy is in fact an act of devotion, Kazantzakis' tribute to a man in whom all men can believe, for he is one of us, and he rises above us.

Jesus as Lazarus, dead once more and not once more to be raised, is the central myth of the novel, but other archetypes also operate here, fertility figures, both Jewish and pagan, whose presence suggests some kind of new life for man. In the biblical pattern, in his dreams in particular, Jesus becomes the new Adam to Magdalene's Eve. Out of the chaos of his initial vision—a world as dark, hot, and silent as the earth prior to Creation—Jesus emerges as Adam in Paradise: "A cool heavenly breeze took possession of him" (p. 5)—the first words of the novel. But the wind shifts and brings to his bed of wood shavings the smells of the village, not Eden but Nazareth and Bethany, man's fallen world after he is expelled from the garden. Later, in the home of Lazarus, he dreams of himself as Adam newly created, his fresh clay ripening in the sun (pp. 279–80); on the way to the monastery, as he passes Magdala, he dreams again of the garden and sex (p. 81); and the snake tempts him in the desert as it did his great-grandfather Adam, insisting that it is Magdalene-Eve whom he must save (p. 256). He resists the temptations of sex and power, of godhead too, and emerges from his ordeal in the desert weakened in body but confident in his true strength. But he is too quickly assured; he has not yet overcome his human desires: the fruit that so quickly revives him on the outskirts of Bethany (p. 266) is from the same pomegranate tree—a fertility symbol long tied to Kore[21]—which stands as a symbol of knowledge at Magdalene's door (p. 85). She appears again in his final dream, again as Eve, the first great martyr, speaking of death with God in the garden (pp. 451–52). Jesus as Adam is all men, tempted by life just when he thinks he has mastered his weakness, saving mankind because of his weakness, himself to be saved by one who supersedes him.

Jesus as Noah offers salvation to men caught up in their wordly pursuits. In the fiery desert where Abraham and Moses first spoke with God, he too hears the voice of the Lord: " 'Son of the Carpenter, a new flood is lashing out, not of water this time, but of fire. Build a new ark, select the saintly, and place them inside!' The selection has begun, friends. The ark is ready; the door is still open. Enter!" (p. 302). The humanist innkeeper Simon has already explained how this new ark can resist the flames: " 'The thing they call Noah's ark, what do you think it is? Man's heart, of course! Inside sits God with all his creatures' " (p. 293). The great flood that assaults the monastery and washes the grain from the threshing floors (pp. 98, 109) marks the end of Jesus' old way of life; he determines now that there is no escape, that he must pursue his own mission. And he will bring the deluge of fire next time, his Sodom the old Jerusalem. In this same desert in which the cities of old are buried, he recalls the wrath of the Baptist and God. "He thought of Sodom and Gomorrah . . . plunged in the tar. Abraham had shouted, 'Have mercy, Lord; do not burn them. Are you not good? Take pity, therefore, on your creatures.' And God had answered him, 'I am just, I shall burn them all!' " (pp. 254–55). Only the new Noah—like the Lot of old, who was probably an Edomite fertility god—can survive this Flood and start life anew for mankind.

As fertility god, the new Jesus will marry the earth (p. 195) and die for all men instead. He will be Boaz, keeper of the grain, to Martha as Ruth (pp. 462, 466); Jacob, keeper of his people, to both sisters as Leah and Rachel (p. 470); the bull slain by Mithra, the corn god, waiting for death " 'like a dark and wounded god' " (p. 448). He will die as the king always must die—Lazarus become part of the soil (p. 374), the cross become a springtime flowering tree (p. 444)—to save the wheat and the people. "Why couldn't the wind of Jehovah fill the dried-out wells of the desert with water? Why couldn't the Lord love the green leaf and feel pity for men? Oh, if only one man could be found to approach him, fall at his feet and succeed, before being reduced to ashes, in telling him of man's suffering, and of the suffering of the earth and of the green leaf!" (p. 140).[22] Jesus finds his own identity in the myths of his precursors. From the young man who does not know why he suffers or what forces pursue him, who cannot know what he is to become or even what he should call himself, he moves confidently on to his destiny, achieves at the end his own salvation and the saving of those who believe in him. At the end he knows why he suffers: because he is man, because he is god, "because Buddha, Christ and Dionysus are one—the eternal suffering man."[23]

V

In Saint Catherine's Monastery, in the Sinai desert, an old Greek monk, who had once known Kazantzatis' father, told Kazantzakis of a "strange temptation" he had had in his sleep.

> I saw myself as a great sage in Jerusalem. I could cure many different diseases, but first and foremost I was able to remove demons from the possessed. People brought patients to me from all over Palestine, and one day Mary the wife of Joseph arrived from Nazareth, bringing her twelve-year-old son Jesus. . . .
> I kept him near me for a month, addressed him ever so gently, gave him herbs to make him sleep. I placed him in a carpenter's shop to learn a trade. We went out for walks together and I spoke to him about God. . . . We spoke of the weather, of the wheatfields and vineyards, the young girls who went to the fountain. . . .
> At the end of a month's time . . . Jesus was completely cured. He no longer wrestled with God; he had become a man like all other men. He departed for Galilee, and I learned afterwards that he had become a fine carpenter, the best in Nazareth. . . . Instead of saving the world, he became the best carpenter in Nazareth![24]

The monk Joachim was surely the model for the fictional Abbot Joachim, his dream most likely the novel's donnée. In it Kazantzakis had found another figure of his lifelong concern, of his own temptation, the man struck by divinity. "Every man," he wrote of that meeting in Sinai, "is half God, half man; he is both spirit and flesh. That is why the mystery of Christ is not simply a mystery for a particular creed; it is universal. . . . The stronger the soul and the flesh, the more fruitful the struggle and the richer the final harmony . . .—the supreme purpose of the struggle—union with God: this was the ascent taken by Christ, the ascent which He invites us to take as well, following in His bloody tracks."[25]

Jesus in the novel is consistently human, the desires and fears of his youth persisting to the end of his life: he is attractive to women and attracted by them; he is frightened to be alone in the desert and rejoices when he is again among men; he is tempted on the cross at the end of his mission as he is tempted in the desert at its beginning. His concern throughout is for man's life on earth— " 'What's beyond is God's affair,' " he declares (p. 224). But he is torn between man and God. In his early fear of divine pursuit, he still yearns for godhead; in his later confidence in his new role, he still fears that he may be mistaken. He recognizes that the raising of Lazarus is the surest sign of his legitimacy, but he is sickened by the dead man's smell and appalled at his own miraculous power: " 'When I saw him lift up the tombstone I became terrified. I wanted to run away but was too ashamed. I stayed there and trembled' " (p. 395). But his humanity in no way diminishes his significance, for "Christ passed through all the stages which the man who struggles passes through. All—and that is why His suffering is so familiar to us . . . and why His final victory seems to us so much our own future victory. . . . If He had not within Him this warm human element, He would never be able to touch our hearts. . . ."[26] The disciples believe Jesus is God precisely because they know he also is man: "All these ends of the world and kingdoms of heaven were not dreams and mere excitement, they were the truth; and the dark-complexioned, barefooted youth next to them who ate, spoke, laughed and slept like other men was truly the apostle of God" (p. 325).

Jesus is most like man in his duality, in the tensions between his body and soul. As some of his followers are tied to the signs of their senses—Philip to his sheep, Thomas the capitalist to his business, and Judas to his patriotism—so he is drawn to the earthly life symbolized by woman; as others among them glorify their souls and demean their physical senses—the monkish spirituality of John is the foremost example of this—so he is impelled to favor his soul: it is a partridge, he says (p. 259), and the body merely " 'the camel on which the soul mounts in order to traverse the desert' " (p. 336). Paradoxically, the partridge-soul is more durable, more worthy of trust in this spiritual desert. But Jesus forgets, and he comes to believe with Magdalene that the soul of man may after all be a woman (p. 329, cf. p. 90); he moves between body and soul even to the end of his life. Then, fittingly, it is sensual Judas who reminds him in his vision of his own teaching.

> "Judas," he said, his voice trembling, "you were always intractable and wild; you never accepted human limits. You forget that the soul of man is an arrow: it darts as high as it can toward heaven but always falls back down again to earth. Life on earth means shedding one's wings."
> Hearing this, Judas became frantic, "Shame on you!" he screamed. "Is

that what you've come to, you, the son of David, the son of God, the Messiah! Life on earth means: to eat bread and transform the bread into wings, to drink water and to transform the water into wings. Life on earth means: the sprouting of wings." (p. 493)

Kazantzakis' heroes often appear to reject their senses, but the beauty of the physical world is too great for them to ignore. However, they achieve no true resolution; they remain torn between body and soul, between the very real life of this world and the hoped-for life of another. So Thomas converted sells two kinds of wares—combs and cosmetics on top, the kingdom of heaven below (p. 206); so a blind minstrel sings alike of naked women and God (p. 284); so life and dream coalesce. When Manoliós in *The Greek Passion* attempts to repudiate this life, we feel that he somehow has erred, that a man of spirit alone is somehow incomplete. This is an error that Jesus does not make. Drawn both to Magdalene and to the monastery, recognizing two opposing paths to salvation, he is both "sweet teacher" and "savage Baptist" (p. 294), apostle of love and of fire. Surely, Jesus favors the spirit, but he is drawn by his nature to demands of the flesh. He would overcome these if he could—and to some extent he does in the end—but the body, he knows, may truly be worthy, the earthly life at its best capable of beauty and a kind of immortality as well. In the sensual atmosphere in which he lives, in a world full of mystical overtones, only nature can resolve the conflict between body and soul, and then only in part. To John, the rabbi quotes an ascetic—a profligate in his youth—who lives on Mount Carmel, his words echoing those of Joachim, the monk from Mount Sinai. " ' "One morning I saw a flowering almond tree and was saved" ' " (p. 429).[27] It is through nature that the senses are raised almost to spirit, through nature that we may achieve that "profound correspondence between body and soul, between earth and man" (p. 467). Manoliós perceives this truth as he goes to his death, but it is lost in his moment of sacrifice; Jesus recalls it even at the end. His sacrifice is a victory for spirit, but not a negation of earthly concerns; he overcomes his bodily limits, but he does not deny them, and so he achieves "union with God." Soul and body coexist in Kazantzakian man not in some Aristotelian mean, but in constant, ever-warring tension; this tension itself is the goal of the fiction—not the resolution of tension. It is apparent in the very structure of the novels, glorifying spirit in theme, but upholding body in substance. The author creates an earth so vital, so capable of beauty, that no heavenly impulse can negate it. Only in *Zorba the Greek*, his most philosophical novel, does he endeavor to resolve the tension and make it an aspect of theme.

VI

There are similar echoes from the rest of Kazantzakis' canon, but again with key variations. Certain metaphors and themes recur in each of his works, but always in new contexts and at times with new meanings as well. Thus, the nationalistic struggle of *Freedom or Death* here becomes universal, and the role-playing and metaphor of *The Greek Passion* are here transformed into reality and myth. The pervasive animal imagery is part of the naturalistic surface of each of the novels, the imagery of fire and wings again derived from *The Saviors of God* and the interplay of dream and reality drawn from the author's own life and his view of the modern consciousness—a balance of tensions and not one of harmony. But these final motifs also have biblical roots.

The intertwined snakes painted above Magdalene's door (p. 84) derive, of course, from the serpent in Eden. They appear again after the storm at the monastery and perform their sensuous, coupling dance. " 'They have fled from your heart' " (p. 151), Rabbi Simeon interprets for Jesus, who has at last overcome his lust for his cousin. But perhaps he has not escaped her completely: it is a snake "with the eyes and breasts of a woman" that tempts him in the desert (p. 255). In a dream he watches a trembling partridge move inexorably toward the snake's open mouth and finally plunge in—man's soul, he believes, succumbing to bodily temptation (p. 259); but the partridge may be the same bird that Magdalene keeps at her door, suspended in its cage from a pomegranate branch (p. 85)—a sign of the body perhaps, and not of the soul. His failure to perceive that body and soul may unite in the partridge, as in man himself, should warn us that he has not yet surmounted his weakness and prepare us for his final temptation. But, then, all symbols blur in the desert.

For this is the same "fiery air" in which the Prophets of old "had cried out to God" (p. 142), on which Elijah had risen to heaven (p. 124); the flames with which the Baptist threatens the earth are those which formerly destroyed the cities of the plain (p. 242). Early in the novel, fire describes the physical and political atmosphere of Zion; later, it serves as a metaphor of its spiritual needs. It is God's fire that has burned out his father and that singes young Jesus (p. 24); it becomes in his hands a means to rebirth, to heal man's soul: " 'Before the kingdom of heaven,' " he proclaims, " 'the kingdom of fire' " (p. 308). In his last temptation it becomes the fire in the hearth at Bethany (p. 459). " 'The great conflagration subsided, I too became a kind tranquil fire' " (p. 476).

Symbols blur in dreams as in reality; they can be sent by the devil as well as by God. "'Whatever you Jews yearn for while you're awake,'" Pilate tells Jesus, "'you see in your sleep. You live and die with visions.'" And Jesus responds by citing the vision of Daniel, of freedom for Israel and destruction for her enslavers; but now the clay-footed statue is Rome, and he is the stone flung by God in order to topple it (p. 382; cf. Dan. 2:31–45). For man always dreams of what he most fears and desires. So Jesus dreams in the desert of sex and power and divinity, as at the end he envisions hearth and home in Bethany. Lazarus rises from death and wonders if he has been dreaming (p. 395); Jesus awakes on the Cross and hastens to Bethany—his is a dream within a dream. He dreams now that the crucifixion itself was a dream and that Martha and Mary are his reality. The visionary prophecy of Daniel, of freedom for man and dominion for God, becomes in his vision a dream of petty domesticity. But he struggles to awake from this last temptation—as earlier he had fought out of his dream of Redbeard and the dwarfs—and aided by Judas, he awakes and dies on the cross, affirming the life he has chosen to lead and denying the one he might have enjoyed. He truly lives and dies with his visions. In the silence at the edge of the precipice, confronting himself across the abyss of human desires and forgetfulness, he has at last sprouted wings, his life a dramatization of all men's struggles, a living metaphor that grows from the rhetorical imagery of *The Saviors of God.*

VII

The Last Temptation of Christ is Kazantzakis' only novel that demonstrates an awareness of Modernist innovations in narrative technique. His other novels are completely chronological and largely omniscient, but the theme of this work demands a sense of subjective time and a limited, sometimes even ambiguous, point of view. It is his most effective union of function and form. Like the New Testament story of Christ, *The Last Temptation* creates a feeling of haste, of the need for speedy salvation. The active preaching of Christ is hardly dated at all in the Gospels and covers at most two years; the career of Kazantzakis' Jesus—his promised union with the earth and the people and God—is similarly timeless, for "Time is not a field, to be measured in rods, nor a sea, to be measured in miles; it is a heart beat. How long did this betrothal last? Days? Months? Years?" (p. 195). But it is not a finite event and cannot be measured so simply.

Time passes swiftly not only in dreams—the entire lifetime of Jesus in Bethany takes place in the single instant of his vision—but in all human life. Measured against the chronology of God, man's life is truly an instant. So he might be expected to ignore the transience of social and political reform and concentrate instead on the soul's eternity. Against the continuity of Jewish history, however, against the long tradition of his suffering people, Judas demands change during his lifetime: " 'I'm a man, and that means a thing which is in a hurry' " (p. 246). And the Abbot adds, speaking like Job to God, " 'We know well enough that one second for you is a thousand years for men. All right, but if you're just, Lord, you'll measure the time with man's measure, not with yours. That's what justice means!' " (p. 102). Jesus endeavors to live by both measures, to dignify man's time on earth and to glorify the heavenly spirit. The result is a form of simultaneity more dense philosophically than anything in Proust, Woolf, or Joyce; it is not simply clock time and the time of the mind that Kazantzakis balances here, but those of man and of God—not a psychological insight with which he is concerned, but a metaphysical premise basic to man's place in the universe—two distinct, coexisting standards that parallel the duality of body and soul.

Point of view in *The Last Temptation* follows a similar pattern: largely conventional, but with one stunning insight. In general, it recalls the limited omniscience of *The Greek Passion*, shifting frequently among characters and settings and from exterior to interior views. We are aware throughout of an authorial presence, not so much Kazantzakis himself—the author as puppeteer, in the Thackeray mode—as some objective observer who is present at all the events of the narrative and who subtly attempts to involve the reader in them. Thus, listening to the disciples sing with their teacher, "your heart skipped a beat: they can't keep it up, you said to yourself" (p. 219). We are able in this way to penetrate into events that even Jesus, who is at their center, cannot fully comprehend. As he is baptized in the Jordan, a white-feathered bird circles his head, crying out "as though proclaiming a hidden name, a name never heard before. . . . He had a presentiment that here was his true name, but he could not distinguish what it was." He is not even certain whether it is a bird or an angel. But we are less limited, for the Baptist understands the language of God, and through him we learn the bird's message. "Today is baptized, he whispered to himself, trembling, the servant of God, the son of God, the Hope of mankind!" (p. 240). The disciples, however, construct a far different version of this miracle.

"And did you all see the dove over his head while he was being baptized?"
"It wasn't a dove, it was a flash of lightning."
"No, no—a dove. It was cooing."
"It wasn't cooing; it was talking. I heard it with my own ears say: 'Saint! Saint! Saint!' "

"It was the Holy Spirit!" said Peter, his eyes filling with wings of gold. "The Holy Spirit came down from heaven and we all turned to stone, don't you remember!..."

"I didn't see anything and I didn't hear anything," said Judas, incensed. "... You had an appetite to see the Holy Spirit, so it was the Holy Spirit you saw. And what's more, now you make these numbskulls see it too. You'll have to answer for the consequences." (p. 287)

And Jesus, when he was baptized, went up straightway out of the water: and lo, the heavens were opened unto him, and he saw the Spirit of God descending like a dove, and lighting upon him:
And lo a voice from heaven, saying, this is my beloved Son, in whom I am well pleased. (Matt. 3:16–17).

The publican Matthew has closed down his custom house and shut his ledger forever in order to follow the master. Now he has opened another book. "How should he begin? Where should he begin? God had placed him next to this holy man in order that he might faithfully record the words he said and the miracles he performed..., to catch with his pen all that was about to perish and... to make it immortal" (p. 326). As a follower of Jesus, he can record certain events at first hand; but for many details, he is dependent upon others, especially upon the remaining disciples. He himself is so disreputable, however, his reputation as tax collector for the Romans and his physical appearance so filthy, that they avoid him whenever they can. He has questioned Peter about the incident of the dove, "but Peter recoiled and turned his face aside to avoid inhaling the publican's breath" (p. 327). And so he is forced to rely upon different sources. He knows the Scriptures intimately, and from the first is aware "how the teacher's sayings and deeds were exactly the same as the prophets, centuries earlier, had proclaimed; and if once in a while the prophecies and Jesus' life did not quite match,... [and] if he occasionally matched things by force, God forgives!... Did not an angel come and bend over his ear to intone what he was to write?" (pp. 348–49). Matthew had begun by writing of the birth of Jesus to poor parents in Nazareth, but the angel had dictated details of the virgin birth—to fulfill the prophecy of Isaiah (Isa. 7:14)—and of the stable in Bethlehem—according to Micah (Mic. 5:2).

But his subject protests this fantastic account. "'What is this?' he screamed. 'Lies! Lies! Lies! The Messiah doesn't need miracles. He is the miracle—no other is necessary! I was born in Nazareth, not in Bethlehem; I've never even set foot in Bethlehem, and I don't remember any Magi. I never in my life went to Egypt; and what you write about the dove saying "This is my beloved son" to me as I was being baptized—who revealed that to you? I myself didn't hear clearly. How did you find out, you who weren't even there?'" So Matthew reveals the presence of his angel, and Jesus relents. "If this was the highest level of truth, inhabited only by God . . . . If what we called Truth, God called lies. . . . 'Write whatever the angel dictates,' Jesus said. 'It is too late for me to . . .' But he left his sentence unfinished" (pp. 391–92).[28]

Matthew's own reaction to his narrative is still more vigorous. When the worn-out disciples confront their one-time master in his vision at Bethany, the chronicler laments not the loss to the world but his personal loss: " 'You should have been crucified. Yes, if only for my sake, so that these writings might have been saved, you should have been crucified!' " (p. 494). One sympathetic critic, attempting to justify Matthew's role on realistic grounds, explains that his belief in his dictating angel "might be described in psychoanalytic terms as an autonomous complex that takes control over a conscious function."[29] But his role in the novel is far too important to be explained on psychological grounds alone, for Matthew as dual point of view is one of the keys to the novelist's inspired use of the biblical story.

In *The Last Temptation* Kazantzakis has transformed the Gospel of Matthew into an eyewitness account of the ministry of Jesus; he has intentionally merged the sophisticated scholar whose Greek-language work, so dependent on Mark, appeared a generation after the death of Jesus, with his probably unlettered namesake who had personally followed the rabbi. Within this reflexive approach, Matthew is both an actor in the events and the source on which they are based, a deviation from traditional accounts and their verification. By blurring distinctions between the two Matthews, as readers of the Bible have frequently done by mistake, Kazantzakis recreates both the sophisticated effects and the air of simplicity of the original Gospel. For Matthew makes use not only of the biography of the gentile Mark, but of the sacred documents of his own Jewish forebears, and blends with them material that is clearly legendary; he can thus have it both ways, both Bethlehem and Nazareth (see Matt. 2:13–23 and 21:11), both Mark's account of the dove (Mark 1:9–11) and echoes from Daniel, the Psalms, and Isaiah. Kazantzakis discards much of Matthew that is most obviously apocryphal—the tales of the Magi and Egypt, for instance, but not the three desert temptations—and borrows as well from other Gospel accounts. He even merges John, the brother of James, with John the Evangelist, who wrote at the end of the century, creating still another point of view, an implicit one to underlie Matthew's—for we know that John will one day write his own commentary and that it will be still more creative and daring than that of his predecessor. The result of all this is a sense of narrative excitement, increased involvement on the part of the reader, our awareness that the story of Jesus may have many more levels than we have previously known.

Kazantzakis brings to his task great knowledge and great sensitivity. He seems to have read all the relevant scholarship. "For a year now I've been taking out of the library at Cannes all the books written about Christ and Judea, the Chronicles of that time, the Talmud etc. And so all the details are historically correct, even though I recognize the right of the poet not to follow history in a slavish way."[30] He has furthermore realized possibilities that have long been submerged beneath orthodox interpretations—he recognizes, above all, as Francis Bayard Rhein puts it, that Jesus in the Gospels is "a man whose personality dominates every scene of which he was a part. Here is no pale, emaciated weakling. Ecclesiastical art has done history a disservice."[31] Kazantzakis' controversial reading brings new vitality to many aspects of these traditional tales. He alludes to the birth of Jesus, so central to the Gospels, only in retrospect, so that Jesus the man comes to the fore; he sees in Lazarus and Matthew new ways to understand the nature of Jesus; he largely invents the relationships with Magdalene and Judas and posits the disciples and Paul as future betrayers; he ends with the crucifixion of Jesus and not the resurrection of Christ. He had traced many of these possibilities in *The Greek Passion,* but *The Last Temptation* is more convincing and moving. Jesus of Nazareth is both more human—more susceptible to temptation—and nobler than Manoliós the shepherd, and so is his betrayer.

It has become almost customary to contend that in *The Last Temptation* Kazantzakis had written merely a variation of his familiar narrative pattern, that in particular he had made the Jews of first-century Palestine into the imagined, heroic Cretans of his father's generation.[32] But this is to miss the significance of the Cretan experience for Kazantzakis. The Galilean surroundings of Jesus do recall the Crete of Captain Mihális, but they function as metaphor and not as substitute reality. All those values that Kazantzakis had found in the history and culture of Crete, those universal values that he summed up as the Cretan Glance, are present in Jesus and in Galilee. His accomplishment is not so much to see this analogy as it is to use one place as a metaphor to illumine the other: through the overlay of Crete, we perceive the full significance of Galilee; because we have known the shepherd Manoliós and Captain Mihális, we can appreciate fully the nobility of Jesus. When Jesus determines to awake on the cross, when he wills the renewal of suffering, he is repudiating—like his predecessors—the fatalism of those who would accept a limited role for mankind and asserting his own worth and integrity. He moves at his death beyond even this, from the limited vision of the disciples and Paul to the peak of human needs and accomplishments, from local politics to universality.

There is a verse in Seferis' *Mithistórima* that sums up the dilemma of existential man in a Modernist age. "But what do our souls seek voyaging/ on the decks of outworn vessels," wonders a shipwrecked and rootless descendant of the Argonauts and the crew of Odysseus.

> But what do our souls seek voyaging
> on rotted seacraft
> from port to port?
> . . . .
> in a country that is no longer ours
> nor yours.[33]

In *The Last Temptation of Christ*, Kazantzakis provides an answer. Through his hero we learn what harbor it is that our souls continue to seek. The Modernists of the West—and Seferis might almost be numbered among them, since his sources are as much Western as Greek—taught us that in a rotting world there is no haven for searching man; but the Cretan Kazantzakis shows us how, metaphorically at least, we may regain the land and redeem ourselves.

1. George Seferis, "Dialogue on Poetry: What Is Hellenism?" *On the Greek Style*, trans. Rex Warner (Boston, 1966), p. 82.

2. Victor R. Yanitelli, S. J., *Best Sellers*, 20 (September 1, 1960), p. 186.

3. Robert Flood, C. S. B., *The Critic*, 19 (October/November 1960), p. 56.

4. Michael Novak, "Inner Struggle of a Romantic Artist," *Commonweal*, 72 (September 16, 1960), p. 502.

5. R. Gartagenes, cited in Anthonakes, p. 145. Gartagenes wrote in 1954, but according to Anthonakes, *The Last Temptation of Christ* "did not appear in Greek until December, 1955. One must conclude that this critic knew German and read it in that language. But there is nothing in his study about *The Last Temptation*. Is it possible that this critic... made this extremely general analysis of Kazantzakis without having read the novel?" This is not a unique possibility in the history of Kazantzakis criticism in Greece.

6. Letter to Börje Knös, Antibes, January 1, 1952, cited in Helen Kazantzakis, p. 507.

7. Letter to Börje Knös, Antibes, November 13, 1951, cited in Helen Kazantzakis, p. 505.

8. Hugh J. Schonfield, *The Passover Plot* (New York, 1965), p. 38.

9. The reluctance of the hero to fulfill his preordained mission is part of the archetype: his "willed introversion," says Joseph Campbell, "is a deliberate, terrific refusal to respond to anything but the deepest, highest, richest answer to the as yet unknown demand of some waiting void within." The answer comes in response to this refusal: "as a result of which some power of transformation carries the problem to a plane of new magnitudes, where it is suddenly and finally resolved." *The Hero With A Thousand Faces* (Cleveland, 1956), pp. 64–65.

10. All references are to the Simon and Schuster edition (New York, 1960), trans. Peter A. Bien.

11. In Thom Gunn's poem "Jesus and His Mother," *Poems 1950–1966: A Selection* (London, 1969), a very human Mary complains to her son, both human and divine, whom she fears will soon be taken from her. Like Kazantzakis' Mary, she has raised her son to be no more than a man, and she possessively resents any other fate for him:

> Why are you sullen when I speak?
> Here are your tools, the saw and knife
> And hammer on your bench. Your life
> Is measured here in week and week
> Planed as the furniture you make,
> And I will teach you like a wife
> To be my own and all my own.

12. In *Those Incredible Christians* (New York, 1965), Schonfield cites the second-century Church historian Hegesippus as claiming that the words attributed to Jesus on the cross by Luke (23:34), "Father, forgive them; for they know not what they do," were actually the last words of James, who was martyred by stoning (p. 213).

13. "It is not Jesus, the man, who might conceivably have been accepted as the Jewish Messiah, but the divine Christ whom Paul encountered in a revelation who fills Paul's concern and to whom Paul is dedicated. He is determined not to know Christ 'from the human point of view' (II Cor. 5:16); his interest in the significance of Jesus' career completely overshadows the details of his career, and his writings give few data about Jesus. . . . The man Jesus, then, has little relevance to Paul's thought." Samuel Sandmel, *A Jewish Understanding of the New Testament* (Cincinnati, 1956), pp. 52–53.

14. G. A. Williamson, *The World of Josephus* (Boston, 1964), p. 99.

15. Williamson, p. 100.

16. Schonfield, *The Passover Plot*, p. 23.

17. The one major European writer who has clearly been influenced by Kazantzakis is Elie Wiesel, the recorder of the Holocaust. In *The Gates of the Forest* (New York, 1972), a young Jewish refugee, pretending to be a deaf mute in order to escape the Nazis, is pressed into service as Judas in the Passion Play of an Hungarian village. His conception of the role is very much like that of Kazantzakis' character: "Meanwhile, as a good actor, Gregor struggled to accommodate himself to the character of Judas. Who was he? Christ's best disciple and closest friend. From one day to the next, and for no apparent reason, his loyalty was shattered and Judas became a traitor. Why? Why this sudden change? According to the Gospels there was an obscure story of money. Thirty pieces of silver. Absurd and inconceivable: The money adds to the mystery rather than explaining it. Christ's companions had no interest in terrestrial things—these had nothing to do with their aspirations. There had to be other reasons, more hidden than these. If the disciple abandoned his Master for thirty miserable pieces of silver, it meant that both men were more vulnerable than they knew" (p. 101). This shifting relationship has intrigued others as well: Professor Schonfield sees Judas as an unwitting participant in Jesus' plot to become the Messiah, his unstable and mercenary character played on by his teacher and friend. Another view, far less scholarly but still more imaginative, sees Judas, Jesus, and John the Baptist as co-conspirators in the messianic plot; his friends dead, in this interpretation, Jesus escapes to India with Mary Magdalene. (The author of this view is

86

Gourgen Yanikian; it is set forth both in a novel, *The Resurrected Christ*, and in a play, *Our Messiah*.) Cf. also Jorge Luis Borges, "Three Versions of Judas."

18. R. H. Lightfoot, *St. John's Gospel: A Commentary* (Oxford, 1956), p. 237.

19. Lightfoot, p. 225.

20. This blurring of one Mary into another is consistent not simply with Kazantzakis' technique elsewhere in the novel (e.g., the two Matthews and the two Johns) but with New Testament technique as well. "That Mary of Bethany was identical with St. Mary Magdalene, seems the most probable opinion; it has the balance of Christian tradition behind it . . . [for] St. Mary Magdalene is described in the collect for her feast as having prayed for the resurrection of 'her brother' Lazarus." Ronald Knox, *A Commentary on the Gospels* (New York, 1952), pp. 153–54.

21. The pomegranate is said to have sprung from the blood of Dionysus, and it was the eating of a pomegranate seed that ensured that Persephone would return each fall to the underworld. Sir James G. Frazer, *The Golden Bough* (New York, 1958), pp. 451, 457. Similarly, the pomegranate is a traditional Christian symbol of Eternal Life. Charles Thomas, *Britain and Ireland in Early Christian Times* (London, 1971), p. 77. Kazantzakis again uses both possibilities.

22. The "wind of Jehovah" to which Jesus refers is literally the fiery wind of the desert, which fills the monastery to which Jesus flees and from which he emerges as potential Messiah; metaphorically, it is allied to the whirlwind through which God confronts Job and to the Holy Spirit. To Kazantzakis, it is both wind and spirit—the "rushing-wind" and the "rush-of-spirit" of a new translation of the Old Testament, one which the novelist cannot have known. "The Hebrew Bible speaks of *ruah* in several different contexts: as the 'spirit of God' which comes over a charismatic leader; as simply a natural phenomenon —wind; and as the *'ruah* of God' which hovers over the waters of chaos and confusion at the beginning of creation. The first two usages are actually mirror-images of the third. *Ruah* does not speak of two separate spheres; rather, it speaks out of a unity which has two aspects. . . . As such it represents a view basic to the Hebrew Bible, one which the West has yet to learn." Everett Fox, "We Mean the Voice: The Buber-Rosenzweig Translation of the Bible," *Response*, 12 (1971–72), pp. 33–34. This seeming coincidence is one more illustration of Kazantzakis' profound knowledge of and insight into the Bible and the processes of myth.

23. Nikos Kazantzakis, *Japan/China*, trans. George C. Pappageotes (New York, 1963), p. 100.

24. *Report to Greco*, pp. 296–97.

25. *Greco*, p. 290.

26. *Greco*, p. 291.

27. The monk had told Kazantzakis how he had been saved from his youthful excesses: " 'One morning I opened my window. Dawn was just breaking, the morning star still twinkling in the sky. The calm sea sighed lightly and tenderly as it broke along the shore line. We were still in the heart of winter, yet a medlar tree in front of my window had blossomed; its aroma was peppery, as sweet as honey. It had rained during the night; the leaves were still dripping, and the whole earth glittered contentedly. "Lord, O Lord, what a miracle this is," I murmured, and I began to weep. It was then that I understood: salvation had arrived. I came here to the desert and buried

myself inside this cell with its humble bed, its jug of water, its two little stools. Now I am waiting.'" *Greco*, p. 299.

28. This relationship of biographer and subject is again evidently archetypal; virtually the same story is told of the Baal Shem Tov (The Master of the Good Name), founder of the Hasidic movement within Orthodox Judaism. See Dan Ben-Amos and Jerome R. Mintz, *In Praise of the Baal Shem Tov* (Bloomington, 1970).

29. Morris Philipson, "As the World Turns," *Midstream*, 7 (1961), pp. 105–6.

30. Letter to Börje Knös, Antibes, November 13, 1951, cited in Helen Kazantzakis, pp. 505–6.

31. Francis Bayard Rhein, *An Analytical Approach to the New Testament* (Woodbury, New York, 1966), p. 53.

32. In a translator's afterword, Peter Bien, who has done so much to make Kazantzakis available to American audiences, speaks of "the essential Greekness of this novel, which although set in the Holy Land, is peopled by Greeks in disguise" (p. 502).

33. In Kimon Friar, *Modern Greek Poetry* (New York, 1973), pp. 291–92.

CHAPTER FIVE

The Companions of Kazantzakis: Nietzsche, Bergson, and Zorba the Greek

"My life's greatest benefactors," Kazantzakis wrote toward the end of his life, "have been journeys and dreams. Very few people, living or dead, have aided my struggle." But if he were forced to designate those who had "left their traces embedded most deeply in my soul," he adds, he would name Homer, Buddha, Nietzsche, Bergson, and Zorba: Homer for the clarity of his vision and style, and Buddha "the bottomless jet-dark eye in which the world drowned and was delivered. Bergson relieved me of various unsolved philosophical problems which tormented me in my early youth; Nietzsche enriched me with new anguishes and instructed me how to transform misfortune, bitterness, and uncertainty into pride; Zorba taught me to love life and have no fear of death." It is Zorba whom he would choose from among them as his primary spiritual guide, "a *guru* as the Hindus say, a *father* as say the monks at Mount Athos."[1] The influence of Buddha, Nietzsche, and Bergson is most apparent in Kazantzakis' first mature novel, his most important philosophical work, the one named for, and inspired by, the untutored Zorba.

Zorba the Greek is also Kazantzakis' most popular work in America, the only one that most educated readers are likely to know of. Many people, in fact, can identify the author's name only if it is associated with that of his character. The obvious reason for this is the fine film made from the novel by Michael Cacoyánnis, with its masterful performance by Anthony Quinn as Zorba. The much less satisfying musical play derived from it attests to the film's success in dramatizing the personalities and events of the original.[2] But Cacoyánnis' interpretation of the conflict between the vital Greek peasant and the ineffectual writer who employs him—the character portrayed in the film by Alan Bates—is itself an oversimplification of the dualities represented by these characters and by several others as well. For *Zorba the Greek* is much more than a simple, heart-warming statement of the superiority of a life of action to the contemplative life, or even of the seeming supremacy of body to intellect; it is an intense investigation of the relation between art and life, of man and his institutions, of his dealings with his fellow men and with God. The film's misreading is to some extent justified by the popular nature of the medium and by its dramatic results, but the persistent critical misinterpretations of the novel are much less excusable. The commentators have emphasized the autobiographical basis of the fiction, as well as its philosophical roots, but few have recognized how ably the novelist has utilized the facts of his life for the purposes of his art, or have understood completely the synthesis he has made of the thought of Nietzsche and Bergson.

The general facts about Kazantzakis and Zorba are by now rather well known, although some dispute remains over specifics.[3] They seem to have met either in 1914 or 1915 among the monasteries of Mount Athos, where both had gone in search of some vague spiritual ideal and had instead been disillusioned by the reality they had found. They were associated again in the operation of a lignite mine at Prastova in the Peloponnesus in 1917, went together to the Caucasus in 1919 and kept up an active correspondence until Zorba's death in Yugoslavia in 1942. These are in general the basic facts of the novel as well, although Kazantzakis has altered the Christian name of the title character—from George to Alexis; the site of his first meeting with the owner of the mine—from the sacred mountain of Zorba's native Macedonia to the port of Piraeus; and, most significantly, the location of the mine itself—from the southernmost part of the mainland to the island of Crete. The character of Zorba, many of his sayings, and some of the major events of the novel are reported as they actually occurred—or at least as Kazantzakis remembered them twenty years afterward—but these few minor changes should alert us to the possibility of other, more basic alterations.

The character of the unnamed narrator is surely based on Kazantzakis himself, but he is not Kazantzakis, not even a reliable spokesman for his views. The author has taken a situation perceived in his own life, transformed it to fit the pattern of thought he had by this time developed, and made it into fiction and not autobiography. Failing to distinguish the man whom Zorba calls "Boss" from his creator is as likely to lead to misunderstanding as to confuse Stephen Dedalus with James Joyce. The critic who makes this mistake clearly lacks the distance from the character that the novelist himself has achieved, for Boss—like Stephen—remains fictional despite his autobiographical beginnings. Just as Joyce has altered the facts of his life to make Stephen fit his conception of the isolated young artist, so Kazantzakis has molded Boss into a dramatic and philosophical foil for Zorba. The film version further converts the thirty-five-year-old Cretan-born writer into a still younger Englishman, a stranger to the traditions of Crete and not their repudiation. The dramatic contrast between Zorba and Boss is thus greater in the film than in the novel, but it now has less philosophical import and indeed distorts the theme of the novel. A similar distortion occurs when we confuse Kazantzakis with his creation.

The facts may at first seem to justify such a connection. The stories of the narrator's childhood on Crete, of his years in Germany and his passion for travel, of his friendship with the Rumanian writer Panaït Istrati and the Cretan aristocrat Yannis Stavridhákis are certainly autobiographical. And the reader suspects that other characters and incidents are similarly based on Kazantzakis' early life on Crete, that the ugly old serving-woman with the desperate yearning for marriage was his family servant (p. 159),[4] that the maternal grandfather who searches out travelers to hear of the world outside his village was his own grandfather (pp. 49–50). The symbolic study of Buddha, which so dominates the narrator's life, is surely the book on which Kazantzakis labored for more than three decades—although he did not begin work on it until several years after the episode of the mine. When the narrator speaks of the influence of certain pieces of art—of Rembrandt's *Warrior* and Rodin's *Hand of God*—on his life and the life of his friend Stavridhákis, he is probably again speaking from life. In the novel, Stavridkákis appears only in his letters to Boss, for it is 1919, and he has gone to the Caucasus as part of a mission to rescue his countrymen from the Bolsheviks and Kurds. The letter announcing his death is certainly factual, for the real Stavridhákis, who had been the Greek consul in Zurich, was buried in Tiflis at the age of twenty-two. But there was likely no need for a letter, for Kazantzakis himself was in the Caucasus: he was the head of the mission, Stavridhákis one of those who accompanied him. Another was George Zorbas. The differences between the fictional Boss and Zorba are certainly based on historical differences, but the character in the novel who represents their synthesis—Stavridhákis, the intellectual capable of action—is not wholly historical; he is a fictional character based on reality, modeled on both the man bearing his name and his friend Kazantzakis. He is all the evidence we need that *Zorba the Greek* is fiction and not autobiography.

The narrator tells us near the end of the novel of his dream announcing the death of Zorba; it is at this point that he determines to write this account, to act out in the one way he can the precepts of his spiritual mentor, to substitute for his early testimonial to the contemplative Buddha a new memorial to the activist Zorba. "Was this not the heart's duty?" Kazantzakis asks in *Report to Greco*. "Did not God create the heart for this very purpose: to resurrect dear ones, bring them back to life?"[5] The stories he tells of the last days of Zorba are virtually the same in novel and autobiography, but this is as likely to prove that *Greco* is fiction as to demonstrate that *Zorba* is fact. As he wrote of his memories when he began work on the novel, "Our many days together crossed in front of me like graceful white doves. . . . The memories ascended a story higher than truth, two stories higher than falsehood. Zorba metamorphosed gradually and became a legend"[6] —what the novelist was to call in an early title "The Golden Legend of Alexis Zorbas." Kazantzakis, Zorba, and Stavridhákis, all real men, all become part of a legend. The art of *Zorba the Greek* is so great and resourceful that we may miss it completely, mistaking it for history. To find the truth of the novel, we must look not to history but to its philosophical roots.

II

In a primitive Cretan village on the shores of the Libyan Sea, Boss and Zorba act out the well-defined lines of their lives, the former carrying his manuscript of Buddha and volumes of Dante and Mallarmé, the latter bearing his own experience and freedom. One lives through his art; the other possesses a life that itself has the quality of art and inspires art in those who observe him. It is not the Cretan-born artist but the Macedonian worker who embodies those qualities of Cretan life that function as metaphor throughout the Kazantzakian canon: his is the life of vitality and daring, of closeness to nature and willingness to confront the abyss. The narrator is moved by his return to his homeland, but he remains essentially alien to its people and customs; he has chosen the strangely mixed way of Western rationality and Oriental contemplativeness, a way of passive observation that comes to life only in his art. "I had fallen so low," he admits, "that, if I had had to choose between falling in love with a woman and reading a book about love, I should have chosen the book" (p. 101). The colossus Zorba rejects the passivity of Boss and his Buddha and intuits instead his own active philosophy, a unique synthesis of the thought of Nietzsche and Bergson. But his way alone does not make up the theme of the novel; for that we need the unseen Stavridhákis, the student who surpasses his master, a man of reason who is able to act.

Kazantzakis tells a marvelous story in his autobiography of his first confrontation with Nietzsche. A girl came up to him in a library in Paris, pointed in amazement to a photograph in a book that she carried, and exclaimed, " 'But it's you—the very image! Look at the forehead, the thick eyebrows, the sunken eyes!' " The photograph was of Nietzsche, the book she then gave him *Thus Spoke Zarathustra*. "That was one of the most decisive moments of my life. Owing to the intervention of an unknown university student, my destiny had laid an ambush for me there in the Bibliothèque Sainte-Geneviève. Waiting for me there was the Antichrist, that great fiery warrior all covered with blood . . . , [creator of] the Superman as the assassin of God."[7] The story is probably apocryphal, for there is evidence that Kazantzakis knew of Nietzsche even as an undergraduate in Greece, and there is a curious parallel between this experience and another, related some years earlier, in which he is compared to Tolstoy.[8] But the figurative truth of the incident is undeniable, for Tolstoy and Nietzsche alike represented for the young Kazantzakis the way to express "a new sense of life," a union of art and philosophy that "transcends the [usual] limits of Art."[9] The German philosopher was to become a major force in the young artist's life.

His dissertation, completed in 1909 for submission to the Faculty of Law of the University of Athens, was on "Friedrich Nietzsche and the Philosophy of Right"; in 1910, he translated *Zarathustra* and *The Birth of Tragedy* into demotic Greek; he followed the path of Nietzsche across Europe as if on a "pilgrimage" and for years kept a deathmask of the philosopher over the doorways to his various homes. Both *The Birth of Tragedy* and *Zarathustra* have been cited as the model for *Zorba*, and the careers of their creators have been closely compared, "not only through the external events of their lives, but also through their fundamental experiences—the loneliness, the tension, the struggle and the creation—and most of all through the relationship between, not to say identity of, their ideas."[10]

Celebrating the anniversary of Nietzsche's death, Kazantzakis himself acknowledges the identity of their goals: "For you had tasted that keenest joy the hero feels, which petty spirits think a martyrdom: to see the abyss before you, to move ahead and not accept retreat."[11] "You saw what man is not permitted to see, and your sight was taken from you; you danced beyond human endurance at the brink of the abyss, and into the abyss you plunged." As for himself, he asks, "Which is the most dangerous way? That is the one I want! Where is the abyss? That is where I am headed. What is the most valiant joy? To assume complete responsibility!"[12] The Nietzschean archetype, however he discovered it, inspired both the life and the work of

Kazantzakis, the Great Martyr's life acting as analogue to his own and such works as *Zarathustra* serving both as literary and philosophical sourcebook and as support for his own developed ideas.

Both men led lives of keen isolation, valuing their vision and art above all other human concerns; both rejected the narrow orthodoxies into which they were born and developed their own humanistic theologies; both were obsessed by their fathers' examples and consistently returned to them in their work. Their lust for travel, their reliance on dreams, their distrust of art and hence of themselves as artists, their ambiguous attitudes toward family life in general and women in particular, their reactions against institutions and governments—here, too, their thoughts and interests converge. Even their styles are similar: the richness of Nietzsche's prose, his ability to dramatize abstractions, his frequently hyperbolic language, are all part of that "Mediterranean style" which the northerner long sought and which from the start, as Prevelákis puts it, "was in Kazantzakis' blood and in the language of his own people."[13]

There are resonances from Nietzsche throughout Kazantzakis, devices and themes that the disciple converts to suit his own needs. Thus, Zarathustra's song to his soul, "Of the Great Longing," becomes a song from the soul to the universe at the end of *The Saviors of God;* man the worm, tied to the Nietzschean flux of this life, turns in the *Odyssey* to a fighter resistant even to God; the cycle of Eternal Recurrence, "the wheel of existence [which] rolls for ever"[14] and binds man to its inevitability, becomes in *Zorba* and elsewhere "the everturning wheel of life" (p. 169), the force of nature through which man can free himself; and the will to power of the Superman is for the freedom-loving Cretans their resistance to the forces of fate. Many of the images that appear first in *The Saviors of God* and later recur in the novels are surely derived from *Zarathustra,* but again they appear with new implications. The cleansing fire, the perilous ascent, the silence at the edge of the abyss confront both Nietzsche's heroic ascetic and his descendant, the colossus of Kazantzakis. But the student dares more than his teacher: the Superman, he says, is an effort to restore hope to a world doomed to Eternal Recurrence, but it is "just another paradise, another mirage to deceive poor unfortunate man and enable him to endure life and death."[15] Kazantzakis' heroes feel no such terror and need no hope; they can accept both life and death, man's decaying humanity and his yearning for godhead. Like their creators, both the Superman and the colossus in his various guises—Captain Mihális and Kosmás, Priest Fótis and Manoliós the shepherd, Jesus of Nazareth and his betrayer, St. Francis and Zorba—reach for divinity but remain tied to mankind. Zarathustra stands at the brink of the abyss and declares to a crowd of cripples and beggars, "My will clings to mankind, I bind myself to mankind with fetters, because I am drawn up to the Superman: for my other will wants to draw me up to the Superman" (*Zarathustra*, p. 164). His words predict those of a humanist Jesus, for, the critics aside, it is not so much *Zorba the Greek* that is modeled on Nietzsche's great work as *The Last Temptation of Christ*.

Zarathustra—"A Book for Everyone and No One"—is built around the semihistorical, semimythic Zoroaster, the Christlike founder of a religion whose very core is duality—the conflict of the forces of light and of darkness. He gathers disciples around him and preaches to them in parables, his language full of Biblical echoes; he is uncertain at first of his mission but perseveres to the end; he is tempted in the desert by sensual pleasure, by lust for power, by the selfishness of solitude, and emerges only when he hears his alter ego cry to the world, " 'It is time! It is high time!' " (*Zarathustra*, p. 155). Like Kazantzakis' hero, he rejects the old ethic and posits a new, more demanding "law-table": *"Do not spare your neighbour!* Man is something that must be overcome" (*Zarathustra*, p. 216). He despises Christianity for its mediocrity and Christ for his easy acceptance of death: "Had he only remained in the desert and far from the good and just! Perhaps he would have learned to live and learned to love the earth—and laughter as well! Believe it, my brothers! He died too early; he himself would have recanted his teaching had he lived to my age!" (*Zarathustra*, pp. 98–99). He declares the death of God from senility and uselessness, suffocated by an excess of pity. " 'Do you know *how* he died?' " he asks the old pope. " 'Is it true what they say, that pity choked him, that he saw how *man* hung on the Cross and could not endure it, that love for man became his Hell and at last his death? . . . Better to be a fool [than such a God], better to be God oneself!' " (*Zarathustra*, pp. 272, 274). It is his best-loved disciple who interprets Zarathustra's dream of death and leads him again to life.

Jesus in *The Last Temptation* has learned to love the earth, and his death—assisted by his best-loved disciple—is an act not of pity and sacrifice but of strength and fulfillment; it is an event that he willingly accepts, a "voluntary death," like Zarathustra's, "that comes to me because *I* wish it" (*Zarathustra*, p. 97). It is quite different from Zorba's. Boss has been speaking of man bent over " 'the awe-inspiring abyss,' " confronting death, accepting it, even coming to like it. And Zorba, in his sixties, reflects for a time and responds, " 'I think of death every second. I look at it and I'm not frightened. But never, never, do I say I like it. No, I don't like it at all! I don't agree!' " (p. 270). When death comes to him, he is standing erect, his nails dug into the window frame, looking out to the mountains. " 'Men like me ought to live a thousand years,' " he says at the end. " 'Good night!' " (p. 310). For Zorba has learned to fulfill his younger friend's yearning, to unite body and soul, to rebel against those natural forces of which he is otherwise a part. In many ways, he too recalls Zarathustra—in his distrust of poets and his preference for action above contemplation, in his desire to will his own fate, above all, in his love of laughter and dancing: he too has "canonized laughter"; he has learned, as even the Superman has not, "to dance as a man ought to dance" (*Zarathustra*, p. 306).

But Zorba the realist would certainly suspect the mysticism running through Zarathustra, just as Zorba the democrat, who can understand and forgive the worst of men's sins, would be opposed to the Superman. He would not agree that his own deeds qualify him as some higher form of existence; he believes that all men are capable of what he has accomplished, that all men can master themselves and give meaning to life. We realize, in short, that he could reject the idea of the Superman yet at the same time be its embodiment. He reaches Zarathustra's position not through mystical contemplation, however, not through the intellectual's desire to be part of a life that he cannot descend to, but through the life force itself, through a kind of Bergsonian intuitiveness. This is the philosophical synthesis represented by Zorba.

III

The eclectic Kazantzakis utilizes Bergson much as he does Nietzsche, selecting those images and ideas that inform and reinforce his own perceptions of life, rubbing metaphorically the "mystic salves" of his teacher in the Collège de France onto the "deep and hallowed" wounds opened by his German precursor. Yet, he admits, "for as long as I remained young, what I desired most deeply was not the cure but the wound";[16] for the young Kazantzakis succumbed to a romanticism that Zorba could never accept. Wound and cure, Nietzsche and Bergson, are nearly indistinguishable in Kazantzakis' mature works. Thus, Nietzsche's doctrine of Eternal Recurrence and Bergson's *la durée*, the time of consciousness, unite to isolate his heroes from their historical contexts (this is true whether events repeat themselves, as in Nietzsche, so that all men in all ages are faced with similar problems, or whether, as in Bergson, events in phychic time are new for each individual despite his surroundings). Thus, too, the Nietzschean hope in the Superman and the *élan vital* of Bergson combine to influence his characters' reactions to these events.

As Kazantzakis uses them, these alien philosophies are perfectly consistent with the metaphor of Crete; partly as source, largely as analogue, they express the same universal beliefs. In Crete or Judea, Anatolia or Italy, the man who attempts to master himself and his life—the colossus—must strive to attain what Ian W. Alexander has labeled the central doctrine of Bergsonian thought, "the assertion of the unity of world and mind in immediate experience," that "limitless aspiration which brings us into communion not only with the whole of mankind but with the universal creativity that inspires all human efforts."[17] Whether Superman or representative common man, he must endeavor to unite mind and matter through the force of his personality and actions; this belief is central to Bergson, implicit in Nietzsche, and carried out in the life of Zorba the Greek.

Even early in his career Kazantzakis had linked Nietzsche and Bergson, expounding both new ideologies to his audience in Greece[18] and translating *Laughter* alongside *Zarathustra*. This brief statement on aesthetics would later help to illuminate the career of Zorba the moralist. "Laughter," writes Bergson, "indicates a slight revolt on the surface of social life. . . .Like froth, it sparkles. It is gaiety itself. But the philosopher who gathers a handful to taste may find that the substance is scanty, and the after-taste bitter."[19] It is a positive moral force as Bergson perceives it—akin to Horatian satire in its effects—directed at individuals in the hope of effecting reform, purporting to deal with the surface of affairs while going in truth to their depths: "Any incident is comic that calls our attention to the physical in a person, when it is the moral side that is concerned" (*Laughter*, pp. 50–51). So it is with Zorba, who seems at first to be concerned with the physical alone. For he can laugh at the most difficult moments, almost as if he does not appreciate the tragedy of old Bouboulína's life or the failure of their mining venture; but we recognize, as Boss himself learns to, that Zorba laughs—even when he laughs at himself—in order to maintain balance in his soul, to forget the evils persisting in life. He may invert Bergson's dictum somewhat, but he never mistakes the moral significance of laughter: the comic spirit for him is not so much, as Bergson puts it, "a special lack of adaptability to society" (*Laughter*, p. 133), as it is a refusal to adapt, an unwillingness to accept those aspects of society that seem to him unjust or absurd. If he cannot remake society in his own more positive image, he can at least go his own way, living within society for the most part but maintaining his independence and self-respect. It is the most valuable lesson that Boss can learn from him.

In the Bergsonian sense, Zorba is the ideal metaphysician, demonstrating in his reactions to life insights and tenets identical to those that Bergson develops. We find in Zorba's untutored mind the same heightening of common sense—of *justesse et justice*—that the philosopher advocates, the same adaptability to new situations and the same reluctance to accept traditional ideas without questioning them. His intuition, like that articulated by Bergson, is not a substitute for intellect but a supplement to it, a combination in fact of intelligence and instinct; it is not so much a form of mysticism, as some have argued, as a rejection of it, not a repudiation of science but a means of subjecting metaphysics to scientific analysis—an insistence that every perception be tested through the experience of living. "The 'intuition' of Bergson," claims Jacques Chevalier, another disciple, "seems in so many respects akin [to] the 'heart' of Pascal.... Reason *proves*, and the heart *knows*.... Intuition is like the heart: it *knows*."[20] Echoing Manoliós and Jesus, Zorba speaks throughout of knowing with the heart: " 'When will people's ears open, boss? When shall we have our eyes open to see? When shall we open our arms to embrace everything—stones, rain, flowers, and men? What d'you think about that, boss? And what do your books have to say about it?' " (p. 94). Zorba is always ready to test his intuitions against empirical evidence; for this reason, he is a truer philosopher than his more scholarly friend. He is no more anti-intellectual, moreover, than Kazantzakis or Bergson—although all three have been so accused; he simply demonstrates the Bergsonian doctrine that all ideas originate in instinctive reactions, that ideas must be acted before they become known. All religion, all freedom, all art, adds Bergson, are functions of the active lives of men such as Zorba: "we are free when our acts spring from our whole personality, when they express it, when they have that indefinable resemblance to it which one sometimes finds between the artist and his work."[21] Nor is such free will mere spontaneity: "At most, this would be the case in the animal world where the psychological life is principally that of the affections. But in the case of man, a thinking being, the free act can be called a synthesis of feelings and ideas, and the evolution which leads to it, a reasonable evolution."[22] So we are mistaken to view Zorba as a child of nature, instinctual and lacking in intellect; he performs that vital first act without which no thought can follow. Boss can achieve such freedom only by building his art on Zorba's perceptions, only by converting individual actions to general ideas.

Separated from Zorba by miles and years, Boss dreams of his death and begins feverishly to write, attempting to capture in art the essence of one who "lived the earth, water, the animals and God, without the distorting intervention of reason" (p. 136), of a man who could work in the mine and become "one with the earth, the pick and the coal, . . . [who] could feel matter with a sure and infallible instinct" (p. 109). Boss writes now with a new élan, evincing the same tension between emotion and discipline that lies at the heart of Bergson: "I worked like the sorcerers of the savage tribes of Africa when they draw on the walls of their caves the Ancestors they have seen in their dreams, striving to make it as lifelike as possible so that the spirit of the Ancestor can recognize his body and enter into it" (p. 310). He creates now with the same spirit as his own creator: as Kazantzakis wrote of the original Zorba,

> I had come to know [him] too late. At this point there was no further salvation for me; I had degenerated into an incurable pen-pusher. . . . But no matter what I wrote—poems, plays, novels—the work always acquired, without conscious effort on my part, a dramatic *élan* and form—full of mutually clashing forces, struggle, indignation, revolt, the pursuit of a lost equilibrium. . . . No matter how much I struggled to give a balanced form to what I wrote, it quickly assumed a vehement dramatic rhythm. In spite of my wishes, the peaceful voice I desired to emit became a cry.[23]

Even this late in his career Kazantzakis remained a romantic, just as Boss as an artist remains superficially unchanged by his encounter with Zorba. Yet for both there are significant changes: they have at last developed, as Zarathustra's animals demand of their master, "new lyres . . . for your new songs" (*Zarathustra*, p. 237).

IV

As he leaves for the Caucasus, Stavridhákis declares to his friend, " 'How long are you going on chewing paper and covering yourself with ink? . . . Don't you preach: "The only way to save yourself is to endeavor to save others?" . . . Well, forward, master. You're good at preaching. Why don't you come with me!' " (p. 5). But the narrator, like Chaucer's persona, is so caught up in his art that he is unable to act. He cannot leave for the Caucasus; he cannot operate his mine without the assistance of Zorba; he cannot court the widow, as his grandfather would have done, or act to save her, as Zorba attempts to. Even years afterward, he is unable to leave Berlin just to see the green stone Zorba found, although he knows that he may never again see its like. " 'In some other life,' " he thinks, " 'I'll behave better than this!' " (p. 123). But in this life he can only make plans—plans for an ideal community in which artists can work freely, plans for his own art. The artists and thinkers whom he admires provide a sign of his character and, implicitly, of the nature of his art: idealists all of them—Mallarmé, Marcus Aurelius, and Dante (not Dante the tough-minded citizen of Florence, but Dante the lyricist, creator of a world Boss can inhabit in place of his own) and, above all, Buddha.

For the two years prior to his departure for Crete, the time of his meeting with Zorba, Boss' life has been dominated by his manuscript on Buddha. He returns to his homeland, in fact, in order to free himself of its burden, in the hope of liberating his soul from matter by writing of one who has similarly been freed. It is an intended blending of function and form far different from the one he eventually achieves under the guidance of Zorba. In Buddha, this "absolutely pure spirit"[24] who served as model for Zarathustra and whom he sees as though through a Nietzschean lens, he seeks escape from all physical concerns. "The true Buddha has no body,"[25] Kazantzakis once wrote, and Pandhelis Prevelakis adds, speaking of his own friend and master, "Beneath the poet, the mystagogue was buried.... Buddhist renunciation filtered through Kazantzakis like an unfulfilled presentiment, a way of living which he had planned but had never carried out. But its cold light often shone in his eyes."[26] Neither mystagogue quite overcomes his dependence on soul, but Boss, like Kazantzakis, learns from Zorba not to feel shame for his body.

Attracted against his will to the widow, the artist sublimates his desire in his manuscript: he envisions instead of his own temptation, the temptation of Buddha, and turns from his life to his art, "painfully endeavoring to transform that violent desire of the flesh into *Buddha*," convinced that he, too, "in fighting against the widow... was obeying a great universal rhythm" (p. 113). But he finally does sleep with her: "That night, for the first time, I felt clearly that the soul is flesh as well, perhaps more volatile, more diaphanous, perhaps freer, but flesh all the same. And the flesh is soul, somewhat turgid perhaps, somewhat exhausted by its long journeys, and bowed under the burden it has inherited" (pp. 237–38). He continues to intellectualize his reactions, but he has come to believe with his guide that the body has a soul of its own. After their great Easter feast on the beach, Zorba—drunk a little from the wine and the food and perhaps from his normal élan—shouts to his boss, " 'Let's go and dance! Aren't you sorry for the lamb we've been eating? Are you going to let it fizzle out into nothing, like that? Come on! Turn it into song and dance! Zorba is reborn!' " (p. 234). Boss will not dance now, but it is on this night that he goes to the widow. And later he will ask Zorba to teach him to dance; he will himself be reborn in their dance, in this new, intuitive union of body with soul.

Even his concept of art changes under the influence of Zorba. Once he thought it a process removed from the pettiness of life, and the artist a figure raised above other men; the lyricism of Dante and the purity of Mallarmé seemed to him then the ideal forms to transmit this vision. It is in this romantic, almost Platonic spirit that his *Buddha* is written. He continues afterward to believe in the power and sanctity of art, but he has now learned from Zorba that life may be both the subject of art and itself great art, that life and art cannot be made separate. Now as he rereads his volume of Mallarmé, he wonders, "Why had these poems gripped me for so many years? Pure poetry! Life had turned into a lucid, transparent game, unencumbered by even a single drop of blood. . . . That is how it always is at the decline of a civilization" (pp. 133–34).

Zorba at one point attacks the lifelessness of those who customarily write books, and Boss defensively sneers, " 'Why don't you write a book yourself, Zorba? And explain all the mysteries of the world to us?' " The peasant responds, " 'For the simple reason that I live all those mysteries, as you call them, and I haven't the time to write. . . . That's how the business falls into the hands of the pen-pushers!' " (p. 217). Any obscurantist might parrot his opinion, and we would surely reject it, for it seems as extreme as Boss' own earlier view—and a good deal more dangerous. Zorba, however, is no enemy of art but an artist himself, the poem of his life purer by far than Mallarmé's verse, his work more true than that of the narrator. We find in Zorba that union of art and life that we so admire in Dante and that Boss had once so badly misread.

It was his passion to play the *santúri* that led the young Zorba to abandon his respectable bourgeois home (p. 12); as a potter he cut off part of his left index finger because it interfered with his work at the wheel (p. 18); even now he tells stories with imagination and fervor, "like a poet in the burning second of creation" (p. 212). "This," thinks the narrator, "is how great visionaries and poets see everything—as if for the first time. Each morning they see a new world before their eyes; they do not really see it, they create it" (p. 136). The creativity of Zorba is expressed in all of his actions, but in his dancing especially. It is in dance that he communicates those feelings he cannot put into words—his acceptance of the needs and desires of others, his hatred of the injustice that shadows existence, his love of life; in dance he glorifies the body and endeavors to surpass its limited abilities. "Watching Zorba dance [on the beach], I understood for the first time the fantastic efforts of man to overcome his weight. I admired Zorba's endurance, his agility and proud bearing. His clever and impetuous steps were writing on the sand the demoniac history of mankind" (p. 291). Zorba is most himself when he dances and at the same time most representative of man.

"There is only one dancer, but he has a thousand masks. He is always twenty. He is immortal" (p. 243). Young Sífakas, the shepherd, comes down from the mountains each year at Easter, to see people once more and to seek communion in dance. Watching him, watching Zorba, Boss experiences the movement of nature and myth, understands the value and dignity of man. "In song and in dance," writes the demoniac Nietzsche, "man expresses himself as a member of a higher community;... he feels himself a god, he himself now walks about enchanted, in ecstasy, like the gods he saw walking in his dreams. He is no longer an artist, he has become a work of art."[27] Boss is able to dance only when everything material in his life has first been accented and subsequently lost—the widow once slept with, now dead; his business once promising, now totally failed; Zorba regretful but ready to laugh. It is not the emotionless Buddha who frees him of the weight of his body, but passionate Zorba; art is liberating, Boss insists, as he increasingly devotes himself to his book, but he himself cannot be freed until he has exorcised Buddha, until "I, too, raised my hand, and ordered the Buddha within me to dissolve" (p. 239). *Buddha*, ironically, is primarily a burden to him, but *Zorba* is a joy as well as a duty. For Zorba expresses in dance both the weight and the weightlessness of the human body, both man's tie to earth and his reach toward heaven; it is Zorba who illuminates the soul in this ultimate act of the body.

Boss is first attracted to Zorba by his knowledge of mining, the exotic soups he can cook, his ability to play the *santúri*. To Boss, these are all practical concerns: " 'You can superintend the workmen. In the evening we'll stretch out on the sand . . . we'll eat and drink together. Then you'll play the *santúri*.' " But his employee warns,

> "I'll work for you as much as you like. I'm your man there. But the *santúri*, that's different. . . .It needs freedom. If I'm in the mood, I'll play. I6ll even sing . . . but . . . I must be in the mood. . . . As regards those things, you must realize, I'm a man."
> "A man? What d'you mean?"
> "Well, free!" (pp. 14–15)

Zorba is free because he respects his own life and the lives of others as well and because he controls the body whose activity he glorifies; his good sense and experience moderate even the most extreme of his attitudes. He is, for example, a great lover of women, patronizing in his view of their weakness and dependency, but he remains sensitive to Bouboulína's needs and is still able to boast of his Russian lover whose independence and strength were as great as his own (pp. 87–88). He has fought against Turks and Bulgarians in patriotic battles, has burned down whole villages and pickled Turks' ears in alcohol—he was even present as a warrior to welcome Prince George to Crete (p. 24); but now, like Captain Katsirmás of *Freedom or Death*, he has risen above nationalism, too:

"There was a time when I used to say: that man's a Turk, or a Bulgar, or a Greek. I've done things for my country that would make your hair stand on end. . . . Nowadays I say this man is a good fellow, that one's a bastard. They can be Greeks or Bulgars or Turks, it doesn't matter. Is he good? Or is he bad? That's the only thing I ask nowadays. And as I grow older—I'd swear this on the last crust I eat—I feel I shan't even go on asking that! Whether a man's good or bad, I'm sorry for him, for all of 'em . . . whoever he is: he has his God and his devil just the same. . . . Poor devil! We're all brothers! All worm meat!" (p. 226)

For all his vitality and love of life, Zorba feels sympathy for man's worm-eaten temporal existence and questions the wisdom and justice of God. " 'Is there a God?' " he keeps asking Boss (p. 105); " 'Who is it who throws these bones to us?' " (p. 184); " 'Who the devil brings us onto this earth and who the devil takes us away?' " (p. 264); " 'And, above all, why do people die?' " (p. 269). His doubts form part of a leitmotif sounding throughout the novel, quite literally from the first page to the last. " 'This world's a life sentence,' " says a stranger in the café in Piraeus where Boss first meets Zorba; " 'Be damned to it' " (pp. 3–4). A rich old man in the village on Crete looks back over his successful life and decides, " 'And yet if I had to start my life all over again I'd put a stone round my neck . . . and throw myself in the sea . . .; even the luckiest life is hard, a curse on it!' " (p. 163). Boss, more intellectually, reaches this same conclusion: he thinks of himself and the widow as "two insects who live but a second beneath the sun, then die for all eternity" (p. 102). "That is life," he concludes, imagining the pleasures of Bouboulína's youth while watching her die, "checkered, incoherent, indifferent, perverse . . . pitiless" (p. 261). Both the old woman and the widow are now part of the earth, part of the cycle of nature that goes on eternally, condemning man to its inexorable movement: "our ultimate ruler," after all, is the maggot that feeds on us.

Yet, despite the irrationality and brevity of life, Zorba stands at the abyss without awe, unafraid of God's judgment, willing even to judge Him, especially for the death long before of his own infant son (p. 247). "For Zorba's dance was full of defiance and obstinacy. He seemed to be shouting to the sky: 'What can you do to me, Almighty? You can do nothing to me except kill me. Well, kill me, I don't care! I've vented my spleen, I've said all I want to say; I've had time to dance . . . and I don't need you any more!' " (p. 291). It is his dance that frees him from the seeming bondage of nature's unyielding cycle. At the end, he leaves his *santúri* to Boss, for Zorba too feels the need for continuance, for some sign of the spirit to survive the body that houses it. Boss cannot go to Serbia for the *santúri* of Zorba, but he can remember his friend in his own art. Zorba survives in this book.

V

Once the narrator attempted to free himself of the burdens of life by writing of the salvation of Buddha. He too could progress beyond his flesh, he believed, if he could capture in prose the state of Nirvana that Buddha achieves: freedom of the need for nourishment and shelter, of the lust to possess cows and oxen and meadows, of the desire for love and companionship (p. 19). " 'Buddha is [the] last man,' I cried. That is his secret and terrible significance. Buddha is the 'pure' soul which has emptied itself; in him is the void, he is the Void" (p. 134). There is much of Zarathustra in this conception of Buddha, and something of Bergson as well: surrounded by his disciples on a mountain peak, the ascetic teaches the abnegation of the world, but he does so with unique vitality and power; the artist too emulates these sources by struggling to free himself through his art. But *Buddha* enslaves him instead; no longer a literary exercise, it becomes "a life-and-death struggle against a tremendous force of destruction lurking within me, . . . a real war, a merciless hunt, a siege, a spell to bring the monster out of its hiding place" (p. 134). As Buddha, the Good Herdsman, observes in the traditional parable, " 'Whatsoever a [man] considers much, ponders much, to that does his heart incline.' "[28] Although Boss is himself an ascetic, very nearly free of worldly possessions, he is not free of his senses: his desire to capture the essence of Buddha is so overpowering that his book becomes his possessor—until he learns from Zorba of man's genuine need for fellowship and love.

Once he thought Zorba spoke with the voice of Māra, the Evil Herdsman, Buddha's antagonist, "the crafty pander" who offers in the place of Buddhist dedication, "a sure, attractive and very human path to tread" (p. 114). But in the end, paradoxically, it is Zorba who frees him from Buddha, not by suggesting a simpler means of living—one cannot live simply with such knowledge of death as Zorba possesses—but by demonstrating a new dedication, a new kind of commitment to life. As Buddha progresses from his earliest animal forms through to Nirvana—freedom from the cycle of life and of death—so Boss, under the influence of Zorba, comes to acknowledge physical beauty and worth. One night, on the island of Aegina, Zorba appears to him in a dream. "I cannot remember what he said or why he had come. But when I awoke . . . I was filled with an irresistible desire to reconstitute the life we had lived together on the coast of Crete, to drive my memory to work and gather together all the sayings, cries, gestures, tears, and dances which Zorba had scattered in my mind—to save them. . . . For I felt my soul to be so united with his that it seemed impossible for one of them to die without the other being shaken and crying out with pain" (p. 309).

He once felt this same way about Stavridhákis. They had agreed, as the young man left for the Caucasus, to warn one another of impending disaster. As Stavridhákis puts it, " 'If ever one of us finds himself in danger of death, let him think of the other so intensely that he warns him wherever he may be' " (p. 7). On Crete, the narrator receives two letters from the Caucasus, the first reminding him of their pact, the second describing the successful end of the mission; only then does he dream of his friend. The telegram announcing Stavridhákis' death of pneumonia arrives soon after Boss sees Zorba for the last time. This association of aristocrat and worker is not simply fortuitous, for Boss from the start has unconsciously connected the two: as he prepares to leave the mainland for Crete, he recalls that earlier departure—"The two mornings mingled," and the face of his friend appears before him (p. 7); so he seeks consolation in reading his Dante and soon feels a presence looming above him—"A mad hope flashed through my brain: 'I'm going to see my friend again.' I was prepared for the miracle, but the miracle did not happen" (p. 9). It is, of course, Zorba who is standing before him, but Boss will not perceive how miraculous this is until he dreams of him, too. Years afterward, when he receives confirmation of Zorba's death, he reads of it "calmly, unhurriedly" (p. 310). He can be calm now because he has learned from that earlier death, because he has dreamed already of Zorba and composed his memorial. And this is no solemn, arcane statement of mystical faith, such as his *Buddha* has likely become, but a forceful, lyrical, universal affirmation, a work both serious and joyous. In the reflexive way of such books—as Stephen Dedalus at the close of *Ulysses*, having found his true subject in Bloom, will write the novel we know as *Ulysses*—so Boss, like Kazantzakis, has abandoned Buddha for Zorba, has written for once of "a great man of the people,"[29] has created *Zorba the Greek*.

It is this configuration of Stavridhákis and Zorba that determines the shape of the novel. Developed initially through various letters—in the communications between the Caucasus and Crete, in a message from Zorba in Candia (Iráklion) to Boss in their village, and in an unexpected letter from Africa, from Karayánnis, a one-time fellow student—their implied relationship helps frame the action and develop the theme. At his departure, Stavridhákis urges action on his scholarly friend, who then returns to Crete and encounters Zorba; the one letter he writes to Stavridhákis is filled with memories of their friendship, with references to Buddha, with an account of that "extraordinary Sinbad the Sailor" (p. 90) whom he has just met. Boss at this point is entirely an observer, able to watch Zorba work and dance from afar while he himself slowly digs into Buddha. Karayánnis' letter arrives as Zorba sets off for Candia to buy supplies for their enterprise; it is as wild and impulsive as its writer, a Zorba gone mad—once a monk in his native Crete, he has abandoned his heritage and immersed himself in his work, in his flesh, in alien Africa. He offers a course so extreme that Boss rejects it almost immediately. In the same post is a long letter from the Caucasus, full of dedication and patriotism and the same reasoned moderation its author had shown before his departure from Europe. It provides a sharp contrast to Karayánnis' message and a strange introduction to Zorba's. "Three days, four days, five days went by, and still no Zorba. On the sixth day I received from Candia a letter several pages long, a whole lot of rigmarole. It was written on scented pink paper and, in the corner of the page, was a heart pierced by an arrow"—a prostitute's stationery (p. 143). "Dear Boss!" it begins, "Mister Capitalist!" and is signed, "Me, Alexis Zorba"; it opens by repudiating all dogmas of nation and religion, closes by equating humanity and freedom and is marked throughout by laughter and folly, by an awareness of the flesh and of its limitations. The extremity of Karayánnis makes Zorba too, even at this early point, seem moderate and wise, but Boss can not yet recognize this truth. "When I had finished reading Zorba's letter I was for a while in two minds—no, three. I did not know whether to be angry, or laugh, or just admire this primitive man who simply cracked life's shell—logic, morality, honesty—and went straight to its very substance. All the little virtues which are so useful are lacking in him. All he has is an uncomfortable, dangerous virtue which is hard to satisfy and which urges him continually and irresistibly towards the utmost limits, towards the abyss" (p. 151). He admires but is still condescending; by the time of Stavridhákis' next letter, however, Boss has learned Zorba's true worth; he has finished mining Buddha by now and is free to participate in Zorba's dance.

When Zorba does finally return from town, twelve days late and reeking of perfume and toilet soap, Boss is afraid to display his emotion: the situation demands anger and righteousness, not the joy that he actually feels. Even the little prank that he plays—lying to Bouboulína about Zorba's intention to marry her—is somehow inappropriate, an act too cruel for Zorba to sanction, but one that might be taken under the influence of Karayánnis. When Boss hears later of the success of Stavridhákis' mission, his first reaction is again to hide his feelings, but by now he has learned something of emotion from Zorba: "Whatever's happening to you? I asked myself mockingly. Were you as patriotic as that then, and never knew? Or do you love your friend so much? You ought to be ashamed! Control yourself and quiet down! But I was transported with joy and continued along the track, shouting as I went" (p. 294). Still, he cannot do quite as Zorba would do, as he rebuffs a goatherd who attempts to share in his joy. He is no Zorba, quite simply, and cannot become one; indeed, there is no reason for him to overturn completely half a lifetime's dedication to art. But he can be more like Stavridhákis; he can learn to temper his art with emotion and action. It is Stavridhákis, not Zorba, who points up the theme of the novel. He appears only through letters and memories (and not at all in the film) and yet, in a sense, he is the dominant figure, for he represents a synthesis that the artist can undertake.

We recognize in Stavridhákis that same balance of passion and discipline found in classical Greek art and philosophy, put forth in more modern times by Nietzsche and Bergson, and demonstrated throughout the continuing folk tradition in Greece. He is the Aristotelean mean between the extremes of action and inaction, of practicality and mysticism, of life and art, which are represented by Zorba and Boss. He understands with Zarathustra the danger of extremes—that killing the senses is not the same as being innocent of them, that chastity may be both virtue and vice, that there may be "lust of the soul" as well as that of the flesh (*Zarathustra*, p. 81). And he knows with Bergson that civilization can survive the enemies that forever confront it only if men of good will learn to mobilize their resources. Stavridhákis is the synthesizer who joins the Dionysian ecstasy of Zorba with the Apollonian dreaminess of Boss, creating a new union in life as the classical tragedians did in their art. The still vital folk tradition in Greece dramatizes a similar union—even the most passionate of its songs display a balance of meter and form. Zorba prefers the warlike ballads of the Klephts, those patriotic brigands of the late Turkish occupation, whose songs are marked by a dramatic tension between their violent subjects and the serenity of nature, which provides their background. Modern Greek poets and dramatists frequently borrow from the folk tradition; its influence helps to explain the seemingly paradoxical tension in much of Kazantzakis' art. It helps us also to understand Zorba and Boss.

We discover from the mad example of Karayánnis that Zorba is much less extreme than he first seems. However, his is still no mean that this artist can achieve: he can do little more than lead Boss away from his former asceticism—a position as extreme in its way as the unthinking sensuality of Karayánnis—and direct him toward the mean of body and soul represented by his friend Stavridhákis. Although Boss will never play Zorba's *santúri*, he does learn to play a new tune on his own lyre. In return, he creates this book as memorial—not Kazantzakis, but Boss, learning from Zorba in fiction as his creator may have learned in real life. It is a memorial to both of his teachers. Stavridhákis laments in a dream that there will be nothing left of his soul to remember him by: "'A few lines of someone else's poetry, scattered and mutilated lines—not even a complete quatrain'" (p. 308). Yet this is his poem as much as it is Zorba's; he too represents a part of the metaphor of Crete.

Three Cretan intellectuals leave their homeland in search of new experience and meaning: in Africa, Karayánnis merely immerses himself in a new provinciality; in the Caucasus, Stavridhákis finds himself and offers an example for his friend; and Boss returns to Crete to learn from Zorba a new freedom and art. In Everyman-Zorba, this "great popular spirit,"[30] he discovers the metaphoric potential of Crete at its most universal.

1. *Report to Greco*, p. 445. A similar account appeared as the preface to the first Greek edition of *Zorba the Greek (Alexis Zorbas)*. It is available in English in *Books Abroad*, 46 (1972), pp. 399–402, trans. Apostolos Athanassakis.

2. Cacoyannis wrote the screenplay and directed the film; as for the highly derivative musical, the book was written by Joseph Stein, with music by John Kander and lyrics by Fred Ebb.

3. The major sources for this period of the author's life are Yannis Anapliotis, *The Real Zorba and Nikos Kazantzakis* (announced in several bibliographies as having been published in Chicago in 1967, this work has not yet appeared in English); Lewis A. Richards, "Fact and Fiction in Nikos Kazantzakis' *Alexis Zorbas*," *Western Humanities Review*, 18 (Autumn 1964), pp. 353–59, which is apparently based on Anapliotis' original Greek study; Pandhelís Prevelákis' previously cited *Nikos Kazantzakis and his Odyssey*; and, of course, Helen Kazantzakis' *Nikos Kazantzakis: A Biography Based on his Letters*. Their frequent differences over details point to the need for a definitive biography: the problem is aggravated by Kazantzakis' ostensible autobiography, which scrupulously avoids specifics about dates and places and sometimes even about people, and tends to merge fiction and fact, e.g., when it places the first meeting with Zorba after the author's first trip to Russia (which took place in 1925) and speaks of their working a mine on the southern coast of Crete.

4. All references are to the Simon and Schuster edition (New York, 1952), trans. Carl Wildman.

5. *Greco*, p. 458.

6. *Greco*, p. 461.

7. *Greco*, pp. 318–19.

8. From his notebook for March 19, 1915, cited in Helen Kazantzakis, p. 58.

9. Kazantzakis' record of a conversation with a friend on Crete, August 18, 1921, cited in Helen Kazantzakis, p. 77.

10. Prevelákis, pp. 23–24. It is Peter Bien, in "Zorba the Greek, Nietzsche, and the Perennial Greek Predicament," The Antioch Review, 25 (1965), pp. 147–63, who contends that The Birth of Tragedy is the primary source for Zorba, whereas Andreas Poulakidas, in "Kazantzakis' Zorba the Greek and Nietzsche's Thus Spake Zarathustra," Philological Quarterly, 49 (1970), pp. 234–44, makes the same claim for Zarathustra. Bien has written further of "Kazantzakis' Nietzschianism" in the Journal of Modern Literature, 2 (1972), pp. 245–66. In this same special issue is an article by Poulakidas, "Kazantzakis and Bergson: Metaphysic Aestheticians," pp. 267–83.

11. Nikos Kazantzakis, England, trans. Amy Mims (New York, 1965), p. 188. An almost identical statement appears in Greco, p. 321.

12. Greco, p. 329.

13. Prevelákis, p. 47.

14. Friedrich Nietzsche, Thus Spoke Zarathustra, trans. R. J. Hollingdale (Baltimore, 1969), p. 234. All other references in the text are to this edition. The image of the wheel, one of the basic symbols of the cycles of nature throughout Kazantzakis' fiction, has been used as a symbol both of Stoic resignation to the inevitability of life and of the Dionysian affirmation of life. This apparent contradiction fits perfectly into the duality that characterizes all of Kazantzakis' thought.

15. Greco, p. 339.

16. Greco, p. 333.

17. Ian W. Alexander, Bergson: Philosopher of Reflection (London, 1957), pp. 100, 58.

18. In addition to his dissertation, Kazantzakis wrote several articles on Nietzsche for the Athenian newspaper Néon Ásti between 1907 and 1909, the precise period in which he studied under Bergson; a more important later article, commemorating the anniversary of Nietzsche's death, appeared in Eléftheros Týpos on August 22 and 26, 1926. There is also a long essay on Bergson in the Bulletin of the Educational Society of Athens for the year 1912.

19. Henri Bergson, Laughter: An Essay on the Meaning of the Comic, trans. Cloudesley Brereton (New York, 1911). All other references in the text are to this edition.

20. Jacques Chevalier, Henri Bergson, trans. Lilian B. Clare (New York, 1928), p. 118.

21. Henri Bergson, Time and Free Will, trans. F. L. Pogson (London, 1910), p. 172.

22. Henri Bergson, Matter and Memory, trans. Nancy Margaret Paul and W. S. Palmer (London, 1911), p. 243.

23. Greco, pp. 448–49.

24. Greco, p. 348.

25. Nikos Kazantzakis, Japan/China, trans. George C. Pappageotes (New York, 1963), p. 249.

26. Prevelákis, p. 25.

27. Friedrich Nietzsche, *The Birth of Tragedy*, trans. Walter Kaufmann (New York, 1967), p. 37.

28. Eugene Watson Burlingame, *Buddhist Parables*, trans. from the original Pali (New Haven, 1922), p. 265. Kazantzakis' library, installed now in the Historical Museum of Iraklion, indicates his scholarly concern for ethics and especially for Eastern mysticism. Among its contents: D. T. Suzuki's *Essays on Zen Buddhism; The Divine Life*, by Shri Aurobindo; several volumes each of Swami Ramdas and Swami Vivekananda; Paul Dahlke's *Buddismus als Religion und Moral;* and *Die Lehre des Buddha* of Georg Grimm. There are also studies of Gandhi by Romain Rolland and Eleni Samios, now Mme Kazantzakis. Other authors and subjects represented here include Confucius, Julian the Apostate, Saint Augustine, Loyola, Saint Theresa, Campanella, Spinoza, Schweitzer, Spengler, Tillich, and Hasidism. As for Kazantzakis' own *Buddha,* the only section translated to date into English is a dialogue between the prophet and his disciple Ananda, which appears in *Greco,* pp. 349–52. One last connection among Buddha, Nietzsche, and Bergson: Anthonakes, pp. 114–16, suggests that Bergson's *élan vital* is akin to the Buddhist concept of rebirth, while the Silence of Kazantzakis and Nietzsche recalls the Buddhist Nirvana.

29. Letter to Börje Knös, Antibes, May 9, 1950, cited in Helen Kazantzakis, p. 486.

30. From the same letter cited immediately above.

CHAPTER SIX

KAZANTZAKIS' *ODYSSEY*
A Modern Rival to Homer

In a Modernist age in which epic deeds no longer seem possible either in life or in art, Crete is that rare modern land where the epic remains a viable form, where the memory of an heroic past—sometimes even a past within the poet's own lifetime—is valued still and still bears meaning for present times; the forms of their ancestors continue to live because the Cretans continue to find them meaningful in their own lives. There is even a sense in which the epic tradition may help to determine their lives, in which memories of Dhaskaloyánnis and of other heroes who fought the Turks may have acted to harden resistance to German invaders or to totalitarian colonels. The tradition lives on even as the island becomes increasingly Westernized.[1] So it was almost inevitable that Kazantzakis too would some day write an epic.

He began his *Odyssey* on Crete in September of 1924, at a time when he "had not yet decided... his own destiny," as Prevelákis puts it.[2] He was then forty-two years old, the author of several verse dramas—including an early, somewhat Romanticized "Odyssey"; of some experimental (i.e., demotic) textbooks; of a large body of translations into the demotic—to these mostly philosophical texts he would later add *The Divine Comedy* of Dante and the *Iliad* and *Odyssey* of Homer; and of two unsuccessful novels, *Snake and Lily* (1906) and *Broken Souls* (1908), which he later dropped from his canon, and *The Master Builder*, which the composer Manólis Kalomíris made into an opera in 1916.[3] When Kazantzakis finally completed the epic in December of 1938—working now on the island of Aegina, off the coast of Attica—he had become a major figure in Greek cultural life, the result largely of his widely serialized travel books and of the controversy aroused by *The Saviors of God*. The *Odyssey*, Kimon Friar reports, "had long been awaited with intense anticipation, and was received with confused bewilderment."[4] Kazantzakis would not achieve a truly international reputation until he returned to the novel in the last phase of his career, but even then the bewilderment over his epic remained.

Yet it was the *Odyssey* which he considered his *Obra*, the central document of his life, and on it he hoped to establish his fame as an artist, among the young in particular; he had long since given up on his own generation. "The aim of the *Odyssey*," he wrote to a friend at the time of publication, "is to be read by the young people at all costs. This book was not written for old men. It was written for the young people and those who have not yet been born."[5] Only now, ironically, have his aims begun to be realized, and perhaps more in the West than in Greece; certainly it has seemed more accessible to students in America than to those in his own country. Simple availability has been one problem: published originally in a private edition, still the general custom for poetry in Greece, it sold only one-third of the three hundred expensively bound volumes; Kazantzakis gave most of the remainder away to his friends. Copies did circulate freely, however, but it was not until 1957, some two decades later, that a second, less expensive Greek edition appeared. Thus, it was not until after the death of the poet that his major work became generally available to the poets and scholars of Greece. In contrast, the American edition of five thousand copies sold out in the first week; since then it has gone into several printings and has sold, including three book club editions, well over one hundred thousand copies.

More serious perhaps for a Greek audience has been the problem of assimilating the epic—even reading it has sometimes been difficult for the poet's own countrymen. For the *Odyssey* culminates a lifetime of fighting for language reform. Written in an unfamiliar meter, simplifying conventional spelling and syntax and abandoning the useless accentual marks common to the language since Byzantine times (retaining only the acute accent for emphasis), with an added glossary of some two thousand words that were familiar to the peasants of Greece but virtually unknown to its scholars,[6] the *Odyssey* was an effort to revolutionize the diction of modern Greek poetry. Even today, there are literate Greeks who claim to find it more readable in English translation than in the original *Dhemotiki*. "The intellectuals of Athens cannot understand this," Kimon Friar has said of the epic which he translated so well; "I give it to the boatmen and fishermen, and they have no trouble."[7] The irony would have delighted the poet.

Most significantly of all, this monumental poem of 33,333 lines—almost three times the length of Homer's great epic—bridged more successfully than any other work of its time the enormous gap between Classical Athens and the Modernist Age, a period during which much of the finest Greek literature existed in a kind of self-imposed limbo, unsure of whether to continue to copy the ancients or to look forward to Europe, certain only of its failure to match up to the models of old. In a sense then, Kazantzakis' *Odyssey* makes possible the liberation of Greek literature from its bondage to the past, providing a way for younger Greek artists to be true both to their ancestral inheritance and to the modern world in which they live. Its potential importance in this regard may be even greater than that of James Joyce's *Ulysses* for the West. Because of its controversial diction, however, because it has only recently become widely available, this potential has been unfortunately circumscribed. Far more influential has been the example of George Seféris, who turned to his heritage in a far different way: his *Mithistórima* looks similarly to Homer for its imagery and setting, but subject and theme here are derived at least in part from the West—the connections are more to Eliot's *The Waste Land* than to the *Odyssey* of Homer. Where Kazantzakis adapts Western ideas to fit the model of his native Crete, Seféris, no less important a poet, has poured the experience of Greece into the alien molds of the West. The result is great verse to be sure, but for lesser poets it is a potentially negative example, one which might very well add a new form of bondage to the old. Finally, just as British and American writers have begun to repudiate Joyce—perhaps to abandon him before they have assimilated his full significance—so those young Greek writers who have been influenced by Kazantzakis may deservedly feel that it is time for them too to go their own way, that they have learned all they can from their master's example.[8] It is a decision of which Kazantzakis, ever mindful of the need for the young to surpass their elders, would have surely approved. The disciple who does not surpass his master, he would say with Leonardo, fails his master.

For his real influence, ironically, we may have to look not to Greece but to the West, for here the young are just beginning to discover Kazantzakis' work, and it is to the *Odyssey* that they most often turn. The *Whole Earth Catalogue* offers a striking example: a periodical developed by students and dedicated to a philosophy of brotherhood, peace, and a balance between nature and man, it lauds the poem that it believes "may well turn out to be the spiritual handbook of the future. In fact," its reviewer continues, "our future may lie within its pages."[9] But the academic admirers of the *Odyssey*, following the lead perhaps of their colleagues in Greece, remain somewhat uneasy; despite student approval (perhaps even because of it), despite an overwhelmingly favorable press when it first appeared in translation (Max

Schuster told Friar "that in his thirty-five years as publisher no other book brought out by his firm had received so many and such laudatory reviews"[10]), scholars accustomed to an art whose goals and limits seem more clearly defined, cannot feel fully at ease before such an apparently unreasonable, such an immense, eclectic, idiosyncratic work. Seféris we can read with ease, for his work appears within our tradition; but to read the *Odyssey* of Kazantzakis requires a major adjustment, demands that we forego our accustomed moderation and reason and accept instead the possibility of Cretan excessiveness: that we accept the vast scope of the epic, its union of metaphysics and gross sensuality, its function as an encyclopaedia of Modernist thought, and, above all, its refusal to compromise. Some critics, of course, will never make the adjustment.[11]

But even those who admire Kazantzakis' novels may have reservations about his epic. Peter Bien, for example, contends that the *Odyssey* fails as art because of its dominant interest in language reform, because the poet's pioneering involvement with the demotic tongue—an issue as much political as it is literary—overwhelms his more human concerns. The English translator of *Report to Greco, Saint Francis*, and *The Last Temptation of Christ* and a sympathetic judge of their philosophical roots, Bien believes that Kazantzakis made of his epic a kind of dictionary of the demotic, that the final four of his seven drafts were designed more to add new words than to improve the verse, that cut off from Greece by his long exile in Europe the writer erred in using a commonplace diction in a basically intellectual poem. Bien would have us turn instead to the novels, beginning in 1940 with *Zorba*, to find the true worth of Kazantzakis: his pride in his nation renewed by its resistance to fascist invaders, living again in Greece and dealing again with Greek characters and scenes, Kazantzakis had at last a setting appropriate to his demotic language. Thus the *Obra*, in this critic's view, is itself merely a preparation for the last, supposedly lesser, works of the author's career.[12]

Bien raises issues of prosody and diction, of values and taste, that cannot be dealt with fairly in a critical study limited to works in translation; they will have to wait for some more definitive book, one addressed primarily to scholars. Yet he may well be correct in asserting that the reformist zeal at work in the epic limited its original audience and impact; but his sense of the incongruity of subject and tone seems rather forced and old fashioned. Kazantzakis himself evidently believed that the language of his people perfectly suited philosophical questions derived from their own history and life, that no arbitrary concept of literary decorum should be allowed to destroy the living language that had evolved along with the people. This, after all, was the core of the entire struggle against the enforced use of the *Katharévousa.*

The problem for English readers is somewhat moot because of the nature and quality of Kimon Friar's translation, surely one of the best of our time. Removed from the start from the controversy over language and syntax, we are further shielded by a rendition in which there are no shocking poetic effects, in which subject and tone seem always harmonious. The result, of course, is not quite the same as the original—Kazantzakis said in praise of his collaborator that it was "not a translation but a recreation" of his poem[13]—so that we will never be able to read this *Odyssey* without thinking also of Friar; still, his rendition does give us an intense awareness of both meaning and sound in the original epic, of its complexity and scope and the depth of its knowledge, especially of the richness of its imagery and language. For this was indeed the result of what the translator has termed a collaboration unique in literature. For several months in 1954 and then again in 1957, shortly before the death of the poet, Friar virtually lived in Kazantzakis' home in Antibes, working with him for many hours each day, in both English and Greek, "on words, phrases, images, meaning, nuance, source, anything that might help me toward a better and more accurate translation."[14] Kazantzakis read the entire manuscript in close detail, until he had approved even those few sections with which he did not agree: a unique sort of man for an artist, one who not only understood the creative needs of the translator, but who remembered those of young poets as well.[15] "Kazantzakis never lived to hold the printed copy of my English translation in his hands, something he deeply longed for, . . . [but] without doubt, had [he] lived a year longer, the availability to the Swedish Committee of what he himself considered to be the one work by which he might live on in the minds of men, would have assured him of the Nobel Prize, . . . which he had come within a few votes of winning several times before."[16]

One thing is certain: whether we prefer the novels with Bien or share the poet's own faith in his *Odyssey*, whether we are unconvinced by its effort to shape a contemporary worldview or see in it the shape of our future lives, we cannot hope to know Kazantzakis—his role as a Modernist artist, his significance as a recorder of local and universal phenomena—unless we first understand his great epic. In it we find the dominant techniques and themes of all of his fiction—the naturalistic and symbolic styles of *Freedom or Death* and the social overtones of *The Greek Passion*, the philosophy of *Zorba the Greek* and the mythic structure of *The Last Temptation of Christ*: in short, that whole sense of Cretan history and life turned in his art to universal values, the Cretan Glance as metaphor of the nature and history of man.

II

The Odyssey: A Modern Sequel is one of the great encyclopedic works of our time, encompassing the major motifs of our civilization and Homer's, bridging the gap of our common heritage not only for Greeks but for all those to whom Homer is both ancestor and guide. Writing like his predecessor in a period of calm between tumultuous epochs, Kazantzakis endeavors similarly to include all the knowledge and history of his own time, to make of his epic too a symbolic chronicle of the glorious past and a guide for action in the troublesome future. "'Blessed be that hour that gave me birth between two eras!'" Odysseus proclaims, as if he were himself the epic poet (III, 742). As Homer employed the surviving folk tales and legends of the Mycenaeans to narrate their greatness and fall, so Kazantzakis makes use of Homer to dramatize both those mythic extremes and our own. But his is a far different work, a revolutionary contrast to the conservative Homer, a direct challenge to that earlier *Odyssey:* it was Kimon Friar who added the subtitle "A Modern Sequel" to the later epic; Kazantzakis called it simply *Odyssey.*

Like Homer, he begins *in medias res,* in the middle this time of Homer, as if in the midst of a sentence: "And when in his wide courtyards Odysseus had cut down / the insolent youths...." Soon after, accompanied by his son, as in Homer, the returned king puts down by guile the revolt of his subjects, the first of many revolts in these new adventures, with implications far more compelling than in the original. For there are commoners at the head of this crowd—more commoners than in all of Homer—and maimed veterans returned from Troy. For them the far-off war, in a cause removed from their interests and needs, is a sign not only of their own king's arrogance but also of an entire society concerned alone with its elite; thus they repudiate also the attitude of Homer, who numbers only nobles and slaves in his social perspective. "'The guileless gods grant freedom only to earth's masters,'" says Helen, referring at this point not to those most fit but to those most nobly born (III, 1260). But Odysseus can no longer accept such a view, and the revolt in Ithaca is the last in which he will act as tradition demands. Each subsequent uprising will have similar social and political overtones, but his attitude toward each will subtly change, building progressively, until in the end the king will join with the rebels, convinced that not only society but all humanity must be purged and reformed.

In Homer, the revolt of his Ithacan subjects provides one more step in the reconciliation of Odysseus with those who have so long awaited him: with his wife, with his son, with the people he once ruled. Kazantzakis replaces these scenes with an account of the returned king's own alienation. Seeing Penelope for the first time after the slaughter of the suitors, he tries to convince himself that she all along has been his lone goal:

> "... she who for years has waited you to force
> her bolted knees and join you in rejoicing cries,
> she is the one you've longed for, battling the far seas,
> the cruel gods and deep voices of your deathless mind."
> (I, 30–33)

But he feels only rage at her seeming connivance with the suitors and cannot even bring himself to speak to her. When he does tell her of his travels, it is only of Calypso and Circe and Nausicaa that he speaks, temptations he ultimately resisted not for her sake but for his own, because he was not a god as Calypso would have it, but a mortal; because his essential humanity was threatened by the gross sensuality of Circe; because his need to reach above himself, his potential divinity, would have shriveled in simple home life with Nausicaa. It is hardly a politic tale to tell even to a wife renowned for her patience, and it could hardly have come from the travel-weary, home-loving husband of the original epic; yet it is Homer's Odysseus who unaccountably tells his wife, immediately upon their reunion, of the prophecy that he must travel again to lands and seas beyond the borders known to the Greeks. When, finally, he does leave Ithaca, this new Odysseus has no farewell for his " 'heavy-fated' " (II, 1117), "his luckless wife" (II, 1446); she sees him last at dawn, "treading on tiptoe through the court... like a thief" (II, 1462).

Telemachus is appalled by his father's indelicacy, by the demands he makes on those he encounters, both by his grasp for, and his rejection of, divinity:

> ... shuddering, [he] spied on the hard knees and thighs,
> the hands that could choke virtue, that on savage shores
> brashly could seize yet cast aside the dread Immortals.
> (II, 198–200)

The prince has fought bravely beside his father against the suitors, but now he counsels moderation and quiet acceptance of life in Ithaca. He is precisely the sort of ruler that any reasonable citizen would desire. And with him, we reasonable men might curse his father, who makes it impossible to follow in traditional paths, to live calmly and well:

> "You set all minds on fire, you plague man's simple heart,
> you drive the craftsman from his shop, uproot the plow,
> until the country bridegroom wants his bride no more
> but longs for travel and immortal Helen's arms."
>
> (I, 1280–83)

An old bard who had known Odysseus' grandfather sings of the ideal monarch, the " 'good man. . . grown old [who] sits like God in the market place' " (II, 1130–32). Laertes has been such a king; his grandson will be another. But Odysseus disdains their ideal, for under such moderate rulers, he knows, men are too easily content, too willing to limit their divine aspirations. It is only when the prince Telemachus endeavors to seize the throne that his father the king elects to abdicate, pleased for once by the initiative of his " 'wretched, well-bred' " conservative son (II, 1122).

Even Ithaca and the symbols of his reign fail the returned king: his people are mundane—" 'a mess of bellies and stinking breath!' " (I, 1069); the assembly he so longed to hold is made up of close-minded and cowardly elders—"was this, by God, the foul fistful his soul desired?" (II, 702). His journey, he has now come to realize, has made him unfit for Ithaca—his goal, paradoxically, more noble than its attainment. To reach it, he had resisted all the faces of death; now, he discovers, "even his native land was a sweet mask of Death" (II, 434).

By the end of the second book of this new *Odyssey*—corresponding in time to the last book of Homer, in which reconciliation is finally complete—the king has collected a new crew of misfits and left Ithaca forever: en route to Sparta, where he carries off Helen a second time, offering her not love but adventure and freedom; to Minoan Crete, where he presides over the fall of its decadent civilization; to Egypt, where he leads a futile, bloody revolt and from which he escapes as Moses leading an army of rebels and misfits. In Africa, at the source of the Nile, he founds a utopian city of craftsmen, warriors, and scholars, a socialist state in which the family is outlawed and the people glorified as a whole, a state destroyed at its birth by a volcanic eruption and earthquake. As he moves further south, now without companions or followers, Odysseus comes increasingly to deny his old worldly concerns, to move away from society and politics, away from his idealism and concern for the flesh. Finally, at the southernmost pole, in a snowy white deathship, his mind and soul leap free of his body, and he becomes free at last even of the need for freedom.

> All the great body of the world-roamer turned to mist,
> and slowly his snow-ship, his memory, fruit and friends
> drifted like fog far down the sea, vanished like dew.

Then flesh dissolved, glances congealed, the heart's pulse stopped,
and the great mind leapt to the peak of its holy freedom,
fluttered with empty wings, then upright through the air
soared high and freed itself from it last cage, its freedom.
(XXIV, 1387–93)

In his movement from body to spirit, from Ithaca to the Antarctic, Kazantzakis' Odysseus creates a new philosophical complex, one built on a base of Mediterrannean archaeology and history, of the fertility myths of Africa and the Near East, fulfilling at last the prophecy of Homer's Tieresias in Hades: that the sailor would travel from his home to a land so far from the sea that its people would mistake the oar on his shoulder for a winnowing fan; that he would experience there new adventures of great moral and intellectual import; that he would eventually die on the sea—"a seaborne death soft as this hand of mist."[17] The oar of Odysseus is a basic symbol of Kazantzakis' poem: from it will sprout man's figurative wings, emblem of his spiritual rebirth, of his human potential for godhead. For this man there will be no Mycenaean funeral games, no burial in the *tholos* tombs of his ancestors: Odysseus will indeed die in mist, his flesh dissolved into spirit, into that combination of mind and soul from which, Kazantzakis believes, the ancient fertility figures were sprung and into which we must evolve if we and our civilization are similarly to be renewed.

III

Drawn by a vision of Helen "withered . . . in idleness" (III, 232) and choking for freedom, the self-exiled king sails first for Sparta and a reunion with her and her husband, his wartime companion. But Menelaus, he finds, has grown comfortable and soft, so content with the outward signs of his reign that he is fit no longer to rule. He represents to Odysseus both cause and result of Mycenaean decay, the symbol of a society grown so far from its roots that it cannot be renewed unless it first is destroyed. The Dorian invasion will provide the new blood. Here Kazantzakis telescopes history and politics, literature and myth, as the Bronze Age, grown rotten with social injustice, comes to an end with the return of the last hero from Troy; as a civilization expires when its king, grown sterile, forgets how to die so that his people may live.

The "guardian lions" continue to stand at the gates of Ithaca and Sparta (I, 419; III, 906), but they are mere relics of a world that is passing. Odysseus, however, with his "lion-stench" (IV, 10) and his " 'lion-soul' " (IV, 764), continues to embody the old virtues of

Mycenae, its restlessness and force in particular. " 'I never thought you'd storm my castle like a lion,' " Menelaus sighs (III, 1208), pleased to see his friend once again yet instinctively fearful of that unregenerate soul. The Spartan himself dreams of leaving his wife and kingdom behind and riding off with Odysseus to new adventure and freedom, of sharing with him the old virtues; but he awakes with no memory of his dream. Waking, his mercantile soul is preoccupied with contemplating his riches—the fruit of his olive groves, of his farms and his flocks. And he confides, " 'If God had not predestined me to rule my people, / I'd be a shepherd browsing flocks on these far hills' " (IV, 392–93). This is hardly the tone to appeal to Odysseus, who has rejected the husbanding instincts of his own father and son and who scorns all talk of predestination—in another ironic reversal, he will later make a king out of Rocky, Menelaus' shepherd. His answer to this confidence is explicit:

> "I think man's greatest duty on earth is to fight his fate,
> to give no quarter and blot out his written doom.
> This is how mortal man may even surpass his god!"
>
> (IV, 411–13)

From this moment on, as Menelaus admires his flocks while he is joying in the difficulty of life, Odysseus abandons his friend, stifles his compassion for his former comrade, and identifies instead with the future enemies of Sparta—the blond Doric hordes from the North. They alone have the vigor of old Mycenae, and they have usurped its lion symbol. Bargaining with the Dorians to settle on unused lands and become his vassals, the Spartan king puffs with remembered pride, and unconscious irony: " 'My strength is like a lioness who has given birth!' " he proclaims (IV, 884). But the invaders have been given the land without even fighting, and we see—through the eyes of Odysseus and the old Dorian chief—the coming order of things:

> The lion had pounced upon his prey, devoured it whole,
> and soon, with his rude tongue had wiped his bloodstained chops.
>
> (IV, 899–900)

Now, accompanied for the last time by his friend, Menelaus walks silently across the bronze threshold of his palace, "guarded by two aging lions" (IV, 909).

Extrapolating from the lion gate uncovered by Schliemann at the site of ancient Mycenae, the city of Agamemnon, which gave its name to Bronze Age Greece, Kazantzakis creates a symbol that suggests both the fall of that people and the reasons behind it: it is not Dorian iron alone that makes possible their victory over a civilization far more advanced than their own. The lion for them is no mere artifice to adorn threshold or gate, but a living symbol of their restlessness and strength, a symbol wrested intact from their self-satisfied antagonists. Here the author imaginatively restructures the extant archaeological evidence, which indicates that the Mycenaeans were indeed unprepared for the Dorian onslaught, perhaps in part because they had grown soft, perhaps even because in their regimented society there was discontent among the subjects themselves. In Kazantzakis' Sparta, the working classes are so poor and dissatisfied that they will surely not fight for their lords—as centuries later the Cretan masses refused to resist the Turks on behalf of their Venetian masters. At the games organized by his host in his honor, Odysseus offends both noble and worker by awarding the prize to the "boys of myriad seed" (IV, 621), bastard sons of Spartan women and men from the North, whose play ignores all the rules and swiftly runs into brutal combat:

> "I give this bitter wreath of manliness and freedom
> not to the poor who thunder idly and spout words,
> nor to the lustrous noble youths who strut and crow
> as though all earth were a dancing floor and mind a garden—
> I crown instead those heads that were blood-broken in battle!"
>
> (IV, 789–93)

From their mixed blood will develop a great new civilization, a series of restless forms that we perhaps erroneously call Classical.

In all of this, Kazantzakis' metaphor is close to historical possibilities. However, there is no real proof, not even from the many excavations conducted since the publication of the *Odyssey*, to support his conception of a peaceful opening to this northern invasion. As it is, we are not even sure of who the Dorians were or where precisely they came from, or just when or how they conquered the kingdoms of Mycenae. We know for certain only that all the walled cities of the mainland—except for Athens—were destroyed by fire, one after the other, starting most likely with those in the North and the West, that the final victims at least had a good deal of warning and that their most careful precautions could not prevent their destruction. Their unpreparedness, it seems, was not a matter of effort or time, but one of people and perhaps of motivation. The crude iron swords of the invaders were not, as we sometimes think, harder than the bronze weapons opposed to them; but bronze was more rare than iron, a sign, among other things, of influence and prestige, and in Mycenae only an elite was actually armed. The armed Dorian masses must have simply overwhelmed them. In this sense too, then, Kazantzakis may be closer than we realize to the symbolic truth of these uncertain events. For when Menelaus invites the newcomers into his realm, he heightens our sense of his own unfitness and of the impending doom of his people.

King and kingdom are inextricably bound in this scheme, the former's vitality (or lack of it) both cause and effect of the life of his subjects. And Menelaus, "like a stout gelded ram with twisted horns" (IV, 379), is spiritually sterile, so that his divided kingdom can bear no more fruit: the land remains fertile, but the people will soon die— " 'because your loins are drained, O king, your heart has shrunk,/ and now new hearts and loins shall inundate the earth' " (III, 1182-83). As the poet perceives them, the Dorians are a kind of fertility force that will eventually renew life in Sparta. For a time, the war in Troy had reinvigorated the old mainland kingdoms—" 'a raging war that opened minds and widened seas,' " in the words of Odysseus (IV, 954)—but now only their own destruction can lead to renewal.

It is strangely fitting that Odysseus, who has already rejected his own preordained role as monarch and symbol, should be the one to recall the ancient order that, in the end, the king must die if the people will live. When he himself finally dies, a lifetime away from his kingdom in Ithaca, it will not be to save that people alone but to save himself and perhaps, in the dying, to save all of us. Like other Kazantzakian heroes, he offers a way of life and of death that has overtones beyond his own being, something more than a mere fertility god can command. For the moment, however, he can do little more than repudiate forever the values retained by Menelaus: by running off with the wife of his host to Crete, home of the oldest fertility rites, ruled over by "the all-holy mother" (V, 278), "dread Mother of men and beasts" (V, 730). His first act there is to barter for clothing and food Menelaus' parting gift, a golden symbol of Zeus, the god of hospitality and friendship who rules Homer's *Odyssey*. It is a long way from Homer's god-fearing Odysseus to this "heaven-baiter" (V, 427), but the road before him remains equally long.

IV

When Odysseus in Ithaca confronts his rebellious subjects, he is welcomed by the elders "with reverential fear." Praise the Immortals, they cry, for now " 'your orphaned island . . . shall bloom once more and the stones sprout with grass' " (I, 370-73). Ironically, as both he and they realize, he has returned not only legitimacy but death to Ithaca. Still, monarch and elders alike retain their faith in the ancient fertility formula: whatever prosperity there may have been during the king's long absence, it is only in his presence that the land can flower in truth. An analogous situation prevails in Sparta, where the sterility of Menelaus in no way affects nature; it simply dries up the souls of his subjects. What Odysseus believes in, in short, is a formula less literal than that of *The Waste Land:* fertility to him is a function of the spirit alone, and not of the landscape. This is nowhere more evident than in the wasteland of Minoan Crete, where Odysseus and Helen are driven by a storm.

But Odysseus realizes that in a sense he has been heading for Crete all along, at least since the old Cretan minstrel, warning him against contentment with Ithaca, sang of that " 'living land whose entrails are still burning, / where still the bull-sun mounts her like a cow each dawn'" (II, 1343-44). The catalogue of ships in the *Iliad* lists eighty vessels from Crete, under King Idomeneus, in the fleet that sails against Troy, a force inferior only to those of Agamemnon's Mycenae and Nestor's Pylos—only a dozen ships followed Odysseus from Ithaca and the surrounding lands. Neither Homer nor his sixth-century Athenian editors, however, are likely to have understood this traditional reference, for by Homer's time Crete had become a back-water, with virtually no remaining trace of its former magnificence. Thus, Idomeneus and the Cretans play only a minor role in the Trojan siege; even at that date, several centuries before Homer, Minoan Crete had begun to decline, so that the brilliant empire that Odysseus and Helen now find is a kind of literary anachronism.

For here, too, Kazantzakis interprets the historical facts—such as they are—with great ingenuity. At a time when most authorities erroneously believed with Sir Arthur Evans that the Mycenaean cities were colonies of Crete, Kazantzakis perceived that they were separate states—contemporaneous for a time but distinct in style and structure—and that although the religion and art of the mainland had been strongly influenced by the Minoans, Mycenae at some point might well have conquered and governed Knossos. Only recently have archaeologists and historians generally come to accept this viewpoint. Kazantzakis also telescopes time, as in Homer, so that Idomeneus and Odysseus appear as contemporaries, although the originals must have lived centuries apart. As a result, he shows us a Crete far more powerful than Homer could have imagined, a purely Minoan civilization at the height of its power and decadence, before its conquest by Mycenae and long before the natural disasters that would destroy it completely.[18] In this scheme, it is Odysseus who conquers Knossos, creating a new kingdom in which both Mycenae and Crete may be potentially renewed, a kingdom with a Dorian presence as well. But he will leave this place too, as he previously abandoned Ithaca and Sparta; his search is for something greater than empire or even national renewal:

> ... many-breasted, shameless, nude, Crete's body spread
> her practiced thighs amid the waves, swarming with merchants
> ... [who] sauntered on the quays adorned
> like birds with peacock plumes and bracelets of pure gold.
> These acrid captains ate and drank till their guts burst,
> they'd seen all, kissed and drained their bodies dry with lust,
> till drenched in fine perfumes, fluttering their feathery fans,
> they swooned now in the firm embrace of their black slaves.
> Their fingers were all rotted, but their rings remained,
> their empty loins were withered, but their thin skulls shone
> with wide-eyed sophistry and brimmed with mocking smiles.
> In their plush homes, the gods, demeaned to bric-a-brac,
> cooped up like parrots in their cages of gold bars,
> were hung in windows where with human voice they squawked
> and cackled back those words which they were taught to say.
>
> (V, 299-314)

The old bard was mistaken: the bull-god no longer mounts the female island. On Crete—a land abundant in riches and so refined in its art that it values form over content, birthplace of the most ancient fertility rites—the gods too have been prostituted to commerce. The time-honored forms continue to be observed, but they are occasions now for popular entertainments and love-games for the ladies of the court. Religion on Crete has degenerated into art, art into deception and perversity: the king has withered but refuses to die, and so arranges the ritual that he will seem to the people to have been reborn. And the Mother Goddess acquiesces in the deception. In the autumn, he must submit to the bull-god in the great cave on Mount Dikte in which Cretan Zeus was once born. Powerful kings in the past often failed to return from the hazardous rite, but when Idomeneus submits his "rotten loins," his "'empty bones'" and "'putrid flesh'" to the god in the cave (V, 570-75), there will be no danger for him—and no renewal. Like Menelaus, he is both cause and effect of his people's decay, but putrescence here is far more advanced than in Sparta. As a street peddler informs Odysseus and Helen,

> "the Bull-God gulped our kings only in ancient times,
> for now they've learned to be on good terms with the gods
> and climb unruffled toward them, bearing golden towers,
> for learn, the gods are merchants now and strike hard bargains."
>
> (V, 584-87)

The myth has been perverted, but its symbolism remains true.[19] The land will be renewed, but only after the death of the king and the scourging of the palace by fire—for "'fire is good when governed by man's inner light'" (VII, 626); and a new, virile king will replace him—Hardihood, the red-haired bronzesmith from Ithaca, promised this post by his captain because he would not sacrifice Helen to save their ship from a storm. And Helen, too, through her part in the ritual, has at last been fulfilled. Idomeneus has chosen her to be his bride, to lie within the hollow cow of bronze onto which he will mount, on his head "the skull of a black bull . . . on which two golden horns stood stiff and flashed in light" (VI, 118-19). But no phallic mask can blunt the truth of his impotence, and his place is soon filled by the blond palace gardener who had once brought her water. Bearing his Dorian child, she is content to remain on Crete, all memories of Spartan aristocracy forgotten, only dimly recalling "those brave youths who died at Troy for her sweet sake" (VII, 944)—a kind of earth mother brought in the end to earth. Once her sensuality, like that of Odysseus, seemed ready to taste all experience, to engulf the whole world, but now she is pleased just to rest with her child in her symbolic garden. She barely sees her old friend as he bids her farewell, and no thoughts pass through her mind. For "woman's flesh is an unable, transient thing" (V, 538), and her soul is caught in her flesh: "man's soul perched, an eagle's nest, high in the head, / and woman's soul lay brooding deep between two breasts" (V, 720-21).

Parting for Odysseus is the more bitter because once he had been tempted to live with Helen, to abandon his crew in mid-sea and make a home of their ship, to "fondle her with pride, / and in her womb entrust a son that one day would surpass him" (V, 163-64).[20] Like Jesus in *The Last Temptation of Christ,* he overcomes this vision of sensual home life and easy immortality, but he cannot help being envious of her gardener. In the heated atmosphere of Knossos, his sensuousness in every respect is more intense than ever before; but here, too, he submits his passions to a certain intellectual control. To the rebellious workers and slaves of Crete, freedom means an opportunity to indulge in the joys of the senses, as their masters have done; to Odysseus, however, freedom to enjoy the flesh is a means of rising above it. " 'My mind is not a gentle lamb that feeds on grass,' " he rebukes a censorious friend, " 'but like a hawk hunts flesh and blood to sprout with wings' " (VI, 722-23). His entire odyssey is an effort to sprout wings, its symbol an artifact mysteriously acquired from a street vendor who suddenly appears and then vanishes, bearing with him knowledge of the court and of human nature—an ivory god "with seven towering heads piled on each other, worn / by myriads of caressing hands and pilgrim lips" (V, 589-90). In it Odysseus sees a universal symbol that he had overlooked in his earlier travels, as well as a concrete sign of his own spiritual journey, of his labor to reach above his body to his soul and beyond—to reach from the bottom-most physical depths of

```
    ... the most coarse head, a brutal base of flesh
    swelled like a bloated beast bristling with large boar-tusks
    and ... fortified with veins as thick as horns
```
(V, 598–600)

up to the etherealized topmost head,

```
    ...crystal-clear,translucent, light
    [which] had no ears or eyes, no nostrils, mouth, or brow,
    for all its flesh had turned to soul, and soul to air!
```
(V, 627–29)

In his long progression from Ithaca to the South Pole, from the atavistic rage with which he slaughters the suitors to the pure spirit of his own death, in his movement away from a selfish concern for his own affairs to a growing compassion for all suffering men, to a final recognition that immortality can be achieved only through individual effort, Odysseus blazes the path that all men must follow who wish to overcome death. To pass beyond death, he discovers, we first must learn " 'that life is not man's highest or even his noblest good' " (VII, 1203). In a series of legends and dreams, Odyssean man confronts and finally conquers death, conquers at least that fear of death that so often vitiates life. In the first of these, to pass the time and to strengthen the hearts of the crew on their first day out of the known world of Ithaca, the piper Orpheus sings of two worms who have courageously survived famine and frost and the flood, and to whom a malignant God has at last sent Death:

```
"Death took his sharpest knives, crawled down into the cave,
crept close beside the two small worms and spread his feet
to warm himself by the hearthstones and spy with greed
on the pair's simple and calm gossip around the fire.
And when the male worm saw him there, his small heart froze,
but he said nothing, for fear his wife might faint with fright,
and when night fell at length and they lay down to sleep
the worm crawled slowly, careful not to waken Death,
and in the darkness hugged his mate in tight embrace.
Death's dry bones glowed with light in the erotic dark
but he woke not nor felt the two warm bodies merge;
the male worm then took heart and in his wife's ear whispered:
'With one sweet kiss, dear wife, we've conquered conquering Death!' "
```
(III, 169–81)

In the sequel that Odysseus sings on the following day—for " 'I, too, lay stretched in that dark cave when Lord Death came!' " (III, 217)—the suffering, Job-like worm climbs a mountain to beat his drum in God's own face: " ' "why, you Murderer," ' " he yells, " ' "must you slay our children? Why?" ' " (III, 405). When God's only answer is the force and rage of His lightning-like old bronze sword, Job-worm turns, draws from his belt his own iron " 'black-hilted sword,/ rushed up and slew that old decrepit god in heaven!' " (III, 430–31). Underlying all the Jobian heroes of Kazantzakis' late novels is this figure of the Nietzschean rebel who slays his worthless divinity.

> " 'And now, my gallant lads—I don't know when or how—
> that worm's god-slaying sword has fallen into my hands;
> I swear that from its topmost iron tip the blood still drips!' "
>
> (III, 432–34)

Finally, just before Odysseus himself slays the corrupt mercantile gods of Crete, his old comrade, Death, "weary from wandering all night long," stretches out alongside him, throws "his bony hands across the archer's chest," and sleeps.

> Death slept and dreamt that man indeed, perhaps, existed,
> that houses rose on earth, perhaps, kingdoms and castles,
> that even gardens rose and that beneath their shade
> court ladies strolled in languor and handmaidens sang.
> He dreamt there was a sun that rose, a moon that shone,
> a wheel of earth that turned and every season brought,
> perhaps, all kinds of fruit and flowers, cooling rain and snow,
> and that it turned once more, perhaps, till earth renewed.
> But Death smiled secretly in sleep for he knew well
> this was but dream, a dappled wind, toy of his weary mind,
> and unperturbed, allowed this evil dream to goad him.
> But slowly life took courage, and the wheel whirled round,
> earth gaped with hunger, sun and rain sank in her bowels,
> unnumbered eggs hatched birds, the world was filled with worms,
> until a packed battalion of beasts, men and thoughts
> set out and pounced on sleeping Death to eat him whole.
> A human pair crouched in his nostrils' heaving caves
> and lit and fed a fire, then set up house and cooked,
> and from his upper lip hung down their new son's cradle.
> Feeling his nostrils tingling and his pale lips tickled,
> Death suddenly shook and tossed in sleep, and the dream vanished.
> For a brief moment Death had fallen asleep and dreamt of life.
>
> (VI, 1271–92)

The vision blurs, and we are uncertain whether this is dream or reality; but the cycle at least is complete: whether Death resides in the caves of man or man in his, the relationship between life and death—between dream and reality—is more intense and immediate than we may like to accept. To Odysseus, however, as to Kazantzakis, it is this connection that gives meaning to life and potential value to individual lives. Mark Twain, in the bitterness of his lonely old age, posited a universe in which all life is dream, all without meaning, in which no one man need bear any responsibility or guilt.[21] To Kazantzakis, solipsism is no such means of escape but a challenge to accept responsibility—for oneself, above all, but for others as well: indeed, for the entire universe.

The fertility myths of Minoan Crete, which the poet bases on traditional patterns derived from the work of Evans at Knossos and from *The Golden Bough*, and the still more original legends conjured by the artist Orpheus, by Odysseus and perhaps even by God, prove above all the need for involvement in life—even if life itself is a dream, especially if it is. But fertility, in what may be Kazantzakis' most imaginative insight into these myths, is not a function primarily of nature, but a stage in the development of the human soul. Leaving behind Crete and experiences far beyond those envisioned by Homer, the hero is only a third of the way through his odyssey.

V

His experiences in Egypt seem at first glance a replica of those on Crete; again, he is involved in rebellion against a decaying empire; again, his enemies are gross sensuality and social injustice. The implications here, however, are less truly mythic and more overtly political than on Crete: the only renewal that is possible in this ancient land is one of the flesh. Perhaps it is pity for suffering mankind that leads Odysseus to join the rebels, perhaps simply his own inner voice; yet he recognizes now that he belongs truly with neither adversary, neither with starving commoners nor with decadent nobles. This realization marks a new point in his political career. The failed rebellion in Egypt—the forces of Pharoah are far too entrenched for the outcasts to depose—represents the last time that he will act in unison with others, but it is not his last political act. He has still to build his own ideal state and then to repudiate that, too.

Abandoning Crete, Odysseus leaves behind him a final warning to Hardihood, the bronzesmith who succeeds Idomeneus as king. " 'If the soul falls once more to belly,' " he threatens, " 'and your slaves/ begin to groan, your lords to roister and carouse,/I'll swoop on this rich land to loot and kill again!' " (VIII, 878-80). In Egypt he begins to learn that all such actions are futile: not simply that Hardihood's rule will inevitably decay and that he too will fall—as he does—but that man cannot be saved through political deeds alone, that salvation lies not in society but in each of its members. The victory of Pharoah is a concrete sign that even the most corrupt social orders may well outlast all their would-be reformers. It is a sign as well that Kazantzakis himself had passed beyond Marxist doctrine into that highly subjective realm that he called Post-Communism, a region in which the individual soul comes before all considerations of State, in which "economic emancipation is but a means for the psychological and spiritual emancipation of man."[22] When his ideal city is destroyed by an earthquake—a demonstration of the true natural order—Odysseus acknowledges finally that he can save only himself. Thus, Christ-like, he may help save us all.

Myth blurs into politics in these middle books, politics into a philosophy of life as the "flame-eyed leader" (XII, 444); the "much-suffering" (XIV, 1069) "demon-driven man" (XII, 127) leads the defeated hordes out of Egypt through the deserts to the south and into the jungles of Africa. Those following him now are the dregs of society, the disaffected and alien.

> "Here on the sands I cut a line with my iron sword:
> behind lies slavery and our fat grain-mother earth,
> before lies liberty and hunger. Weigh both well.
> He who has never killed or stolen or not betrayed
> or murdered in his mind, let him now rise and leave!
> Who in his heart of hearts still whispers, 'I like this earth,
> and spacious is man's head to hold me'—let him leave!
> We in the wilderness shall shape a rutting god
> stifling with liberty and hunger, blood and brains.
> Place your hearts well within the scales and search your loins:
> we too won't bear that man who can't bear God's grim face!"
>
> (XII, 70–80)

African tribesmen teach them to hunt, initiate them into their rituals, fall on them for their prey. They halt at last at the source of the Nile—the Ithacan is presumably the first European to reach this fabled place—where they will build their city. But Odysseus must first climb the holy mountain, and for seven days—roughly corresponding in their progression to the seven-headed god of the Cretan peddler—he communes like Moses, like Jesus, like Zarathustra, with God in His solitude.

In Book XIV, Kazantzakis develops what his translator calls "the core of his ascetic philosophy, further amplified and more clearly systematized in . . . *Spiritual Exercises: Salvatores Dei.*"[23] But this is not the end of the hero's spiritual development, for he does not yet understand all the lessons to be learned on the mount. He has yet to overcome hope. True, Odysseus does forever repudiate tradition (" 'Earth has no need of you, the past does not return' "—XIV, 342); he does merge with, and finally free himself from, the force of his ego, of the race, of mankind as a whole and his prehuman ancestry, of the lowliest creatures of earth (" 'for I have hidden wings,/I grow with the wild hawks and dance with the swift gulls./ . . . But night has fallen, the aery chase has ended now . . . ' "—XIV, 868–72). He has himself become almost godlike, his soul very nearly freed of his body, but he is not yet fully reconciled either with his own nature or with that of the universe. Only at the end of Book XXIV does he possess the insight to confront the abyss without expectation of success.

> The wheel of earth within him turned, and his god glowed
> nor seemed a mighty beast now nor almighty foe
> to break a lance with on the earthen threshing floor,
> nor yet a bridegroom to merge sweetly with man's heart.
>
> (XIV, 1063–66)

Down below, at the base of the mountain, his shipmate Kentaur, the very type of sensuality, has similarly learned to transcend his body in his newfound concern for the welfare of others. But sensuality in him has turned to a kind of sentimental idealism. "The spirit of love" (XIV, 1391) that motivates him now is the final reach that these others, earthbound still, can achieve; it is a great accomplishment indeed, but Odysseus must go further still.

He comes down off the mountain to formulate his ideal plans for his ideal state, plans derived, as Friar points out, "from various elements in Plato's *Republic,* St. Augustine's *The City of God,* and More's *Utopia,*"[24] plans for a socialist state in which there will be no family life to distract man from his higher duty, in which the old and useless will be allowed to die and give place to the virile and young, in which workers will be honored and above them the warriors and highest still the intellectuals and artists—"the mind-battlers, the full fruit of strife" (XV, 544). The "great lawmaker" (XV, 581) does not hesitate to build this new world afresh, "to re-create the very world God shaped" (XV, 649). "'If you would rule the world,'" he perceives, "'model yourself on God'" (XV, 602). His error is not here, in this seeming *hubris,* but elsewhere, on the mount, where he has failed to perceive the signs of his inevitable failure.

Surely he had warning enough. For on that mountain peak he had seen his ancestral fates, each one impelling him forward. First Tantalus, "that unappeased, unsated soul" (XIV, 385), had cried out in pain, "'I see betrayal in your eyes—you want to plunge roots now!'" (XIV, 390). Then Heracles, "the much-wounded form" (XIV, 432), "'man's great daemonic soul'" (XIV, 398), had urged, "'The final labor still remains—kneel, aim, and shoot!'" (XIV, 425). Finally, there was Prometheus, whose refusal to bow to the will of Zeus is recalled by the worm's resistance to God; "'the hard flint of the mind,'" Odysseus calls him, "'that soul who raised my low brow toward the sun'" (XIV, 539–40). He too, in a marvelous extrapolation from traditional myth, warns his "grandson" against being too easily content:

> "I've not illumined or saved the world! My life went lost!
> God's lightning flash turned into brain, and the brain rose;

I, too, rushed up like God, seized clay, made men,
licked them with flame, thrust in their brains a spark of light,
placed knives within their fists and hopes within their hearts
then spread my deep arms wide and loosed them on the earth:
'Children of earth and fire, belovèd clay, push on!'
But all my troops forsook me and my sons betrayed me,
now see to what I've come, O Grandson, where spite cast me:
I'm nailed to memory's sleepless rock and shout in pain.
Alas, I could not finish life's most glorious task!"

(XIV, 555-65)

Thus far Odysseus too has come, but to him remains the ultimate task:

"Beyond all flame and light, beyond even Death, my son,
the final labor, the last ax, still gleams with blood."

(XIV, 580-81)

But Odysseus misreads the signs: they point not to his ideal city, not to an act of society, however much it may remedy injustice. Odysseus is being too easily satisfied, more like sentimental Kentaur than he would care to acknowledge. He needs not further companions, as he seems now to believe, but solitude, movement beyond, rather than entry into, social concerns. He must sink no new roots; for no city, no matter how high its towers or utopian its structure, can protect man from the hostile forces that threaten him everywhere. The city must fall, for it bears the seeds of its own destruction; its founder—indeed, each of its inhabitants—must go his own way: he must in the end become himself like God, "'that dark beast... who mounts eternally'" (XIV, 1034). The final act of men within society is superseded by the final act of man without.

On the mind's death-scorched rock, narrow, ephemeral,
struck by all times and spaces, thrashed by all the gods,
the daring Act hews down the woods, builds sturdy ships
and strives to cross the abyss like a dark sea, to save
its precious cargo, its much-wounded, bleeding God.

(XIV, 1349-53)

His city fallen, Odysseus becomes an ascetic, famed throughout the continent, and begins his final journey southward to the sea.

VI

The complex myths of Mycenae, of Minoan Crete, and of Egypt—once-mighty empires that bear witness to the inevitable decay of all institutions and to the need in our time for a new fertility—give way in these final books to a more simple and obvious form of allegory.

There are no great mythic adventures in this part of the narrative, no powerful nations to be reformed, no people to be uplifted. The hero encounters now not whole cultures but individuals, character types representing the last temptations that he must resist on his slow, difficult ascent to pure spirit. Politics are behind Odysseus forever, simply another temptation that has been overcome; before him now is the need to master himself, to overcome all the needs of the body, to dissolve into mist. The one great flaw of the epic is here: Books XVI–XXII are clearly necessary to the development of the overall theme, and there is no falling off in the power of the verse; yet, somehow, there seem to be too many episodes too closely related, episodes so highly allegorical that they are barely believable, and we may justifiably wonder why they could not be more effectively condensed. The poet had cut the more than 42,000 verses of the original version to the 33,333 that now stand; perhaps he should have cut further, given us, say, eighteen books instead of twenty-four.[25]

It is not that we object to the symbolic technique per se, or even to its repeated use in the poem, for we have seen it before, often in perfect balance with the narrative as mythic and political statement. From the start, for example, we recognize that the members of Odysseus' crew are primarily symbolic types, representing on the one hand the traditional values of Ithaca and, on the other, the changing nature of the world outside. Kentaur the good-natured sensualist, Orpheus the poet deluded by his own song, and humane Captain Clam, "a shaggy, battered old sea-wolf" (II, 744), are characters who would be at home in any Kazantzakis novel, who might almost have appeared in Homer. Theirs are the most enduring qualities of human nature that Odysseus will need to surpass. The other crew members, however, seem purely symbolic: Granite, a chieftain's son who has surrendered his inheritance after killing his brother in a fight over a woman, embodiment of the old order of affairs; burly Hardihood, the bronzesmith who has learned to work also in iron, a transitional figure; and Rocky, the shepherd from Sparta, the new breed that will inherit the earth for a time. Virtually indistinguishable in personality, as in name, these latter figures represent broad historical forces that are outside human nature. But Odysseus must move beyond them too.

We discover a similar progression and a similar need in the other symbolic groupings that Kazantzakis creates. The fabled worm becomes a Cretan peasant. The athletic games of Menelaus' Sparta turn into the Cretan ritual in which spirit contests against flesh. The three temptations of Homer's Odysseus—Calypso, Circe, Nausicaa—become the three daughters of Idomeneus: one a rebel against her father's rule, another a temple prostitute in the service of that rule, the third a virgin desired by her father for the fertility rite. (It is Phida, the eldest, who beheads the king with the sacred two-headed *labrys*; his reign has grown so sterile that he can provide no son to make the sacrifice for him.) The Cretan princesses, in turn, devolve into the rebels against Pharoah, three young men who encompass the qualities of revolutionaries everywhere (based on Lenin, Stalin, and Trotsky) and Rala, a young Jewish girl like those the poet had known in Germany; she throws away her life in the unsuccessful rebellion, but they live on to begin anew: rebellion goes on eternally, the poet implies, but not for Odysseus: the fiery yet gentle death of Captain Clam foreshadows his own. The seven-headed god of the Cretan peddler, the three daggers with which Odysseus is struck in a dream (symbolizing love of woman, love of power and involvement in the affairs of the world, and, finally, love of life itself as opposed to death), the repeated dreams that pursue the characters[26]—these, too, we recognize as essentially allegorical and accept them as such; they are supplements to the central action and do not detract from it. But the characters that Odysseus meets after the fall of his city are themselves the principal action, and the allegory that they help to develop is simply not compelling enough to maintain our interest through some ten thousand lines of verse. Yet they do point the way to the final voyage of the great sea-worn "light-archer" (XIX, 940), the leader of men become in his age a solitary wanderer.

These allegorical figures represent in their negative example the final spiritual stage that Odysseus must cross, an extended series of last temptations. Among them are the Indian prince Motherth, recalling the Buddha in his embrace of nothingness, and the courtesan Margaro, who continues to affirm the values of love and of hope: Odysseus has learned to reject both extremes; even his asceticism is a basically positive act and not a denial of his essential humanity. But he knows full well the dangers of that humanity: the unnamed blind hermit who seeks hungrily for an answer to the meaning of life dies without answer, unable to accept the fact that there is no answer, that life (earth/nature) is both question and answer. But Odysseus is content:

> "What shall I do with this complaining life of ours
> that sometimes makes me laugh and sometimes makes me sigh?
> I rub it with my fingers like a laurel leaf
> until my flesh and mind both smell of laurel leaves."
> Thus freed of man at length, the soul of the saved master
> whistled a lonely shepherd's song in the sweet wilderness.
>
> (XIX, 1012–17)

A minstrel sings of Prince Elias, who unlike the hermit has sought immortality through warfare and song, whose lyre is dipped in the blood of the seven sons who have died alongside him in battle. He sings on but curses life, for he has understood all too well that earth implacably annihilates life. Listening to the minstrel's cruel song, Odysseus declares that he is in truth its subject and that the son is a fiction. Coldly, the black singer responds that in the reflexiveness of art and of life they may all be one:

> "What do I care about your life, ascetic archer?
> What do I care what's false or true, what's yours, what's mine?
> It may well be, you fool, I've sung my own pain only!"
>
> (XIX, 1421–23)

It may well be, the archer perceives, that the pain of all lives— hermit's, warrior's, minstrel's—in the end is the same, that this definitive answer to the riddle of life is no different from the riddle itself. At his own death, he sees in "'the crystal air'" the "'blood-soaked lyre'" of Prince Elias; "'I'll pluck its chords,'" he says, "'and play Life's great refrains to keep Death entertained'" (XIX, 1266–68).

Captain Sole, whom he next encounters, seeks foolishly like Don Quixote to achieve the impossible; the Lord of the Tower, who follows him and seeks only personal pleasure, is devoid of ideals: they represent two further extremes of civilization that Odysseus denies, although there is something within him of each of them. Once torn between his humanity and his need for renewal, between his eroticism and compassion on the one hand and his self-centered yearning for the soul on the other, he is withdrawn now both from the naive idealist and from the hyper-sophisticated hedonist. He is closer in fact to the primitive, to the eleven sons of an African chieftain who have just killed their father in a time-honored fertility rite. Determined, however, to break the traditional pattern—not to kill off each other in a fight for the kingship, to leave untouched the wives of their father—they have begun their own slow movement toward civilization. And Odysseus in his mind, splattered with the dead chief's blood, seems to move backward toward them—"'Somewhere in dreams or in the slaughter's vertigo / I hid in this dark wood, I saw these dragon-sons / and with them slew our father, and with them broke in dance'"—and to move forward at the same time, to reach for pure spirit and to recall primordial instinct. For "'Time gapes unhinged'" on this continent (XX, 1204–7), and the progression of the young chief is a microcosm of his own. To the primitive mind, he is the bearer of time, the source of civilization, but he brings with him also age and death and decay. He has become in a sense a force of nature, at one with the earth, himself now part of the unanswerable riddle. He is ready now for the final temptation—the example of Christ.

As he builds the boat that will take him to the South Pole, Odysseus, an old man now, sees on the shore a band of fishermen and among them "a slender virgin-lad with flaming fawnlike eyes" (XXI, 1130). Christ-like, the young black fisherman responds to his comrades' cries for justice by urging them to be patient, by rejecting their call for fiery rebellion. He preaches love of one's brothers and love of the one true God, " 'the pure soul that broods on the world's sacred egg' " (XXI, 1303), the God whose grace alone can lead to eternal life and to man's eventual union with the divine. The injustices of this life are unimportant, he tells them, for " 'Body and mind, both land and sea, are smoke and air, / only this final One still lives and reigns as God' " (XXI, 1301-2). On earth, the eternal soul is alone supreme; " 'the body's but a bridge to pass through chaos' " (XXI, 1314). Odysseus is moved by his words but easily refutes them: body and soul, he says, this world and the next, are equally good:

> "Good are your words of love, but my mind walks the earth
> with a bold stride, alone, and has no need of balms.
>
> . . . .
> And I, too, pity both the soul and flesh of man,
> and all the earth, our wretched mother, and God the father;
> I pity them all and sing, I pass, and they pass with me."
>
> (XXI, 1333-40)

His parting gift—what he has learned in his lifetime—is shattering both to the lad's denial of this life and to the Christian faith in the afterlife: " 'That man is free who strives on earth with not one hope!' " (XXI, 1351).[27] Ironically, that same heroic figure who in *The Last Temptation of Christ* is compelled to resist the temptations of divinity and humanity alike, himself becomes in the *Odyssey* the final, most alluring temptation of all: the gentle Negro fisher-lad blurs into the Negro Tempter, sign of the Archer's final victory in life. Kazantzakis is ever willing to reverse himself and to extend metaphors as well as men beyond their apparent limits.

Thus Odysseus sets sail for the Pole, epicenter of all spiritual life,[28] bearing with him only some pomegranates presented by an aged whore, the souls of the dead kept alive in his memory, and the Christ-like image of the Tempter to be hung on the mast, "as scarecrow for the lower world" (XXIV, 1369). For days and months he sails, through mist, through dream, through time. Finally, in Silence, mind and body stripped of all life's accretions, he becomes one with God, "all end and all beginning, present, future, past" (XXIV, 1331), fades slowly into mist.

At length the myth grew drowsy, curled by the hearth asleep,
and the world folded its vast wings and dropped its head;
. . . .
the prodigal son now heard the song of all return
and his eyes cleansed and emptied, his full heart grew light,
for Life and Death were songs, his mind the singing bird.
. . . .
All the great body of the world-roamer turned to mist,
and slowly his snow-ship, his memory, fruit, and friends
drifted like fog far down the sea, vanished like dew.
Then flesh dissolved, glances congealed, the heart's pulse stopped,
and the great mind leapt to the peak of its holy freedom,
fluttered with empty wings, then upright through the air
soared high and freed itself from its last cage, its freedom.
All things like frail mist scattered till but one brave cry
for a brief moment hung in the calm benighted waters:
"Forward, my lads, sail on, for Death's breeze blows in a fair wind!"

(XXIV, 1335–96)

VII

From the small beginnings provided by Homer and the Cyclical
Epics, by Dante's insight into the wanderer Odysseus as symbol of
man's everlasting search for forbidden knowledge,[29] by old legends
in Herodotus and elsewhere of voyages by Phoenicians and Greeks
beyond the Pillars of Heracles, Kazantzakis has created an epic that is
rich in myth and in symbol, in speculation about the nature of man
and his universe, in plans for expanding the force of our spiritual
lives. In many ways, his effort is more daring than Homer's, and in
many ways it is more successful. Both poets organize masterfully a
vast body of complex and often contradictory material; both attempt
in a sense to transmit all the knowledge of their times and to dramatize the universality inherent in seemingly local incidents. Out of the
inevitable aftermath to a petty conflict between historically minor
kingdoms, Homer was able to fashion in the *Odyssey* a document of
universal import—not simply to tell us all there was to know in his
time about the civilization of Bronze Age Greece, or to suggest its
continued impact on his own era, some four or five centuries later. In
Odysseus he created a character who would stand for future ages as a
relevant symbol of man's enduring intellect—in both its positive and
its negative aspects—what W. B. Stanford has called "the untypical
hero." But Kazantzakis' endeavor is far more comprehensive than
this—more comprehensive because, on the simplest level, we know
more today than Homer did about the Bronze Age in the Aegean,
because in addition Kazantzakis' world is not confined to the Aegean
and the immediately surrounding areas, because there is no longer a
single, unified body of custom and lore that is shared by all readers:

Freud, Jung, Frazer, Marx, Nietzsche, Bergson, and all those others who have molded our century, and whom Kazantzakis has used in his *Odyssey*, present together a cultural image that is infinitely more diverse and far-reaching than is apparent in Homer.

For Homer, a single theme—hospitality and its abuses—can serve as determinant of all the principal events and provide a kind of continuing norm against which to judge characters and acts. Zeus, after all, is the god of hospitality, and in this peripatetic, sea-faring society no principle is more highly valued—and no man is more outcast than the one who abuses the obligations of guest or of host (Paris, Polyphemus, the suitors). The rules hold good even today throughout Greece. So much of Homer is dependent upon the Greek experience that whatever universality arises from the original *Odyssey* seems a direct outgrowth of that experience. But Kazantzakis, no less steeped in the culture and values of Greece—perhaps because the lesson of Crete gave him no choice—is less limited to insular Greece for his themes. Moreover, there is an almost picaresque quality to Homer's great epic; surely there is pattern to the hero's wanderings, yet we may suspect that certain landfalls at least are largely coincidental, more a function of plot than of the development of theme. The movement of Kazantzakis' hero, however—in myth and in symbol as well as in spiritual development—is an artfully wrought progression that has about it an air of inevitability, as if the long journey from Ithaca to the Antarctic were one that all men, symbolically at least, must undertake. Perhaps, finally, Kazantzakis in his much longer poem does nod somewhat more than Homer, but his narrative on the whole is wonderfully sustained, as entertaining in general as anything in Homer, often deeply moving when we hear it read aloud. *The Odyssey: A Modern Sequel* is derived from Homer, to be sure, but it is not bound to or intimidated by the original. Kazantzakis is not Homer's imitator but his rival.

Certainly there is no work in modern times—not even *Ulysses* or *Finnegans Wake*—that more effectively dramatizes the intellectual and spiritual forces that have shaped our era or that gives us a better sense of what we are and what we might yet become. For Kazantzakis' Odysseus is very different from Homer's—different as well from the heroes of Joyce, Dante, Tennsyson, and others who have used him as symbol of enduring contemporary man. It is not simply that the literary background to this latest Odysseus is denser than in any of his predecessors, or even that the philosophical overtones emanating from him are more profound and compelling. The difference has to do with the nature of myth: this Odysseus, unlike the others, is both self-conscious subject and creator of myths, as well as, in the end, the

destroyer of outmoded mythologies, even of those in which he himself has a part, especially of those in which he is protagonist.

Early in his travels, Odysseus is willing still to play at becoming
god. It is a few days out from Ithaca, and his ship has put in to land in
search of food and water. There, alongside a stream, "pushing a curly
bull-calf in the stream to cool it," a young maiden appears before him.

> "A god has chanced to find me by this stream," she thought;
> "I bend and bow low to his grace, his will be done."
> The swift mind-reader felt the maiden's fear and joy:
> "Yes, you've divined it, lovely lass, I'm a sea-god
> who saw you far off from the waves and leapt ashore
> so that the thighs of god and man might meet in love."

In return, he offers her immortality.

> "... in nine months' time, I swear,
> I'll lie upon your lap once more and touch your lips;
> an infant god shall suck your breasts, your house shall shine."

This is pure opportunism, of course, hucksterism almost; yet in this
anthropomorphic world, a world so ripe with fertility that any natural
object—swan, bull, or falling leaf—may be the source of new life,
somehow it works: as the girl follows him back to the ship, "flowers
sprang up from sterile sands wherever she passed" (III, 483–547).

By the end of his travels, however, Odysseus is less willing to play
at the god-making game, for the gods, he has come to realize, " 'are
like countless birds that pass above our heads / and the mind soon
confuses their harsh cries and wings' " (XXI, 461–62). Becoming a god
is no substitute for being a man. On the south African coast, he learns
of a band of exiled Cretans and the icon of the "great god" (XXI, 445)
that they carry with them, a god whose worship has spread like
human fire among the African tribesmen.

> "... that Cretan demon of the sea
> with all his visible attributes and secret name:
> A sea-cap like an upright prow, a flaming beard,
> a curved bow in his huge hands as he stoops to kneel;
> some in their prayers call him 'Savior,' and some 'Slayer,'
> but in their secret hymns the priests cry out 'Odysseus!' "
> The archer frowned and bit his tongue, that from his lips
> his savage mocking laughter might not burst in peals,
>
> . . . .
> "I've been reduced to a god and walk the earth like myth!"
>
> (XXI, 467–511)

The man who misuses myth in order to play at divinity is like the
artist who believes in his own false creations. Orpheus the piper,
"wine-dreg of God" (V, 424), misleads the Cretan king with his song in

order to keep the rebellion alive; his art is deceptive but useful in the overall scheme.[30] Later, however, he himself is misled by the rhythms of his voice, by the miracles that he appears to have called forth, by the tale he has concocted of a new, healing god; thinking to become god himself, he forsakes the friends who need him and thus loses his value as both artist and man. But no such fate can befall Odysseus, the artist and mythmaker.

The poet's Prologue to the Sun invokes man as artist controlling his own destiny;[31] the final words of Odysseus enjoin us all to follow the difficult path of the man who would be free of the prisons of life and of death alike; the Epilogue, spoken this time by the Sun, mourns the loss of the free-spirited man, commemorates his going:

> Then the earth vanished, the sea dimmed, all flesh dissolved,
> the body turned to fragile spirit and spirit to air,
> till the air moved and sighed as in the hollow hush
> was heard the ultimate and despairing cry of Earth,
> the sun's lament, but with no throat or mouth or voice:
> "Mother, enjoy the food you've cooked, the wine you hold,
> Mother, if you've a rose-bed, rest your weary bones,
> Mother, I don't want wine to drink or bread to eat—
> today I've seen my loved one vanish like a dwindling thought."
>
> (14–22)

Whether he dissolves into mist like Odysseus or remains to deal with the affairs of earth, man as artist can create his own mythology, can control the progress of his life and the life of mankind. Odysseus impels us to be the masters of our own myths, to make of our lives a work of art that is worthy of belief. This is the central theme of *The Odyssey: A Modern Sequel* and indeed of all Kazantzakis' life and art.

1. "In Greece itself, where, in the mountains of Crete and of the mainland, the 'oral society' is only now giving way under the influence of the press, the radio and the school, old *traghoudhía* [songs] of resistance to the Turks were laid under contribution for the composition of new or only slightly adapted songs and ballads of the guerilla resistance to Germans and Italians." A. R. Burn, *The Lyric Age of Greece* (New York, 1967), p. 160.

2. Prevelakis, p. 17.

3. The composer Bohuslav Martinu similarly based an opera on *The Greek Passion*. It was first performed in 1962.

4. Introduction to *The Odyssey: A Modern Sequel* (New York, 1958), p. ix. All subsequent references to the text of the poem are to this edition.

5. Letter to Stámos Diamantarás, Aegina, January 6, 1939, cited in Helen Kazantzakis, pp. 365–66.

6. Friar points out in his invaluable introduction that "the traditional meter in

which most of modern Greek folk songs and long narrative poems are written, comparable in English to blank verse . . ., is the fifteen-syllable iambic line of seven beats. To the educated Greek Kazantzakis' abandonment of the traditional meter, and his use of an extremely rare measure for the *Odyssey*, that of the seventeen-syllable unrhymed verse of eight beats, came as an unexpected and shocking disturbance" (p. xxvi). "That venerable verse," Kazantzakis wrote of the classical meter, "seemed to me too worn-out; it lacks the breath of life and is no longer capable of containing the fiery contemporary spirit which is suffering and struggling and longing to break the limits stifling it; longing to create a broader, deeper rhythm. These two additional syllables give the epic an unexpected amplitude, majesty and, at the same time, disciplined violence." Letter to Börje Knös, Paris, June 14, 1947, cited in Helen Kazantzakis, p. 468. It is worth noting that Homer's line also contains seventeen syllables. Friar's English version is similarly unrhymed but in hexameter lines.

7. Cited in an interview in Athens, July 18, 1966.

8. Speaking of Kazantzakis and other novelists of the older generation, Vassílis Vassilikós said to his friend, the American critic Leslie A. Fiedler, "frozen meat, put them back in the refrigerator." As reported in a letter from Fiedler to the author, February 3, 1972.

9. Thomas Edwards, "*The Odyssey: A Modern Sequel*," *Whole Earth Catalogue* (January 1971), p. 29. Ironically, the *Catalogue* itself would soon, voluntarily, cease publication, perhaps foreshadowing the demise of the student culture that it helped to represent.

10. Kimon Friar, "A Unique Collaboration: Translating *The Odyssey: A Modern Sequel*," *Journal of Modern Literature*, 2 (1971–72), p. 244.

11. Much of the American criticism of the *Odyssey* has tended to extremes, e.g., the admirer who calls it a work of "sheer evil genius" (Walter M. Abbott, "Poetic Praise of the Seven Deadly Sins," *America*, 100 (January 3, 1959), p. 405). The most absurd view perhaps—one so extreme that we may wonder what book the reviewer has read—is this anonymous comment from *The New Yorker*, 34 (February 7, 1959), p. 144: "the Homeric heroic tradition is totally submerged by a violence and a vitalism that come straight out of the nineteenth century. The narrative is not symbolically planned (as in Joyce's 'Ulysses'); the scenes follow one another in a kind of endless daydream, and the adventures often run over into situations that have more relation to Jules Verne than to Homer. . . . The entire ambitious work seems curiously dated—the eccentric product of a European literary and philosophical tradition that is almost entirely obsolete, and in which even the shock and erotic elements now seem artificially revived rather than creatively produced." As Helen Kazantzakis commented to a visitor who had observed that some Westerners have trouble with Kazantzakis because he seems at times larger than life: "No, he is not larger; they are just smaller." Interview with Helen Kazantzakis.

12. "The Demoticism of Kazantzakis," in Edmund Keeley and Peter Bien, eds., *Modern Greek Writers* (Princeton, 1972), pp. 145–69. See also Bien's book *Kazantzakis and the Linguistic Revolution in Greek Literature* (Princeton, 1972). Helen Kazantzakis has strongly denied Bien's assumptions about the final drafts of the *Odyssey*, contending that the poet always sought for "the most pan-Hellenic word" and insisting that he was never out of touch with Greece—especially with its language—for long periods. Interview in Geneva.

13. Letter to Friar, Antibes, April 16, 1955, cited in "A Unique Collaboration," p. 226.

14. Friar, "A Unique Collaboration," p. 223.

15. "Because he had translated so much himself, Kazantzakis knew profoundly the problems of the translator, and he constantly encouraged me to take much more liberty with his text than I felt I could. Indeed, when I objected that in the beginning of his epic Odysseus completely ignores his wife Penelope, contrary to the rapport between them at the end of Homer's *Odyssey*, he told me I was right and asked me to create and write a scene between them myself. This, of course, I did not do." Friar, "A Unique Collaboration," p. 232.

16. Friar, "A Unique Collaboration," p. 244.

17. *The Odyssey* of Homer, Book XI, trans. Robert Fitzgerald (Garden City, New York, 1963), p. 189.

18. The dates of Minoan Crete's greatness and fall remain very much in question, as do the causes of that fall. Evans dates the destruction of the palace of Minos at 1400 B.C., more than a century before the height of Mycenaean civilization; according to Blegen, however, it was some time after 1200 B.C. that Knossos was destroyed by Dorian invasion, more than two centuries after it came under the aegis of Mycenae. The legendary date for the capture of Troy, probably more or less accurate, is 1184 B.C., some two or three centuries before Homer. A recent theory, based on excavations on the nearby island of Thera (Santoríni), suggests that the destruction of the palaces of Crete was caused not by Mycenaean or Dorian invasion but by natural disaster—a tidal wave caused by an earthquake on Thera. The entire area is obviously very much in flux; what is astonishing is Kazantzakis' insight into the area long before much evidence had been developed.

19. "The tradition plainly implies that at the end of every eight years the king's sacred powers needed to be renewed by intercourse with the godhead, and that without such a renewal he could have forfeited his right to the throne." Frazer, *The Golden Bough*, p. 326.

20. When he first sees Helen on his return to Sparta, Odysseus denies that he had ever been one of her suitors—"he had never longed to embrace lascivious Helen," he contends (III, 670)—thus rejecting that version of the myth in which he is the author of the pact that binds the unsuccessful suitors to eventual war against her abductor. His denial is probably related to his belief that she may be a kind of spiritual exemplar; thus he questions her with fascination about the growing legend that only her "empty shade" had been present at Troy (III, 839), while her physical form waited out the war elsewhere, most likely in Egypt. She answers ambiguously, yet she "rejoiced to hear/how swift her legend spun on fantasy's fast spindle,/for it had been no shade that stretched out on soft divans, / no shade that cried out with delight in tight embrace" (IV, 1097–1100). Another modern variant of the legends surrounding Helen in Egypt, more humorous but with some of the same philosophical undertones, appears in John Barth's "Menelaiad," one of the related stories in *Lost in the Funhouse*. Cf. H. D.'s *Helen in Egypt* and Seféris' "Helen."

21. See especially *The Mysterious Stranger* (1898).

22. The passage is from Kazantzakis' famous "Apologia," written in 1924

after his arrest by the Cretan authorities for alleged radicalism; cited in Helen Kazantzakis, p. 569. Typically, Kazantzakis chose neither extreme but created a new one of his own. As he indicated to his future wife some months before visiting Russia, "I've finished the essay on MetaKommunismus that I wrote you about. . . . It's a big rupture with Communism—not in a backward direction, of course, but terrifyingly forward. All my Communist friends will be furious. Those who are in agreement will misinterpret once more." Athens, December 13, 1926; cited in Helen Kazantzakis, p. 155.

23. Friar, p. 795.

24. Friar, p. 798.

25. When his companion would protest that the epic was overly long and its episodes repetitive, the poet would reply, unperturbed, "Don't forget that I am Oriental—Orientals repeat themselves." Interview with Helen Kazantzakis. But Kimon Friar has argued that this is not such a defect. "I can't agree with you," he has written this author, "that the flaw of the epic lies after Book XVI. Indeed, I infinitely prefer the *Odyssey* in the later half, after the engulfing of his Ideal City, after the action of the first part. It seems to me that the figures he meets are not so obviously symbolic as you make them out to be, and that the poetry not only does not fall off but increases in power and beauty." Eretria, Evia, Greece, December 12, 1972.

26. Most of the dreams, of course, are those of Odysseus, e.g., as when he dreams of Telemachus and Nausicaa back in Ithaca and of their rebellious son, the spiritual child of his grandfather and not of his docile parents. He thus continues the traditional pattern: Odysseus too abandoned the path of his father, Laertes, and took instead that of Autolycus, his much maligned grandfather. It is not mere metaphor then when Kazantzakis refers to El Greco as "grandfather." This pattern is further developed in a reflexive dream that comes to Telemachus, almost the mirror image of one of his father's dreams. "Longing to exorcise his father and make him fade / once more like spinning foam on the night-wandering wave," he dreams instead of Odysseus as an eagle, soaring high with his son clutched in his claws. "An eagle's heart rose in his chest, his claws grew hard, / and on the ancient eagle's neck he swayed with pride./ 'Father, my wings are strong now, drop me from your claws!'" But he is terrified by the swift descent, resists the paternal challenge and forces himself to awake: "all seemed a dream,/ a crazy thought new-hatched in the deceiving night./ But wild sleep now escaped him: all night long he heard / two monstrous eagle wings that beat above his head" (I, 430–58). There are obvious echoes here of *The Last Temptation of Christ*—albeit ironically—of the myth of Daedalus and Icarus and of both primitive and Freudian/ Jungian attitudes toward dream.

27. "I do not hope for anything," reads Kazantzakis' tombstone in Iráklion, "I do not fear anything. I am free."

28. "The mystic 'Centre,' or the 'unvarying mean,' is the fixed point which all symbolic traditions concur in designating as the 'pole,' since the rotation of the earth takes place around it. On the other hand, the pole is also identified with the zenith. . . . The 'unvarying mean' is, nevertheless, the cause of all change. The Chinese *Book of Changes* shows that the continuous metamorphoses of matter are generated by the great pole—a Oneness located far beyond all duality, beyond all occurrence, and equated with the 'unmoved mover' of Aristotle." J. E. Cirlot, *A Dictionary of Symbols* (New York, 1962), pp. 248–49.

Cf. Edgar Allan Poe's *Narrative of Arthur Gordon Pym* and André Gide's *Urien's Voyage* for other allegorical uses of the sea journey to Antarctica.
29. See *The Inferno*, trans. John Ciardi, Canto XXVI.

> not fondness for my son, nor reverence
> for my aged father, nor Penelope's claim
>
> to the joys of love, could drive out of my mind
> the lust to experience the far-flung world
> and the failings and felicities of mankind.

By substituting this "personification of centrifugal force" for the "centripetal, homeward-bound figure" of Homer, Dante "made Ulysses symbolize the anarchic element in those conflicts between orthodoxy and heresy, conservatism and progressivism, classicism and romanticism, which vexed his own time and were to vex later epochs more tragically. When he condemned this Ulysses he condemned what he thought to be a destructive force in society." Yet there is at the same time a "paradoxical feeling of admiration which is evident in Dante's portrait of the doomed hero." W. B. Stanford, *The Ulysses Theme* (Oxford, 1954), pp. 181–82. Giovanni Pascoli's *Ultima Viaggio* (1904), following the tradition of Dante, has Odysseus leave Ithaca after ten years and begin to retrace his voyages. Instead of fond memories, however, he finds no trace that he has passed there before—a most nihilistic conclusion to so active a life.

30. VII, 1128. The episode described below is in XIII, 510–700. An earlier scene on Crete dramatizes the illusory and potentially misleading quality of art. Back from the charade in the Diktean cave, Idomeneus has ordered a goldsmith to immortalize the event:

> "God stood on high and I stood straight on earth before him,
> the great sun hung low to my right, the full moon left,
> so that their double beams met in my dazzled eyes.
> God spread his hands and gave into my trust the firm
> round disk of earth with all its souls and mighty laws.
> I did not move, and held the whole world in my palms;
> God questioned, and I stared straight in his eyes and answered.
> I questioned too, and he replied like a true friend.
> Gather your wits, O goldsmith, teach your crafty hands
> how to immortalize this meeting in pure gold.
> Make infinite what lasted but a lightning flash on earth!"
>
> (V, 1202–12)

31. Prologue, 17–22:

> Great Sun, who pass on high yet watch all things below,
> I see the sun-drenched cap of the great castle-wrecker:
> let's kick and scuff it round to see where it will take us!
> Learn, lads, that Time has cycles and that Fate has wheels
> and that the mind of man sits high and twirls them round;
> come quick, let's spin the world about and send it tumbling!

CHAPTER SEVEN

SAINT FRANCIS
or Asceticism

The same pattern of myth that functions so creatively in *The Last Temptation of Christ* is little more in *Saint Francis* than a dead formulation. The goal, to be sure, is the same: "to match the Saint's life with his myth," the author declares in the prologue, "bringing that life as fully into accord with its essence as possible."[1] But Kazantzakis perceives in this source a far different essence; his Poor Man of God calls forth those ascetic elements—elements destructive to life and to literature—that are implicit in all of his work but that are elsewhere balanced by the appeal of nature and the senses. Narrow-minded and ignorant, fearful of learning and women alike, closed—despite his disclaimers—to paths that are different from his own, the Saint Francis of Kazantzakis is not a free man at all but a victim of fate; essentially humorless, he is "God's buffoon" in epithet only; attempting in his arrogance to emulate Christ, he plays instead an absurd Don Quixote to the Sancho Panza of Brother Leo, his fictional biographer. His transformation from supposed rake to veritable saint is unconvincing; the ascetic strictures he offers are so opposed to normal living that they are bound to repel us; we suspect that no sane man would follow such a fanatic and that no sane age could produce one. Where Kazantzakis' Jesus offers possibilities of universal salvation—if not quite in the orthodox way—his Saint Francis is the most parochial of heroes, and the novel is the least successful of Kazantzakis' fictions.

This potential exists of course in the historical saint from Assisi, as it does in the career of Jesus of Nazareth. But Kazantzakis in *The Last Temptation* endows his subject with the freedom to fail in his mission, for he is prey to the failings of all men. He thus overcomes the narrow asceticism—that substitute for orthodox divinity—which attracts most of Kazantzakis' heroes but which Francis alone succumbs to. He alone rejects nature, rejects the evidence of his senses, rejects life in this world. No matter how Boss or Odysseus or even Manoliós or Jesus may claim to scorn the flesh and favor the spirit, we recognize their inherent vitality, the persistent force of their language and imagery, the appeal that nature and sensuality continue to exert in their lives. Saint Francis purports to honor the body as well as the soul, but we do not believe him. He is moribund, from the start, of excessive holiness. Kazantzakis for once has fallen into the trap of his own philosophy and given us not the excessive color and metaphor that he frequently feared but too little of them, not a work that might offend certain sensibilities by its over-abundance but one whose thinness diminishes his own tensely rich aesthetic. It is almost as if he set out to demonstrate, by negative example, the need for duality, for the flesh as well as the spirit in the lives of men. If *Saint Francis* is indeed the companion novel to *The Last Temptation of Christ*, as some have contended, it is so only ironically: its poverty illustrates the richness of the earlier work; its lack of life points up the other's vitality.

And yet this must have seemed to Kazantzakis an ideal vehicle to dramatize his complex aesthetic, for Francis of Assisi was surely suited to be one of the Saviors of God. In the dichotomy between his early and later life, in his appeal to the oppressed and impoverished masses of people, in his use of the vernacular for his teaching, in the apparent final betrayal by his organized followers, even in his relationship with his domineering father, the historical Saint Francis seems the very type of the Kazantzakian hero. He too makes the difficult ascent up the mountain of human fears and desires—the Nietzschean mountain of dreams—and confronts himself and God across the abyss of human experience. In his legendary communion with the animals, he receives the same sign that Zarathustra has seen, on his mountain, at the end of his search: "Then the doves flew back and forth and sat upon his shoulder and fondled his white hair and did not weary of tenderness and rejoicing. The mighty lion, however, continually licked the tears that fell down upon Zarathustra's hands, roaring and growling shyly as he did so. Thus did these animals."[2]

Kazantzakis obviously believed that in the soil of Umbria he had found still another analogue for Crete, that in the insane age in which Francis lived—this "time of crisis," as Paul Sabatier has labeled it[3]—apocalypse was so near at hand that for the first time in a milennium salvation as he understood it seemed possible. Yet the novelist omits almost entirely the texture of history and myth that would illuminate this age and tie it metaphorically to Crete: he does give us Sultan and Saint and Pope (that is, the Sultan of Egypt, the founder of the Dominican Order, and Pope Innocent III, each of whom figures in the life of Francis), but they are more symbolic than real, and there is little else in his narrative that is even vaguely historical: little, for instance, of the Church's role in thirteenth-century European society, or of the widespread injustices of the time and the heretical movements that they spawned, no real sense of the urgency of Francis' ministry not merely for his own salvation but for the renascence of society as a whole. Of Francis, the central figure of the age, Kazantzakis elects to show little more than the private man, largely aloof from the society around him, increasingly oblivious to the political implications of the revolution he has begun, caught up in his own personal struggle: nothing, in short, of the metaphor of Crete as he has so fruitfully developed it, but merely an unwitting parody: the Cretan glance turned inward.

This emphasis derives in part from what was almost certainly Kazantzakis' principal source, Sabatier's controversial *Vie de S. François*, which reintroduced the saint of history to Europe after six centuries of legend. From Sabatier the novelist derived his central premises that Brother Leo was Saint Francis' first and most important biographer,[4] that the early Franciscans were in almost constant opposition to the organized Church—"The priest of the thirteenth century is the antithesis of the saint," Sabatier proclaims; "he is almost always his enemy"[5]—and that under the guidance of Elias of Cortona, once one of Francis' most trusted disciples, the Order was wrested away from its founder and converted into an arm of the Establishment.[6] The naive Leo, embodiment of Franciscan simplicity, and Elias the intellectual, who plays the dual roles of Saint Paul and Judas, represent the opposite poles of Francis' struggle to biographer and novelist alike.[7] A third pole in the fiction, however, is entirely Kazantzakis' invention: Sister Clara, who leads the Poor Clares, Second Order of the Franciscan world, acts in the novel as the saint's greatest temptation, a sort of Umbrian Magdalene.[8] She represents the chauvinist Kazantzakis' ultimate statement on the status and the role of women and provides as well valuable insight into his male protagonist.

II

"'Women must take a different road if they wish to reach God,'" Francis tells Clara. "'They must marry and have children, allow their virtue to flower and bear fruit not in desert solitude, but in the very midst of the world of men'" (p. 228). Yet Francis admits Clara into his desert order, for he recognizes that although women's strength is inferior to men's, although they constantly need comforting and pity, they too have a role to play in the pursuit of God. It is their love alone, he lectures the sisters, that can return to Satan " 'his original, radiant face,' " that can make God's adversary into an archangel once again (p. 252). Listening in silence, Clara's followers for the first time realize "what an infinitely divine gift it was to be a woman, and also what a responsibility" (p. 253). But it is a responsibility lesser than men's, for Francis does not quite trust these women: they are too susceptible to the distracting appeals of natural life: " 'because you are women, and your hearts do not steel themselves easily against the beauties of the world. You look upon them and they please you. Flowers, children, men, earrings, silk garments, stunning plumes: my God, what snares! How many women can possibly escape?' " (pp. 250–51). And how many men will they entrap with them? And yet, as condescending as he appears to be, Francis is also terrified of women. " 'Women,' " he declares, " 'are wild, savage beasts. Only God Almighty is capable of subduing them. Only He!' " (p. 242).

His ambiguity is his creator's ambiguity: the condescension and scorn, the sentimental idealization, and the stunning sexual fear— these qualities he shares with most of Kazantzakis' heroes, although Francis is probably the worst male chauvinist of them all, the one whose attitudes toward women are most unnatural. But there is nothing in his relations with Clara that we have not seen elsewhere in the fiction. Viewed first as a temptress and then as a sister and finally as Francis' nurse and in a way his successor, she is never a real companion to him, never truly his equal, for she is not allowed to develop into more than a symbol. Kazantzakis is clearly interested in women, and they provide some of his most compelling characterizations. But none of them is quite complete; each is eventually forced into a symbolic mold: they are more important as part of a philosophical construct than as human beings. It is for this reason that the whores Magdalene and Katerína abruptly vanish from sight precisely when they threaten to become most interesting. Should they continue to live—and to offer new possibilities of sensuality combined with worshipful domesticity—Jesus and Manoliós would hardly be able to continue their inexorable movement toward martyrdom. And so they must be killed off. It is as if Kazantzakis, like his male protagonists, does not quite trust these women who claim to be converts; they seem almost to accept their inferiority too easily, for they have been so alive until now.

The young daughter of Captain Mihális, who from puberty on avoids the presence of her domineering father; Zorba's Bouboulína, who needs constant protection from a forgetful, uncaring world; the widow who sleeps with Boss and is killed by the townsmen; the sisters Mary and Martha, the first to recognize Jesus and the last to tempt him; the peasant girl who gratefully bears the child of the godlike Odysseus; Helen of Sparta, who abandons her throne for adventure and then gives up adventure for her Cretan babies and garden; the homebodies Penelope and Nausicaa; the outsider Noëmi, Kosmás' bride; Rala the revolutionary; and the sensualists Margaro, Lenió, and the Cretan princess Diktena—Kazantzakis' women willfully acknowledge their inferiority to men. They themselves seem to recognize that they are too easily satisfied with life as it is and that they thus represent too great a threat to men's aspirations to change life. Even the positive values accorded them are suspect: they obviously provide the continuity necessary to life, but this may mean only that there will be another generation of Cretan men to go off to die in the mountains fighting the Turks; and we are told repeatedly that these idealized creatures possess souls more sensitive than men's, more closely attuned to God and humanity. But this is hardly more than a rationalization, an acknowledgement by Kazantzakis—who knew and respected and worked with and learned from many individual women—of the flaws of his own chauvinism. But he is a Cretan nevertheless, and his philosophy, with all its Nietzschean and Bergsonian overtones, is essentially a Cretan philosophy. And on Crete the primary function of women is to sustain their men in the assuredness of their own superiority. Is this a sign that they are actually as strong as or even stronger than men? Kazantzakis seems at times to hint at this possibility, but it is an imperative of his aesthetic that women—whether they are sensual or religious, sweethearts or mothers—are archetypal temptresses, one more hazard in the path of those men who would change the nature of human existence. And so his women, no matter how strong or individualistic they might have been, are ultimately reduced to symbols. As for Sister Clara, she never rises above this level: Kazantzakis' weakest female character is in a sense his archetype.

Whether we call it chauvinism, therefore, or see it merely as part of an almost allegorical technique, Kazantzakis' handling of women is patently a flaw in his fiction and perhaps in his philosophy as well—certainly in the union of idea and action that he strives to attain in all of his work. For it puts the philosophy before the fiction, the message before its medium, because it violates that marriage of function and form that does characterize Kazantzakis' art at its best. We notice this flaw in *The Last Temptation of Christ* and in *The Greek Passion*. But in those books the movement of history and politics and myth, and the development of character and act as well, are so powerful that although we are aware of, and upset by, the sudden disappearance of the female protagonists, we are nonetheless carried along by the continuing action. In *Saint Francis,* however, male and female are both so weak that we are disturbed by what amounts to their absence from the very beginning. What this indicates, in short, is that in Kazantzakis, fittingly, it is the vitality of the man and his surrounding circumstances, and only secondarily that of the woman, that determines our reaction to the work as a whole. We are unmoved by Sister Clara because we have never been truly touched by Saint Francis: the real flaw is not so much the chauvinism as it is a pattern of metaphor and myth which never rises above the pedestrian, which is totally and monotonously predictable, which can attain no life of its own. The failure in *Saint Francis* is far more fundamental than a simple case of Greek male chauvinism.

III

Practical, close-to-the-earth, moderate in all his affairs, Brother Leo is the perfect prism through which to view the idealist and extremist Saint Francis. It is as if Sancho Panza were to look back on his liaison with Don Quixote a few years after the death of his friend. A religious mendicant long before Francis takes to the streets and his closest companion throughout his ministry, Leo suffers along with his master but never wholly adopts his philosophy; he is simply not cut out to be an ascetic. Even years afterwards, he is forced to admit, "the problem of food, wine, and all the other comforts continued to torment me—yes, and though I am ashamed to admit it, I do: also the problem of women" (p. 277). He torments his flesh, yet dreams of roast suckling pig; he blasphemes against the God who keeps him perpetually hungry, yet he dines on scraps of stale bread and continues to search for God; he continues also to dream of the few earthly feasts that he has enjoyed in his lifetime: "God grant that what Francis says is true and that hens are eligible for Paradise. If so we'll kill one each Sunday—for the greater glory of the Lord" (p. 291). Leo is also the thoroughly practical man who saves his companion, despite the latter's repeated protests, from death by fire on their travels and from death by starvation on Monte Alvernia; he saves him because he is unable to see his friend " 'rising into the air' " (p. 308), because he cannot "discern the invisible world behind the visible one" (p. 287), because he refuses to believe that it is better to die than to live. To Francis, who is a saint like Don Quixote,[9] "the stones which people threw at him were like a sprinkling of lemon flowers. But I, I was a man, a reasonable man, and a wretched one. I felt hunger, and the stones, for me, were stones" (p. 108). Leo's reasonableness and simple humor seem strangely out of place in this deadly serious business of theirs.

Like the Bishop of Assisi and the Pope in Rome, Brother Leo counsels moderation and by his example reminds Francis continually of their essential humanity: "'we're all human. You forget this fact; I don't. It's as simple as that'" (p. 106). But Francis rejects this counsel; there can be no moderation for him in this world. "'Brother Leo,'" he says, "'with the world in the state it is today, whoever is virtuous must be so to the point of sainthood, and even beyond; whoever is a sinner must be so to the point of bestiality, and even beyond. Today, the middle road is no more'" (p. 22). Only through extremist actions can one save the world and himself.[10] To be moderate, as Francis sees it, is almost to be anti-Christian: "'You are extraordinarily prudent, Brother Leo,' he answered me. 'What you say is sensible, but to a fault. In other words, you still cannot take the leap, can you? Are you going to walk on the ground forever?'" (p. 210). Tied to the earth like Sancho Panza, Leo can perhaps see the abyss before him—"God or Satan . . . the double abyss" (p. 38), as well as the twin precipices of God, Hope or Despair (p. 152)—but he will take no such hazardous leap. "What could I say—that whoever loves God does not love anything else, does not pity anything in the world; that his soul is burning, and that even mother, father, brothers and sisters are enveloped in its flames and consumed, as are joy, suffering, wealth—everything?" (pp. 327–28). Leo will remain behind to record for a needful world the career of his saintly master, the man who, like Don Quixote, "most faithfully mirrors the fate of man."[11]

But Francis is in truth no Don Quixote: the flash of insight that he receives at the close of his life is not of his foolish failure but of his foolish success, a worldly success achieved in precisely those terms that he has spent his life endeavoring to renounce. Even at the end he fails to perceive the extent of his foolishness. "How can I ever know what he was like, who he was?" his chronicler wonders. "Is it possible that he himself did not know?" (p. 29). The narrator's uncertainty may be still more ironic than it appears, for Kazantzakis himself does not seem to recognize fully the dimensions of his hero's self-ignorance. Novelist and character alike are convinced that the founder of the Franciscan order has been betrayed by his followers, but we recognize in fact that he has betrayed himself; the fictional Francis is likewise convinced that he has chosen his own path freely, but he is truly a tool of some almost Turkish conception of fate; he is convinced finally that he has reconciled in his person the major dualities inherent in life and in nature, but he has simply repressed these conflicts, and not always successfully so.

"'The body of man is the bow,'" preaches Saint Francis, "'God is the archer, and the soul is the arrow'" (p. 178): the soul is surely predominant, but the body too has a role, he admits; it too is a worthwhile factor in God's scheme of existence. Thus Francis appears to reconcile the basic duality that confronts each of Kazantzakis' heroes. He clothes his own body and those of his followers in earth-colored robes and on his return from his travels kisses the ground of Umbria in springtime. "Didn't he know that the earth had a seductive attraction for men, and that a blade of grass, a goldfinch, a lighted lamp, a sweet aroma were enough to make us never want to abandon this world of clay?" (pp. 354–55). And so he warns Clara's women against admiring nature too closely: "'If you bend down to smell a flower, my sisters, you will find [Satan] there; if you lift a stone he will be hidden beneath and waiting; if you see a blossoming almond tree he will be crouching in the branches, ready to pounce upon you'" (p. 250). Life on earth is bearable, he contends, only because God will soon let us depart from this prison (p. 252), and "'Man's body,'" he claims, "'is a cross . . . upon [which] God is crucified'" (p. 316). Thus, in a subtle progression, the avowedly tolerant Francis actually abjures both body and nature[12]—pours ashes onto the lentils that he enjoys overly much (p. 143), purports to see truly only after losing his eyesight (p. 254), takes delight in his suffering and aches to "'obliterate'" his flesh "'so that my soul may be left free to escape'" (p. 285). At his death he apologizes for his neglect to body and nature alike. "'Forgive me, Brother Donkey,' he said; 'forgive me, my old ramshackle body, for having tormented you so much. . . . And you, my revered Mother Earth: you must forgive me also. You gave me a splendid, radiant body, and now look what mud and filth I am returning to you!'" (p. 375).

His words echo those of Jesus, Manoliós, and Odysseus, those other Christlike Kazantzakian figures, but there is an instructive reversal in their actual roles. When they claim to abandon nature and deny the flesh, we do not fully believe them, for we recognize their enduring vitality—and we see this contradiction as a sign of their strength. Odysseus turns into pure spirit, but he does so in extremely sensual verse; Manoliós goes joyfully to his death but glories as he walks in the life of nature around him; and Jesus on the cross is relieved to discover that he has not abandoned his mission, that he has not given in to the powerful appeals of human husbandry, but he still refuses to scorn the body or even to deny its essential nobility. They add spirit to body, for they are fertility figures and something more: they are recognizably human as well. But Francis can promise us no rebirth—spiritual or otherwise—because he has no life of his own to begin with. Him we refuse to believe when he claims to be responsive to nature and to respect the needs of the flesh. Ironically, he comes closest of all to Kazantzakis' ideal conception of the ascetic hero—and it is for precisely this reason that he fails as a man.

Jesus and Manoliós believe as deeply as Francis in the supremacy of
the soul and in the possibility of life after death, but neither needs to
deny this life in order to justify the next one. Kazantzakis' fictional
practice, in dealing with them, is so vital that it effectively counteracts
his ascetic philosophy. Francis, however, is so doctrinaire, so fanati-
cally opposed to all celebrations of this earthly life (art and learning
notable among them), that we are forced to conclude that he is
motivated less by strength than by weakness. He is opposed to learning, we suspect, not only in reaction to the doctrinal excesses of the
medieval Church ("'Satan inhabits our minds, God our hearts. The
heart is illiterate; it has never opened a book'"—p. 230), as was the
historical Saint Francis,[13] but also in fear of what it will lead him to
discover within himself. Agonizing over his artistic task, Leo reflects
his master's dilemma and echoes his fear: "the letters of the alphabet
frighten me terribly. They are sly, shameless demons—and dangerous!... They come to life, join, separate, ignore your commands,
arrange themselves as they like on the page—black, with tails and
horns.... They deceitfully expose what you did not wish to reveal,
and they refuse to give voice to what is struggling, deep within your
bowels, to come forth and speak to mankind" (p. 23). In Francis'
equally dogmatic rejection of sex, we note a similar terror of self-
discovery, and we may well suspect that the fabled dichotomy between his early and later lives is much less great than it seems, that
close to the surface of the youthful rake lies hidden the fanatical
monk, just waiting for the chance to burst forth. The arrival in Assisi
of the mendicant Leo provides his opportunity.

Francis speaks often of freedom, of man's need to choose his own
path, to resist the thrust of his times (p. 263), even to combat his God
(p. 349). But what he means by free will sounds strangely to us like
fatalism: "'If someone asks you who is free, Brother Leo, what will
you reply? The man who is God's slave! All other freedom is bondage'" (p. 273). This fatalism seems the guiding principle of his entire
career, even as he resists the Bishop and Pope, his possessive mother
and overbearing father, even as he gives in to those followers who
would pervert the meaning and purpose of his revolution. Where
Jesus, Manoliós, and Odysseus are men following the paths of men
and free therefore to master their fates, Francis, who seeks to imitate
God, seems foredoomed from the start. His very lack of self-
knowledge makes his failure inevitable. Even the language used to
describe his adventures is somehow flattened, as if the novelist
realized that the richness of metaphor and myth that characterizes
those other lives would be out of place in this one. Thus, when
Francis cries betrayal, when he accuses the learned colossus Elias of
distorting his message and converting his movement into a secular

force (whose goal, Elias admits, is " 'the spiritual domination of the world' "—p. 331), we are apt to distrust his judgment and lay the blame elsewhere, to see in Francis' own acts the seeds of betrayal—it is he who nurtured Elias and made possible the spread of the order within the traditional terms of the Church—almost as if, in emulation of Christ, he requires an act of betrayal, as if, indeed, betrayal has been his goal all along. Yet, even so, it may be that he has misjudged his condition, for we have long since known that he needs no external Judas, that in self-repression and fatalistic acceptance of what he calls God's will, Francis from the start has betrayed himself. He is the one Kazantzakis hero who fails throughout to know himself, who is unable throughout to learn from, and grow within, his ordeal, who repudiates the lessons of Crete.

IV

"Saint Francis was the last medieval soul and the first of the Renaissance," Kazantzakis once wrote.[14] " 'I love him because by means of love and ascetic discipline his soul conquered reality—hunger, cold, disease, scorn, injustice, ugliness (what men without wings call reality)— . . . subdued reality, delivered mankind from necessity, and inwardly transformed all his flesh into spirit.' "[15] Over his desk the writer kept prints of Dante, that other transitional figure,[16] and of Giotto's Saint Francis, and his novel, we are hardly surprised to discover, was planned during, and written shortly after, a serious illness, its avowed Franciscan purpose to "transform illness into spirit."[17] Kazantzakis' choice of this subject and mode reflects in part his admiration for Dante and in part his own long-time association with Assisi and his experience as translator of Joergensen's biography;[18] it reflects as well the long-established role of Saint Francis in the history of Cretan religious art.[19] But primarily his choice reflects a more intensely personal source, one that offers revealing insights into his art, if not necessarily into his psyche. To borrow a metaphor from C. G. Jung,[20] we might say that Saint Francis serves for the artist as a kind of archetypal shadow, a reflection of what might loosely be described as "the negative side of [his] personality."

"The shadow," Jung writes, "is a moral problem that challenges the whole ego personality, for no one can become conscious of the shadow without considerable moral effort. To become conscious of it involves recognizing the dark aspects of the personality as present and real." A creation of the individual rather than the collective unconscious, potentially much closer to consciousness than those more famous Jungian projections the anima and animus, the shadow can, "with insight and good will, . . . to some extent be assimilated into the conscious personality." It is difficult to do so, however; even to recognize the shadow's existence is an act requiring great moral courage. Yet "this act is the essential condition for any kind of self-knowledge." *Saint Francis* is in a sense an acknowledgement by Kazantzakis of the existence within him of this negative force. This is not a psychoanalytic determination: we are not dealing literally at this point with the state of the author's psyche, and we need not consider how well he does or does not know himself. Metaphorically, however, the concept of the shadow does help us to understand both the attraction that the seemingly shining figure of Saint Francis holds for Kazantzakis and the negative results of that attraction. For Francis, paradoxically, does represent a dark side of sorts for Kazantzakis, the side turning away from life and toward (creative) death, that aspect of his personality which lured him away from the natural life celebrated so forcefully in his other novels and into a shadowy underworld of the soul. What Kazantzakis elsewhere characterizes as "spirit" is, perhaps unwittingly, a vital creative force that partakes almost longingly of physical life and coexists with the body in a dialectic so tense and so rich that it is far greater than the mere sum of its parts. We are drawn to this force because we recognize that it is the result of an unplanned union, that philosophically he cannot deny their continued significance for him as man and as artist. Perhaps he does not realize himself the effects of this union—certainly he never fully acknowledges it—but it serves him as a liberating force, one that frees him, ironically, from the bonds of dogmatic asceticism; it may well be one of the major strengths of his fiction. *Saint Francis* is the sole work of Kazantzakis that dogmatically denies such a union, opts totally for asceticism, and insists throughout that the inward life of the soul is patently superior to the external life of the body; it is his sole work that degrades the body and its sensual appeals, that prefers longed-for shadow to manifest substance. It is in its way a death song to life and to art.

And so the renascence that Saint Francis brings about in the world of Nikos Kazantzakis is an ironically inverted one, for it offers in truth not a rebirth at all but a way out of life, a self-indulgent, self-defeating surrender to the monk and the priest. Of course Kazantzakis should have foreseen this before he began work on the novel: it was the historical saint, after all, who re-Christianized Europe. Similarly, had he known something more of Saint Francis' role in the development of religious art in the West, the artist might again have been less fatally attracted to him. "Those crosses painted in the 12th century depicted Christ as alive with eyes wide open. . . . This symbolized

Christ's triumph through the cross. With the coming of St. Francis (1182–1226), however, the type slowly changed. [He]... preached rather the suffering and death of Christ. Therefore the painters who came after him... gradually painted Christ as a dead figure upon the cross with head bowed."[21] It is this dead Christ—manifestation of an equally dead Saint Francis—that dominates this one lifeless work by one of the most vital authors of our time.

But he is not alone. El Greco too was drawn almost mystically to the great Western holy man, and the Saint Francis theme, "to which he reverted again and again, almost obsessively," is realized in his paintings in much the same manner as in his descendant's novel. "For the essential characteristic of his St. Francis is that of being lifted completely from his historical context. Nothing is left of his native Umbria."[22] All that remains of this world is what Kazantzakis calls "this ephemeral life of preparation" for the world to come.[23] Misled by El Greco's example, the novelist can almost be excused for failing to realize that the metaphor of Saint Francis is antithetical to the metaphor of Crete, that his Christlike career lacks for our time not merely the immediate political significance of the original but, indeed, that it is lacking almost totally in universal appeal. The Franco Zefferelli film based on the life of Saint Francis—entitled "Brother Sun, Sister Moon," it is at once more lyrical and more realistic than the novel—makes it clear that the implicit social message of the Poverello, arising out of the huge gap between the rich and the poor in thirteenth-century Europe, will inevitably be betrayed by his own emphasis on the life after death. The last words of dialogue in the film make precisely this point: "Don't worry," one courtier in Rome says to another concerned about the Pope's acceptance of this newest religious reformer; "His Holiness knows what he's doing. This is the man who will speak to the poor and bring them back to us."[24] "'I thought of my shivering brothers throughout the world,'" says Kazantzakis' Francis, "his teeth chattering. 'I am unable to warm them; therefore I decided to join them in being cold'" (p. 337).

His spiritual program seems no more practical. It is not their own souls alone that they are seeking to reach, he tells Brother Leo, "'but the soul of all mankind'" (p. 122), and when he cries out in the midst of his suffering "that cry had within it all the joys and sorrows of mankind" (p. 351). Yet Francis appears to recognize himself that his is no universal solution; thus he sends back the horde of villagers who would follow him right now to the kingdom of heaven. "What could he do with them, where could he take them, how feed them? And what would become of the population of the world if everyone became a monk or nun?... Many of the ploughmen grew angry. 'First you light a fire for us and then you try your best to put it out. Either what you first told us is correct and we must renounce the world if we want to be saved—or it isn't. If this is the case, friend, leave us in peace. Go somewhere else!'" Desperate, Francis tells them to give away their goods, to be chaste and to pray and to await his return. "'Wait,' he implored them, 'wait, I shall come back,'. . . he continued to shout as he departed from the village with immense strides. . . . 'Impostor! Liar! Parasite! Swindler!'" shout the rock-throwing peasants behind him (p. 275).

His is not a path for all men to follow, no universal prospect at all. It is a path blazed by one man, designed for one man. But that man is wrong too in assessing his goal. Francis may well intend to suffer for all men, as Jesus does; he may well lay claim to being a unique moral exemplar. But he is no savior; he cannot save even himself. For Francis in his arrogance abjures not merely life but that path through life that Kazantzakis elsewhere points out to his heroes. Where they seek their own divinity—a mythic goal that all men might attain—he seeks in the orthodox Christian manner to reach out to, and to imitate, a preordained God, not a human achievement at all but one that repudiates true human potential, a sign not of mythic creativity in the way of the Cretans but of arrogance and egocentricity, a foolish endeavor to rise above humanity through nonhuman means and so a falling below what is human. The fictional Francis does offer, as his creator perceives, a new form of reality, but it is even more negative than the one it replaces, a still more damning necessity from which man must be saved. Neither Francis nor Kazantzakis is aware of this failure; the novelist to the end is unable to recognize fully the negative results of this ascetic image. "It is often tragic," Jung writes, "to see how blatantly a man bungles his own life and the lives of others yet remains totally incapable of seeing how much the whole tragedy originates in himself, and how he continually feeds it and keeps it going. Not *consciously*, of course—for consciously he is engaged in bewailing and cursing a faithless world that recedes further and further into the distance. Rather, it is an unconscious factor which spins the illusions that veil his world. And what is being spun is a cocoon, which in the end will completely envelop him."[25] For the fictional Francis the cocoon envelops a foolish and useless life; the tragedy for his creator is simply a failed work of art. The shadow of Saint Francis hovers over each of Kazantzakis' heroes, but it is dispelled by the brightness that each creates in his life. Even here, moreover, the prospect is not fully dark, for Saint Francis does succeed in demonstrating, albeit by negative example, the force and conviction and beauty of those other Kazantzakis protagonists who do achieve, in the metaphoric context of Crete, a sort of divinity, who become god-like in a sense because they remember that they are no more than human, and no less so.

1. All references are to the Simon and Schuster edition (New York, 1962), trans. P. A. Bién. Kazantzakis explained to his wife as he began work on the novel, "I'll not be writing literature or making a psychological analysis either. What interests me are the unsuspected forces existing in the human soul which, either out of cowardice or for lack of an ideal, we allow to sleep and perish.... The old hagiologists emphasized the Poverello's state of beatitude, neglecting the arduous path that leads to this beatitude. It must have been a hard struggle; and it's precisely this struggle that moves me." Cited in Helen Kazantzakis, pp. 519-20.

2. *Thus Spoke Zarathustra*, pp. 334-35.

3. In his *Life of St. Francis of Assisi*, trans. Louise Seymour Houghton (New York, 1917; originally published in 1894), p. xii.

4. It is true that Kazantzakis had translated Johannes Joergensen's *Saint François d'Assise: Sa vie et son oeuvre* (Paris, 1924; traduits du danois par Teodor de Wyzewa), that he tells in detail in *Report to Greco* of his momentous, almost mystical encounter with Joergensen in Assisi and that he learned from this source that Sabatier's claim about Brother Leo as the saint's first biographer had since been disproven and that Sabatier himself had admitted his error. Yet he also found in Joergensen a certain scholarly justification for making Leo his narrator ("aucun des disciples de saint François n'a joué un rôle plus important et plus décisif que le frère Léon dans la formation de l'image que la postérité s'est faite de la personne de saint François," p. xxxix) and, in addition, an imaginative stimulus for his narrative decision: Sabatier's error, writes the Danish scholar, "n'en a pas moins été très fructueuse, en provoquant ou en stimulant les recherches nouvelles"—it has been fruitful too, we might add, in stimulating new fictional insights.

5. Sabatier, p. xiv.

6. None of these premises has held up to the critical scrutiny of the intervening seventy-five years, although their usefulness to the fiction remains obvious. (1) The *Speculum Perfectionis*, for instance, which Sabatier believed was Leo's work, written within a few years of the saint's death in 1226, is now seen as "an ingenious rearrangement made in 1318, a rearrangement of an earlier miscellany containing tales of Francis, contributed some by Brother Leo, some by other hands." F. C. Burkitt, "St. Francis of Assisi and Some of his Biographers," in *Franciscan Essays*, 2 (Manchester, 1932), pp. 20-21. (2) Similarly, it is clear that Francis worked largely within the confines of the established Church and that he was himself the first organizer of the Franciscan Order, although hardly on the elaborate scale of his immediate successors—such, at least, has always been the Church's contention: "Clearly, Francis had no master plan for the order, but he did project it and, according to his abilities, contribute to its formation. He also approved of the order's evolution from primitive beginnings to its juridical establishment. His unwavering devotion to the Church is noteworthy, especially when con-

trasted with the contemporary heretical sects, the Cathari and Waldenses." L. Hardick, *New Catholic Encyclopedia* (1967), 5, p. 30. (3) As for Elias, finally, he remains "perhaps the most difficult character to estimate in all Franciscan history," but he is evidently not quite the villain that Sabatier would make him: "there is nothing to show that Elias was other than a good religious during the lifetime of St. Francis, else it is hard to understand how the latter could have entrusted him with so much responsibility and how he could have merited the special death-bed blessing of the Poverello." Paschal Robinson, *The Catholic Encyclopedia* (1909), 5, p. 384. There are even those who argue that Elias was himself "the leader of the rough simple laymen which formed the Assisan provincial party" and that he was deposed not by conservative reformers anxious to return to the original Franciscan ideals but by outsiders who wanted to adapt the order to the more sophisticated world beyond Umbria. Harold E. Goad, "Brother Elias as the Leader of the Assisan Party in the Order," *Franciscan Essays*, 2, p. 80. Even Elias' detractors acknowledge, moreover, that the most profound changes within the order—"from a spontaneous lay fellowship into an Order of clerks and priests"—were made not by him but under his successor, Aymon of Faversham. John R. H. Moorman, *The Sources for the Life of S. Francis of Assisi* (Manchester, 1940), p. 87.

7. "The typical Franciscan priest," says Sabatier, "is Brother Leo. . . . Of a charming simplicity, tender, affectionate, refined, he is, with Brother Elias, the one who plays the noblest part during the obscure years in which the new reform was being elaborated. . . . In the inner Franciscan circle, where Leo . . . and many others represent the spirit of liberty, the religion of the humble and the simple, Elias represents the scientific and ecclesiastical spirit, prudence and reason" (pp. 137, 206).

8. Sabatier too derides the accepted view of Francis' repugnance to women, but he would hardly countenance Kazantzakis' symbolic distortion: "the relations of St. Francis with women in general and St. Clara in particular, have been completely travestied," he writes. "Hence this portrait, in which St. Francis is represented as a stern ascetic, to whom woman appears to be a sort of incarnate devil! The biographers even go so far as to assure us that he knew only two women by sight. These are manifest exaggerations, or rather the opposite of the truth." Nonetheless, he admits, "there are souls so pure, so little earthly, that on their first meeting they enter the most holy place. . . . Such was the love of St. Francis and St. Clara" (pp. 148–50). In the Franco Zefferelli film "Brother Sun, Sister Moon," there is a hint of physical attraction between the young Francis and Clare. But this turns, not unnaturally, into spiritual love, perhaps because the film's Francis shows no fear of the woman or of his own feeling for her.

9. In *Report to Greco*, Kazantzakis makes the connection explicit, calling Francis "another supernal Don Quixote, with equal artless simplicity, equal purity and love . . . " (p. 383). At the same time, he identifies his friend Albert Schweitzer with the Italian saint.

10. The Cathari, however, are too extreme even for him. " 'It seems to me,' " Francis tells one of their number, " 'that you scorn the world far too much' " (p. 168).

11. Nikos Kazantzakis, *Spain*, p. 43. In his poem "Don Quixote," Kazantzakis calls out to this savior of God,

You are the youngest, favorite son of God,
his dearest treasure and his purest gold,
his ultimate bastion: firm, impregnable;

. . . .

You are his only worthy champion! Rise,
and from man's foul condition snatch your God. . . .

Translated by Kimon Friar and reprinted in *Spain*, p. 154.

12. It is strange for us to encounter a Poverello to whom the birds do not sing. It is evident that Kazantzakis meant his hero to be drawn to nature but to reject it for a higher beauty; it is apparent also from his letters and journals that he himself loved the landscape of Umbria. But little of this comes across in the novel. What does emerge, ironically, is a saint in the pre-Franciscan Catholic tradition. "Other saints have seemed entirely dead to the world around them, but Francis was ever thoroughly in touch with the spirit of the age. He delighted in the songs of Provence, rejoiced in the new-born freedom of his native city, and cherished what Dante calls the pleasant sound of his dear land. And this exquisite human element in Francis's character was the key to that far-reaching, all-embracing sympathy, which may be almost called his characteristic gift." Robinson, p. 227. This, of course, is precisely what the fictional Francis lacks.

13. Again, the novelist strangely limits the bounds of his fiction, diminishing further his historical model. "Yet strong and definite as the saint's convictions were, and determinedly as his line was taken, he was never a slave to a theory in regard to the observance of poverty or anything else; about him, indeed, there was nothing narrow or fanatical. As for his attitude toward study, Francis desiderated for his friars only such theological knowledge as was conformable to the mission of the order, which was before all else a mission of example. Hence he regarded the accumulation of books as being at variance with the poverty his friars professed, and he resisted the eager desire for mere book-learning, so prevalent in his time, in so far as it struck at the roots of that simplicity . . . and threatened to stifle the spirit of prayer, which he accounted preferable to all the rest." Robinson, p. 225. Latent within Kazantzakis' Francis is not so much a desire for simplicity as a fear of the intellect, the same fear that Boss, Kosmás, Mihélis, and even Odysseus at times express, the same sense of priorities that led the Cretan rebels to convert irreplaceable manuscripts into gun wadding.

14. Published originally in an epilogue to J. Pierhal's *Albert Schweitzer: das Leben eines guten Menschen* (Munich, 1955), and subsequently in Helen Kazantzakis, p. 536.

15. *Report to Greco*, pp. 378–79, as spoken to Joergensen in Assisi.

16. In *Paradiso*, canto xi (Dorothy L. Sayers, trans.), the Dominican Saint Thomas Aquinas speaks admiringly to Dante of the great man of Assisi, who stirred the earth " 'By touches of invigorating power / From his great strength' " (11.55–57) and " 'Roused up . . . godly motions in men's hearts' " (1.78), who received from Christ the stigmata, " 'that last seal / Which two years long his body lived to wear' " (11.106–8). Dante's Saint Thomas speaks largely of Francis' worldly denial, but, even in Paradise, he concludes with the betrayal by Francis' followers and implicitly with the shepherd's own failure.

"But now his flock feel such a gluttonous whim
For fancy foods, they range o'er wood and glen
Dispersed, and so it needs must be with them.

And all the more, the farther from his ken
The sheep run wild at random through the rough,
Do they return dry-uddered to the pen.

Some, fearing to be lost, cling—true enough—
Still to their shepherd, but they're few indeed;
To cut their cowls would take but little stuff."

(11.124–32)

17. Helen Kazantzakis, p. 519. *Saint Francis*, the novelist wrote Prevelakis, "is one of the works you won't like, and I'm puzzled as to how I wrote it. Well, is there a religious mystique inside me? Because I felt great emotion when I wrote it." Antibes, December 6, 1953, cited in Helen Kazantzakis, p. 549.

18. In *Report to Greco*, Kazantzakis speaks of the aged Countess Erichetta as his closest friend and advisor in Assisi. Of her Joergensen reportedly said, " 'If she had lived in Saint Francis's time, she might have become his Saint Clare' " (p. 382).

19. "Together with the Virgin," Saint Francis has long been "one of the most popular objects of devotion in the island of Crete, where his worship was a powerful factor of reconciliation between Orthodox and Catholics." El Greco, the greatest of Cretan devotional painters, left behind "over one hundred and twenty pictures of St. Francis—running from large altar paintings to small devotional images, from autograph works to studio replicas—... one of the keynotes in El Greco's entire output. Childhood memories may partly account for this fact." Paul Guinard, *El Greco*, trans. James Emmons (New York, 1956), p. 86.

20. As elaborated in *Aion*, in *Psyche and Symbol: A Selection from the Writings of C. G. Jung*, Violet S. de Laszlo, ed. (Garden City, New York, 1958), pp. 6–9.

21. Philadelphia Museum of Art, commentary on "Christ on the Cross," by the unknown Master of Saint Francis, North Umbria, c. 1280.

22. Guinard, p. 86.

23. In the Prado is an El Greco "Saint Francis" that Kazantzakis particularly admired, "passionate and pale ... shining luminous in the blue shadow. The 'pauper of God' holds a skull in his hand. He stares at it, as the mask he will wear to make God laugh, when God finally deigns to send his great marshal, Death, to summon him to His court. In the meantime, throughout this ephemeral life of preparation, Brother Francis holds the skull, his future mask, and studies his role." *Spain*, pp. 124–25.

24. "Two years before he [Pope Innocent III] had accorded his approbation to a group of Waldensians who under the name *Poor Catholics* had desired to remain faithful to the Church; he therefore gave his approval to the Penitents of Assisi, but, as a contemporary chronicler [Burchard] has well observed, it was in the hope that they would wrest the banner from heresy." Sabatier, p. 100.

25. Jung, p. 8.

CHAPTER EIGHT

THE FRATRICIDES
Symbol, Act, and Civil War in Greece

Saint Francis, disembodied, is a stunted growth in an arid landscape; it fails almost willfully, cut off as it is from the reality and metaphor of Crete. *The Fratricides*, conversely, is an effort to rejoin body to spirit, to find anew an accustomed fertility, to return to the homeland: its setting is the Greek Civil War of 1946–49. Kazantzakis' final novel is at once the most topical and the most obviously symbolic of all his fictions, the most clear-cut image in the iconography of his life and art. Rooted in contemporaneity—there are even references to "Uncle Truman" and Point Four aid (p. 107)[1]—*The Fratricides* exists primarily on a much deeper level. Each character, each act—played against the backdrop of the modern Greek tragedy—has its symbolic equivalent elsewhere in the canon: the novel at times seems almost a dramatization of *The Saviors of God*. Thus physical description in *The Fratricides* is inseparable from metaphysical statement; Epirote Castéllo, like some village in the White Mountains of Crete, becomes a microcosm of the entire world; and the brother-killing that fills these hills provides forceful comment on the human condition at large. It is a minor work at the end of a rich and varied career, a work filled with familiar echoes and with obvious structural flaws, but it serves admirably to define the boundaries of Kazantzakis' art and to place him in terms of the Modernist tradition that dominated his era.

The novel begins in symbol: the sun sets over Castéllo, and within the stark, stone houses darkness reigns. We recognize from the start that this is a landscape abandoned by God and deprived of humanity. "Not a single house had a tree in its courtyard, or a songbird in a cage, or a flower-pot in the window, with perhaps a root of basil or a red carnation; everywhere, only stone upon stone. And the souls who lived within these stones were hard and inhospitable. . . . Their bodies and their souls were the color and the hardness of stone; they had become one with it, soaked by rain, tanned by the sun, covered by snow; all together, as though they were all people, as though they were all stones" (pp. 7–8). Castéllo is the barren present of the Greek people; their joyous past is caught in the memory of the Black Sea town of St. Constantine, where Father Yánaros was born and from which he and his flock were driven by the Turks, a place where "love and peace and happiness reigned over the people, and the beasts, and the crops in the fields. The earth was fertile, wheat and cornstalks grew high, olive trees were overladen with the blessed fruit, heaps of melons lay in the fields. . . . Yet this good life did not corrupt the people" (p. 11).

There, in Thrace—in contrast to the divided villagers of *The Greek Passion*—the people were saved from corruption by the annual enactment of an ancient ritual, one older even than Christianity and its Passion Play, "stemming perhaps from ancient idolatry" (p. 10). If they are condemned to sterility and fratricide here and now, in Epirus, it is because there are among them no firewalkers to dance on the burning coals and emerge cool and refreshed—bodies shimmering and souls redeemed—to act out as Zorba does the seasonal combat between man and his God, to purge themselves and those whom they represent by this act of challenge and faith. In his youth, Father Yánaros was the leader of the *Anastenárides*, those firewalkers,[2] and now once again—in this strange land and in his old age—he endeavors to dance on the fiery coals ignited by the Civil War. Perhaps, finally, he is able to redeem himself, but his act is a practical failure: cut off from ancient tradition and bound by their familiar roles in society, Reds and Blacks alike are as incapable of spiritual renewal as they are of political harmony.

Looking up to the icon of Saint Constantine the firewalker, an image that he himself has painted, Yánaros explains the symbolic significance of fire: " 'God is not cool water—no, He's not cool water to be drunk for refreshment; God is fire, and you must walk upon it; not only walk, but—most difficult of all—you must dance on this fire. And the moment you are able to dance on it, the fire will become cool water; but until you reach that point, what a struggle, my Lord, what agony!' " (p. 136). It is a necessary struggle, a necessary agony: only when we can dance on the burning coals can we save God and ourselves. This is the most precise explanation in all of Kazantzakis' fiction of the central symbol of fire, and it is appropriate here because the narrative method of *The Fratricides* is itself a kind of verbal iconography.

There is a sense, to be sure, in which all of Kazantzakis' art is akin

to that of the Byzantine icon-makers, as if all his novels were enact-
ments of the varied possibilities—realistic and symbolic alike—
inherent within the traditional forms (and in *The Saviors of God* as
well). The protagonists of *The Greek Passion*, for instance—especially
those who play the Apostles—recall not so much literary or historical
models as they do Byzantine paintings of Saints John, Peter, and
James and of the betrayer Judas. Mihelís-John, son of the archon,
"born to wealth and position, . . . deeply sensitive, bewildered by
treachery, neither of the village nor apart from it"; Yannakós-Peter,
"the sturdy merchant-pedlar, . . . warm-hearted, naïve and impetuous"; "thin, crabbed" Kostandís-James, "willing to share, but confused in spirit"; and Panayótaros-Judas, "a wild, undisciplined man
crazed by lust, hating all, waiting only for revenge"—their descrip-
tions (in the cast of characters that precedes the narrative) seem almost
a verbalization of the traditional artistic forms, of El Greco's Apostles
in particular. Highly stylized and bearing their customary symbols
(cup, keys, staff and crook in the paintings, social positions and
character traits in the novel), they emerge in art and fiction alike as
realized personalities, individuals who encompass and yet surpass
their symbolic limitations.

Other characters too, in other novels by Kazantzakis, function as
what might be called personal icons, those private symbols through
which the artist attempts again and again to dramatize his complex
philosophical position: well-meaning intellectuals out of touch with
their roots and unable to act with decision; domineering fathers who
stifle their wives and their sons; and, most notable of all, the colossus
figures, from Odysseus to Zorba and Captain Mihális, from
Panayótaros to Judas to Father Yánaros. Each character functions
uniquely within his respective fiction, yet it is clear that each represents also some minor aspect of a total aesthetic, a unified view of
society and life that underlies all of the novels, no matter how different they might otherwise be.

There are also the masks created by certain of Kazantzakis' revolutionary heroes (Odysseus, Manoliós, the "frenzied shaman" Toda
Raba from the early French novel of that name,[3] even the leper's mask
worn for a time by the young Kazantzakis himself—for his life is also
in part a creation of his art). Death masks all, or rather, masks of the
new life that follows upon the destruction of the old, they are presented expressly to us as narrative symbols. Thus the African Toda
Raba destroys the old gods of his people and fashions a new one, "its
mouth huge, its skull bald, a threat in its eyes": Lenin.[4] Kazantzakis
would eventually reject this icon too—at least he would repudiate the
uses to which it was put by its true believers—but in this early work

the icon of Lenin serves as the central symbol of his fiction and thought. Other icons serve similarly in the later works: the seven-headed ivory god of the *Odyssey*, the banner that proclaims to all the motto of *Freedom or Death*, Zorba's *santúri* and rare green stone, even the snow-covered mountain to which Saint Francis retreats. Each image encapsulates uniquely that blending of symbol and act that is the essence of Kazantzakis' philosophy and of his art. Helen Kazantzakis has spoken of her husband's dual careers in similar icon-ographical terms: "Like the Orthodox saints whose various deeds are recounted on our icons on several superimposed planes, he conducted at one and the same time a literary offensive paralleling his political activity."[5]

This literary duality is not unique to Kazantzakis of course. In Greek fiction in general—in both prose and verse—as in Greek myth, a surface realism and an underlying level of metaphor have customarily coexisted.[6] We find it in the early Akritic Songs, in the *Achilléid* of the fifteenth century and the *Erotókritos* of the seventeenth, and we find it also in such contemporary novelists as Vassílis Vassilikós: the plant whose tentacles spread through the city of Thessaloniki (in *The Plant*, 1961) is not merely a symbol of the young hero's growing sexual awareness—it is an actual plant as well; and the snapshots that torment the young man grown older, exiled from the city and from his love (in *The Photographs*, 1965), are not simply physical reminders of the past—they serve as symbols of all he has lost, his love and himself. But Kazantzakis goes beyond this comparatively simple joining of varying planes of meaning; his iconography parallels the traditional Byzantine modes because it too is based upon—and at the same time demonstrates—an elaborate system of social and metaphysical relationships. It is such a symbolic system that is worked out in *The Fratricides*.

II

To Father Yánaros, himself a painter of icons, all icons are real and immediate, and not simply man-made representations of divine possibilities. He carries them before him during the central events of his life—in the fire dance, in the forced retreat from his native village, in his advance upon the warring Reds and Blacks in Castéllo; he creates them as ideal forms of his own vision of Greece—Saint Constantine the dancer wearing like Elijah "a ring of flames" for a crown (p. 49), the mournful Virgin emblematic (as in *Freedom or Death*) of a people persecuted and divided (p. 143), and the Pancreator, like Yánaros an exile: " 'Christ is a refugee, on this earth, too, so I will paint Him as one' " (p. 141); Yánaros might almost be said to become an icon himself. " 'The holy icons,' " he calls them, " 'our forefathers' " (p. 144).

But if the icons are signs of the past, they may serve as emblems of the present and future as well. The Chapel of the Forerunner has been demolished in the bombing; against its desolate walls seven women are executed for aiding the rebels. " 'One day,' " Yánaros thinks as he watches them die, " 'a new church may be built over these ruins of the Forerunner, for the seven female forerunners!' " (p. 172). The symbolism is heavy and obvious: it is not that the Reds are the new Messiah, or even so much that Yánaros favors the Reds— although, like his creator, he is certainly hostile to the established order.[7] But the old priest does recognize the youth and vitality and idealism of the rebels, the freedom with which they act and which the best of them promise to bring to all Greece. He recognizes as well the justice of their cause, but he knows like Kazantzakis that they are only men and that their cause must be limited by men's limitations. At their best, the rebels recall still greater revolutionaries of the past. And so Captain Drákos, the dragon-like son of Yánaros who leads the Reds on Mount Aitorákhi, the eagle's peak, remembers what it was to be a Communist in Greece in the days just prior to the Civil War: "Drákos remembered those dangerous days and the flaming nights in out-of-the-way taverns, in the deserted houses and the dark cellars of Salonica. This must be what the catacombs were like, and the first Christians... their eyes must have burned like this... , and this must be how they gathered to decree how they would destroy the old world and build a new one" (p. 198). At their worst, however, the Reds are no different from the Blacks whom they fight: they are subject to the same materialistic desires, to the same atavism in warfare, to the same blind obedience to established authority, to the same crimes against the human spirit. Thus they violate their oath to Yánaros and take vengeance on the village that he has surrendered peacefully to them, even to the point of killing the priest who defies them still. It is the son who orders the death of his father, yet we know that he also is too individualistic to be allowed to survive for long. In this modern Greece, as on Crete under the Turks,[8] it is the best and strongest who perish, the worst and weakest who live after them and set the tone of the nation. And while the Reds may not be the Messiahs whom we await, it is clear at least that we must all continue to fight the Blacks of this world. In politics as in religion, Kazantzakis tells us through his symbols, there can be no new resurrections for men as a whole; only the individual man is capable of salvation.

Father Yánaros' attempt to resolve the conflict between brothers is therefore as foolish and futile as Kosmás' death in *Freedom or Death*, or that of Manoliós in *The Greek Passion*, or that of Saint Francis. Yet, when he recites "the holy words of the Resurrection" to both villagers and rebels (p. 240)—the enemies joined for an instant by means of the ancient liturgy—we recognize that nowhere in Kazantzakis' canon are religion and politics more closely aligned, that here, in the words and deeds of this village priest, is the clearest exposition in all the fiction of what it means to be free,[9] the most patent synthesis of symbol and act.

Every physical deed associated with Yánaros is similarly laden with symbolic potential, yet none is merely an abstraction. It is no figurative mountain that the old priest ascends to the rebel camp, no hypothetical line that separates men from beasts, no simply representative village that he endeavors to free.[10] Unlike Saint Francis, Yánaros rejects with scorn withdrawal from life; to be an ascetic, for him, is to act. " 'Today prayer means deeds. To be an ascetic today is to live among the people, to fight, to climb Golgotha with Christ, and to be crucified every day' " (p. 21). He lives by symbols indeed, but never by symbols alone, for his is a world heightened by varying levels of meaning. Even God in Castéllo is no mere abstraction but a concrete act: to an illiterate fisherman, He is a hungry seagull diving for souls; to a potter, a wheel that fashions the clay of man, that " 'turns without stopping; turns and twists us; molds and makes us into whatever shape it wants: pitchers, jugs, pots, lamps. Into some of these they pour water, into others, wine and honey; some are for cooking, others for shedding light. . . . And if we break, what does He care? He turns, turns, and shapes new pots, and He never looks back' " (p. 78). Each man, we perceive, can be in his own way a maker of icons; each village can serve as microcosm of the world: the fratricide in the mountains of Greece is the destruction of our brothers throughout the world. Symbol and act indeed are one in *The Fratricides*, and Father Yánaros, its hero, is an icon representing the divine potential within all men: paint him in the midst of fire, a flame ascending.

III

The Fratricides, written at the close of a long and distinguished career, strangely recalls two works that appeared early in that career, *Toda Raba* and *The Rock Garden*, both composed originally in French, both outside the mainstream of Kazantzakis' fiction.[11] Like them, it is loosely constructed, concerned in large part with political goals, more allegory at times than narration—closer, it would appear, to the philosophical system expounded in *The Saviors of God* than to its alleged fictional sources; like them too, it seems more autobiography at times than novel. All three works, moreover, resemble the travel books for which Kazantzakis was famous in Greece: episodic in their movement and highly personal in their approach, closely observed from a viewpoint just beyond the center of the action and revealed through the voice of the experienced traveler-journalist whose roots appear to be in no single locale but who creates wherever he goes an intensely realized spirit of place. Kazantzakis may be said to have developed the travel journal as a genre within Greek literature, and travel played an important part in his life—" 'I'm a migratory bird,' " he once told his wife, " 'neither laborer nor fisherman. I wait for an auspicious wind.' "[12] But it is hardly likely that so diffuse a subject could provide either matter or form for significant Modernist fiction.

None of Kazantzakis' work, it is true, possesses the carefully wrought structure that is characteristic of Modernist fiction in general; even his best planned novels are marked by excesses of form that would not have been tolerated by such writers as Joyce, Mann, Kafka, or Proust, novelists who worked within the more orderly Western tradition. But in none of the major efforts of Kazantzakis are these flaws more than a mild distraction, for they are rapidly subsumed by the rush of the narrative and the force of the metaphor that underlies it. It is only in these three minor, peripheral endeavors—the first two completed before the author had come to think of prose fiction seriously, the last unrevised at his death—that the problems of structure appear irreconcilable, only here that the narrative breaks down and the metaphor appears incomplete. These are the least well integrated and the most episodic of all his novels, the most dependent on circumstance, the least consistently developed in terms of the metaphor of Crete—even the symbolic technique of *The Fratricides* seems somehow unrelated to Crete. As for *Toda Raba* and *The Rock Garden*, whatever unity they possess is provided by the author's persona, his thinly disguised voice within the narrative, a kind of spiritual picaro. But the several personae of *The Fratricides* contribute further to the breakdown of structure in that work.

The "I" of *The Rock Garden*, a European who has come to the Orient in order to immerse himself in Buddha, to give in to those mysterious smiles "that mesmerize and murder hope on earth,"[13] discovers instead the still harsher realities engendered by the conflicts among the old Buddhist ways, the new Chinese nationalism, and the surging imperialism of Japan. The people whom he encounters are involved on all sides of these struggles—the narrative reads at times like Malraux's *Man's Fate*—but we recognize quickly that their significance to

him is not human or even political, that they are important to the
narrator primarily as steps in his spiritual progression, as part of an
elaborate series of symbols through which we must move (and comparable to the separate stages of the Buddha's progression). The rock
garden within which the narrative concludes is admittedly metaphorical,[14] but we have long since come to realize that this is in fact its sole
level of reality, for neither the persona nor his creator is able to evoke
convincing characters or believable actions. When he proclaims at the
end that "I dig in the earth, this field of ours. I see with my eyes, I
touch with my hands," we know without being told that he refers not
to the physical senses or to the literal earth but to a different reality:
"from the inorganic mass to the plant, from the plant to the animal,
from the animal to man" (p. 251)—to the by-now-familiar reality of
The Saviors of God. Our awareness that the narrative consists in very
large part of strategically placed passages from *The Saviors of God*, and
that many of its more immediate observations appear also in the
travel journal *Japan/China*, hardly convinces us of its separate life as a
novel.

A comparable situation exists in *Toda Raba*, where again the protagonist is more a spokesman for a philosophical position than a
realized character. But Yeranós the Cretan is even closer to his creator
than is the unnamed "I" of *The Rock Garden*. He speaks for
Kazantzakis as artist—"He was trying to express and to save his soul
through the medium of words, and at the same time to express and
save the souls of the people around him. His frail body was being
consumed by the spirit" (p. 15); as the latest in a long line of
revolutionaries—"And now in his maturity, Yeranós suddenly felt an
old Cretan inside him, his grandfather, red fezz turned around, singing this same refrain at the top of his lungs . . . Liberty! Liberty! / The
Muscovite is on his way down!" (p. 16); as follower of the mythic
Odysseus—"I am one of Ulysses' sailors, with heart on fire and mind
pitiless and clear. . . . 'Eh, companions! [the captain shouts.] Open
your eyes, your ears, your nostrils, your mouths, your hands; open
your minds, fill your entrails'" (p. 94). Yeranós writes in the air an
epigraph to his life that Kazantzakis would later assume for his own:
"Ah, let my own life become this song: 'I have ceased to hope, I have
ceased to fear, I am free!'" (p. 115). He serves as well as a kind of wish
fulfillment for Kazantzakis, who even at this stage in his career was
isolated from both political left and right. And so the secret report to
the Cheka declares admiringly that the Cretan "was a complicated
soul. He went to the heart of everything with a blinding clarity. He
observed fairly and defended Communism with ardor, but at the
same time despised it; he thought it too narrow to satisfy his soul" (p.

168

136). The long trip that Yeranós and his friend, Azad, take through the Soviet Union is clearly an account of the odyssey of Kazantzakis and the Greek-Rumanian writer Panaït Istrati;[15] the speech that Azad makes before the international congress expresses the disillusionment of both artists with the materialism of the new Communist state. Although both may be termed "romantics," there is a clear dichotomy between the visionary thinker Yeranós and the man of action Azad, a dichotomy that foreshadows the conflict between Boss and Zorba. Still later, Azad-Istrati would serve as the model for Captain Drákos in *The Fratricides*, while Yeranós-Kazantzakis provides one of several sources for the captain's father: their collective role, "to work out a metaphysical synthesis of man's struggles on earth" (p. 15). Not until he had learned more about the art of fiction, however, would Kazantzakis himself succeed in enacting this metaphysic. This is the Cretan Glance, the worldview that ultimately distinguishes him from all his Modernist contemporaries. It fails to emerge in *The Fratricides* simply because the protagonist alone is able to unite the physical and symbolic worlds; as we move further away from him, the synthesis falters increasingly. The great structural flaw of *The Fratricides*—the quality that aligns it with *Toda Raba* and *The Rock Garden* and not with the more mature novels—is that we are too often drawn away from Yánaros.

IV

By the time he began work on *The Fratricides*, Kazantzakis had long since proven his mastery of narrative technique and had developed in full the literary and philosophical metaphor that he called the Cretan Glance. Yet here too, in a surprising reversion of form, we find structural and thematic flaws that recall those of the early French novels, flaws that probably could not have been corrected even by further revision. The plot, for example, is often erratic and dependent on circumstance—it is almost as an afterthought that we are informed that the rebel leader is the son of the village priest, as well as a former comrade of the Royalist captain in the Albanian War. There are symbolic possibilities in each of these cases (the long-standing rivalry with the father, the sudden yet questionable change from hero to villain that may beset any man), but the coincidences seem too great for belief. In addition, there are various peripheral tales interpolated within the main narrative—tales of Italian charlatans and Jewish mystics, of visions of Christ and of visions of Russia, even tales within tales. These too may be significant on the level of symbol, but they tend as a group to disrupt the flow of the action and impede credibility. It is evident, in fact, that the basic narrative approach of *The Fratricides* is indirect, sometimes annoyingly so, as the author shifts back and forth in his omniscience—from character to character, from time to time—not to create a sense of simultaneity, as a Modernist novelist might, but simply as an old fashioned storyteller does, revealing details only when they seem pertinent to him, demonstrating at all times his control over events. We might rationalize such an outmoded technique when it provides us with a fully convincing reality—as it does, for example, in *Freedom or Death*. But that is not always what happens here. Instead, as in *Toda Raba* or *The Rock Garden*, Kazantzakis seems at times to be so concerned with some ultimate level of truth—some potential symbolic truth that overrides all other realities—that he is apt to neglect the accompanying need to create a believable physical world. This is particularly true when the point of view shifts away from Yánaros. The novelist might have learned a lesson from his creation: even the painter of heavenly icons must rest at times on the earth.

Because Yánaros is so compelling a character, because he does unite the physical and symbolic realms, we are inclined to overlook those distortions of structure and theme that appear in his presence. Thus we are not overly concerned to discover that the village priest—visionary, ascetic, yet capable of action even now in his old age—serves as a barely disguised mask for his creator, himself near the end of his life. But the novelist creates other personae as well, and with them we become aware of the distortions. Several characters, among them Drákos, are confirmed in their radicalism by Jewish teachers, as Kazantzakis himself evidently was;[16] and the eventual disillusionment of Drákos with the Communist movement, his refusal to subordinate himself to any authoritarian force, is an obvious reflection of the novelist's own earlier rebellion. These masks in a sense are predictable. But there is one persona in the novel who comes as a total surprise and whose presence causes a truly disturbing shift in the narrative focus.

This is the young soldier Leonídas, whom we meet only after his death through the journal that he leaves with the schoolmaster. The journal begins on the twenty-third of January and ends abruptly on Holy Monday night, hours before the young man is killed. His death heralds the holy spring, as his life echoes in brief the life of his creator: he is what Kazantzakis might have been had he similarly been caught up as a young man in a brutal dehumanizing war, had he been born a generation sooner (and thus been old enough to fight the Turks in the mountains), or a generation or two later (and so possibly been sacrificed himself in the Civil War). Gentle, intellectual, humane,

Leonídas speaks sensitively of Homer, quotes Solomós, and longs for the day when he too will be free to write his verse—very different perhaps from the verse that a young Kazantzakis might write: an ode to woman, sensuality, and the immortality to be gained through art. Leonídas is capable of forwarding the vision of universal brotherhood that inspires so many of Kazantzakis' heroes, but he falls before he can even begin to carry the torch.

Although Yánaros never reads this journal or even learns of its existence (and therefore, realistically, there is no way that we should be reading it either), it posits the intellectual basis for his final rebellion. From Leonídas we learn of the dehumanizing effects of the combat, of the man of culture who reverts atavistically to his prehuman ancestry, of the man who can kill his brother and brutalize his brother's wife and child, although he knows that in doing so he acts like a beast and not like a man. Leonídas could take the leap, if he lived, that Yánaros fears he is too old to take—the ideal Marxist equivalent of walking on fire—the universality of dancing not only for Greeks but "for the Chinese, the Hindus, the Africans" as well. "I can't," Yánaros falters. "My heart has room only for the Greeks. Can it be that I've aged—I . . . who boasted that I was twenty years old and that I'd conquered old age? No, I could never take such a jump now!" (p. 181). Leonídas—a soldier for the Blacks with no antipathy for the Reds, a man who perceives the truth of their brotherhood—is young enough still to take the leap, to bridge the abyss that separates brothers. But he too is a prisoner of history, a victim of the "sweet fratricide" (p. 9) that demeans us all. There will be no redemption from either his life or his death; the spring in which he dies is a false one.

Leonídas' role in the development of the theme of *The Fratricides* is manifest: he serves to complete our view of Yánaros as symbol and maker of symbols; he is the missing intellectual half. His structural presence is another matter, however. For his journal draws us away from Yánaros and so furthers the disintegration of form in the novel. Because we encounter him only after his death and because we know that he can exert no direct influence on the protagonist (even indirect influence is unlikely, since the schoolmaster who does read the journal disappears almost immediately afterwards), we recognize that no movement can possibly flow from his journal, that in the absence of the protagonist the young soldier can provide no alternative creativity in the midst of the war, that in this part of the novel at least an unbridgable gap has been driven between symbol and act. Leonídas' narrative function is entirely symbolic, entirely intellectual and passive—as if we were back again in the early French novels, as if his creator had forgotten the lesson of Zorba.

Someone, however—and it might be Yánaros, or even Drákos—must provide us with this special knowledge, must complete the symbol, for it is an integral part of the theme. From the dead soldier's journal we derive a terrifying sense of the war's ambiguity, of its capacity to inspire both the best and worst of men to bravery and brutality alike, of its ability to entrap and dehumanize even the most idealistic of men, of its symbolic potential as a source of a new creativity. "Can it be," Leonídas wonders, "that this war was necessary so that our souls might take on a new power?" (p. 121). He sounds almost like Kazantzakis urging the symbolic powers of fire, that purgative and redemptive force that can destroy corrupt, old civilizations and create from their ashes vital, progressive, enlightened new ones. From the Civil War, ideally, there should arise a new Greek civilization free of the accretions of centuries of servitude, restored at once to the glories of the past and to a still more glorious future. We are perhaps entitled to expect that here, in *The Fratricides*, will be found the ultimate development of the symbol of fire as it was predicted first in *The Saviors of God* and in the *Odyssey* and as it was subsequently projected in each of the intervening novels. But this is not what takes place; the symbol is explained but never developed—aside from the fiery coals of Yánaros' dance, there are virtually no overt references to fire within the novel. Perhaps it is the fault of the loose narrative structure, perhaps the great distance from Crete and its metaphor, perhaps simply the realities of the Greek Civil War that convinced Kazantzakis that no creative renewal would take place here, that for modern Greece at least fire was merely a useful literary symbol and not a potential creative force. In the situation of villagers besieged by Turks and betrayed by fellow Greeks, in the case of a prophet killed by his enemies and about to be disowned by his followers, in the useless death of a man of good will who throws away his life as a gesture—in such seemingly hopeless instances, in his earlier novels, Kazantzakis can still find cause for optimism. But the fratricide in Greece leaves him no hope. It is no coincidence that each persona in *The Fratricides* fails in his task, that none leaves behind him a meaningful legacy: that the young Royalist soldier does not achieve manhood, that the middle-aged guerilla captain is turned on by his own people, that the old village priest is killed at the command of his son. They are destroyed in a sense by their very ideals; those who survive the war, the novel suggests, may well be devoid of ideals. The recent history of Greece does little to convince us that Kazantzakis was wrong in his despair.

As Father Yánaros tells his congregants, in what seems almost a parallel to the paths taken by the various personae, there are three separate roads to freedom. The first is the way of God, but " 'God is out. . . . He does not interfere in our business; He gave us a brain, He gave us freedom, He washed His hands of us!' " The second road is similarly closed—" 'The second road is our nation's leaders, damn them! All of them—all the leaders,' " Red and Black alike. Only the third road to freedom has not yet been closed, and this road—the road of the people—" 'hasn't opened yet. We have to open it with our labor, pushing onward to make it a road. . . . This road begins with the people, and ends with the people' " (pp. 153–55). It is a road whose construction has yet to begin. The attempt by the villagers of Castéllo to begin it is a bloody failure. Kazantzakis acknowledges in *The Fratricides* that the people as a whole are not really capable of creating their freedom. In a time of political and social upheaval, of the rise of totalitarian states and the breakdown of traditional values, of an absence of meaningful new values to replace them, the people, Kazantzakis suggests, are powerless. Only the individual can act with freedom, and he can save only himself. Expressed with finality in *The Fratricides*, this belief—at once political and symbolic—goes back to the author's earliest work. In *Toda Raba*, for example, Yeranós-Kazantzakis is about to embark with his friend Azad on an odyssey through the Soviet Union: "Two men with hearts ripened by suffering . . . their souls have been gripped by a deep agony. The world they lived in seemed to them empty and faithless, abandoned to the dark, brutalizing forces of matter. One day . . . [they] had the sensation they were standing on the edge of an abyss; with a shudder of anguish they thought they saw the world plunging headlong toward this abyss. Their tortured hearts suddenly grasped the painful, inexorable meaning of our time: that we are faced with the end of a civilization."[17] Viewed as a dispassionate, radical, but non-Communist observation, this statement in *Toda Raba* might almost serve as one major aspect of the Modernist creed. But Kazantzakis in his fiction, even in *The Fratricides*, reconstitutes for himself the world that will replace this decadent one of ours, and it is always a world in which human values somehow are relevant, somehow survive. Civilization heads inexorably toward the abyss; individual men may confront the abyss and thereby gain dignity, freedom, and personal salvation. This persistent belief, echoing even within the despairing depths of *The Fratricides*, is the most evident distinction between Kazantzakis and the other Modernist masters.

1. All references are to the Simon and Schuster edition (New York, 1964), trans. Amy Mims.

2. Literally "the sighers," the term refers to the traditional dancers of Thrace and Macedonia, who, even today, dance on burning coals in order to commemmorate the feast of Saint John.

3. *Toda Raba*, trans. Amy Mims (New York, 1964), p. 16. All further references are to this edition.

4. *Toda Raba*, p. 17.

5. Afterword to *Toda Raba*, p. 205.

6. It is instructive that there is no Greek term that corresponds to our word "novel," with its historical implications of realism as distinct from romance (as noted in Richard Chase's *The American Novel and Its Tradition*). The term usually used is *mithistórima*, which emphasizes that opposing combination of myth, history, and narrative that is characteristic of the Greek romance. There is no tradition of realism per se in post-Classical Greek literature.

7. Much has been written about Kazantzakis' attraction to, affiliation with, and eventual rejection of, Marxism. He has been accused of being both communist and fascist, assailed by both right and left—even at the same time, it seems—and supplied as well with a number of epithets between these extremes. It is important to recognize, however, that—although he would tell his Communist friends who criticized his independence, "I am Marxist with my loins" (interview with Helen Kazantzakis)—his philosophical system is much too complex to be characterized so facilely, for he was no man to join a party and be content to follow its dictates. Ultimately, as Helen Kazantzakis and Pandhelís Prevelákis among others have pointed out, the writer appears to have moved beyond the Marxists to a position that he called "Meta-Communism," a position as much metaphysical as it was political. Perhaps the best scholarly expositions of Kazantzakis' politics are by Minas Savvas, "Kazantzakis and Marxism," in the special Kazantzakis number of the *Journal of Modern Literature*, 2 (1971-72), pp. 284-92, and by Peter Bien, "Nikos Kazantzakis," in *The Politics of Twentieth-Century Novelists*, George A. Panichas, ed. (New York, 1971), pp. 137-59. For a somewhat fictionalized account of the novelist's early attraction to the Russian Communists and of the grounds for his later rejection of them, we need only to look at *Toda Raba*. The point, finally, is that Kazantzakis adopted no political position per se that was distinct from his views of spiritual renewal. And for these we must examine *The Saviors of God* and the novels.

8. The comparison is not wholly arbitrary: a sensitive young government soldier who has kicked and beaten the wife of a rebel thinks with some guilt, and with an unspoken but obvious analogy to Crete: "If that woman could, she would set fire to the barracks and burn us all. That baby's no longer going to suck milk from its mother's breast; it's going to suck hatred and scorn and revenge; and when it grows up, it, too, will take to the hills—a rebel; and he will finish off whatever his mother and father left undone; we will pay heavily and rightfully for this injustice" (p. 103). One suspects that the same thought might have occurred centuries earlier to an Arab or Venetian or Turkish soldier on Crete.

9. Yánaros is one of those Kazantzakian figures with what appears to be direct visionary access to God. And he is not content to be a passive observer of God's majesty and strength; his demands go far beyond Job's. " 'Speak to me with human words,' " he insists, " 'so I can understand. You growl, but I am not an animal to understand what you say. You chirp, but I am not a bird;

You thunder and flash but I am not a cloud—I am a man: speak to me in the language of men.'" And the Lord, who is obviously a Marxist-Christian Existentialist, responds in what may be Kazantzakis' clearest exposition— aside perhaps from *Zorba the Greek*—of what it means to be born a man and free:"'Father Yánaros, are you not ashamed? Why do you ask me for advice? You are free—I made you free! Why do you still cling to me? Stop the penitences; get up, Father Yánaros, take responsibility upon yourself; do not ask advice from anyone; are you not free?'" (pp. 147, 149).

10. "The blessed hour has come," Father Yánaros thinks as he prepares to surrender the village, "the world will be judged by this day. Even if Castéllo is a miserable little village—the world will be judged by today" (p. 218).

11. If it seems strange that the passionate advocate of demoticism should write these two early novels in a foreign language, the reason, according to his widow (in an interview with this writer in Geneva, July 1971), is simple: his desire to find an audience in France, where he was living at the time and where he could not expect to find a translator for books written in Greek.

12. Helen Kazantzakis, p. 240.

13. All references are to the Simon and Schuster edition (New York, 1963), trans. Richard Howard, p. 8.

14. The rock garden is a metaphor for the human heart, as Kazantzakis makes clear in *Japan/China*. "If I were to form my heart in the shape of a garden," he writes, "I would make it like the rock garden of the monastery Ruan-zi, in Kyoto. Not even a single green tree, not even a flower. The trees and flowers exist outside the high fence. . . . So-Ami, who designed it in the sixteenth century, wanted to represent with this garden a tiger that fled holding its babies in her teeth." Viewing the garden in the twentieth century, the outsider is convinced of the truth of its metaphor. "Only, instead of a tiger in the imagined garden of my heart, I would place there godliness" (p. 115).

15. For an account of Kazantzakis' friendship with the ill-fated Istrati, see Helen Kazantzakis, pp. 272–99, and chapter 26 of *Report to Greco*. Also of interest is Mme. Kazantzakis' (writing under her maiden name, Eleni Samios) *La Verdadera Tragedia de Panaït Istrati* (Santiago, Chile, 1938).

16. In *The Fratricides* Kazantzakis seems to wish to repay some of his accumulated debt to the Jews, an obligation perhaps more moral and metaphorical than it was literal. "This man enamored of Judaism," his widow has called him (Helen Kazantzakis, p. 88). In both *Report to Greco* and in his letters, he attributes a major part of his education into the modern world—particularly his political education—to the young Jewish women of Polish and Russian descent with whom he became intimate soon after his arrival in Berlin: he immortalizes them as Rahel in *Toda Raba*, as Rala in *The Odyssey: A Modern Sequel*, as Noëmi in *Freedom or Death*. Kazantzakis took vicarious pride in the fact that El Greco chose to live in the Jewish quarter of Toledo (Helen Kazantzakis, p. 146), and he himself often claimed to be partly Jewish. As he wrote years afterward to one of his Berlin friends, "There's a very large drop of Hebrew blood in my veins and this drop produces an effervescence and commotion in all my Hellenic and Cretan blood. I am obsessed and possessed by the Hebraic destiny." The obsession evidently went back a long time; he tells in this same letter of convincing his father when he was just ten to let him take Hebrew lessons from the rabbi of Chanía. But his relatives pro-

tested, and the lessons soon ceased. (Letter to Leah Dunkelblum, Antibes, March 23, 1951, cited in Helen Kazantzakis, pp. 495–96.) The claim about his ancestry is obviously metaphorical (ecumenically, he also contended at times that he had Arabic blood), an attempt perhaps to create within himself a symbolic union of the disparate Arnoldian forces of Hebraism and Hellenism. In the wider sense, it seems to be related to Jorge Luis Borges' equally metaphorical claim to be partly Jewish—an acknowledgement of sorts of the heightened significance of the Jew as metaphor in the literature of the Modernist era, as a sign of moral stability (however he may wander and suffer, even because he must wander and suffer) in an increasingly unstable world.

17. *Toda Raba*, p. 116.

CHAPTER NINE

Kazantzakis and the Modernist View of Literature and Life

"A revealing parallel may be drawn between Kazantzakis and D. H. Lawrence. Both were Dionysian, demon-driven men, placed instinct and the promptings of the blood above the ordered deductions of the mind, celebrated the primitive and atavistic origins of the human spirit, were insatiable travelers who in landscape and inscape discerned the contours of God's or Nature's purpose, turned to the physical universe for their imagery and away from urban mechanics and subtleties, extolled strife and crucifixion as the unavoidable and necessitous law of life and even of love, were impatient with refinements of craft and entrusted themselves to the demonic outpourings of creative inspiration, placed the prophet above the man of letters, were obsessed with messianic drives and dreams."[1] We might add to Kimon Friar's astute comparison that ultimately both Kazantzakis and Lawrence must be judged as men of letters and not as prophets or men of affairs, as they might have desired; that they were equally controversial both during their lifetimes and afterwards—equally attacked (although from different viewpoints) for the alleged murkiness of their political thought; that, romantics both, they intuited a realm of the spirit that existed beyond the senses, perhaps even to be reached through sensuality. Working independently of each other, they created at about the same time the personal travel essay as a modern literary genre; they even developed similar habits of writing and rewriting—not so much a careful line-by-line mode of revision, such as that practiced so fervently by Joyce, as a process of overall change: a tendency to rewrite in entirety rather than to revise. It is partly because of such work habits that both writers have been accused of shoddy craftsmanship, that both have been vigorously attacked for the stylistic and formal excesses of their prose ("hyper-bolic," "redundant," "pedantic").

The comparison of Kazantzakis and Lawrence seems somehow in-evitable (especially if we consider the writer who seems almost their mutual descendant, Lawrence Durrell), but it can easily be pursued beyond the point of meaningfulness. For they are ultimately very different writers, very different men: the system that Lawrence de-veloped only gradually in his fiction is in the end profoundly inimical to the thought that Kazantzakis expounded almost at the start and then elaborated again and again in his novels, although always from some new perspective. In the mysticism that he drew from his blood, Lawrence came finally to submerge individual worth within some new form of mythic community—very nearly a racial ethic: "the blood of the individual," he writes omnisciently in *The Plumed Serpent*, "is given back to the great blood-being, the god, the nation, the tribe."[2] To Kazantzakis, however, it is necessary to advance beyond the group, beyond even the race. To Kazantzakis, the individual is paramount. In his visionary view (not mystical at all, because it insists on the primacy of humanistic values and is based on great scholarship as well as on personal experience), the ultimate spirit of place is the inner spirit, and its sources are personal and positive. As Kazantzakis perceives the disintegrating world around him, it is not simply nega-tive options that remain open to man but significantly positive ones: it is not simply from the earth and his blood that man derives his integ-rity, not so much that society is demeaned but that the individual rises above it, not an ancient or borrowed body of myth that orders his life but one that is close to his life, that grows in part out of his life. In Kazantzakis' view, there is the potential of dignity and even heroism for man, and it comes from within. His heroes share obvious parallels with Lawrence's, but the final implications of their lives are very different indeed.

From Nietzsche (tempered, of course, by Bergson and the Cretan experience), Kazantzakis drew not so much the idea of a superman—of a leader of men, like Ramón in *The Plumed Serpent*, whose power is almost divine[3]—as the concept of struggle itself, of man's need to ascend beyond not only society but his own limitations, as well as those imposed on him by the universal order of nature. No man can save all other men in Kazantzakis' scheme, no matter how pow-erful he may be; each man can save only himself, and each man is free to define himself. Kazantzakis and his heroes choose exis-tentially to define themselves in human terms—as rebels, as artists, as men of intellect and the senses, as Cretan patriots capable of heroic and despicable deeds, as men who rise above their limitations not by denying their humanity but by affirming it. The myths that they together create are in no way like those of Lawrence's heroes. And so we may have been deceived by the obvious: to place Kazantzakis appropriately in the context of the Modernist movement, we must look not to Lawrence, the artist who seems so akin to him on the surface, but rather to one who appears far distant, to an artist whose life and work and values would seem at first antithetical to his, to Lawrence's great enemy, James Joyce.

The comparison with Joyce is rather surprising, since he and Kazantzakis seemingly preside over opposite ends of the Modernist spectrum. Joyce is, after all, the most innovative of novelists, whereas Kazantzakis (aside from his subtly reflexive use of Matthew as a secondary point of view in *The Last Temptation of Christ*) seems almost Dickensian in his narration; certainly, as far as narrative technique is concerned at least, he, like Lawrence, is closer to the Victorians than to his own contemporaries. Nevertheless, as unexpected as it may be, the parallel between Kazantzakis and Joyce does offer revealing insights into both writers—into their lives, into their work, into the use of their lives in their work. We can begin with the same sort of list as with Lawrence.

"Self exiled in upon his ego,"[4] the artist creates his fiction from the materials of his life. From the potentially heightened experiences of his youth, from even the pettiest details surrounding his family and friends, from the nation and religion that once nurtured him, he fashions image and metaphor for his art. As a young man he leaves his island homeland behind and comes before long to consider himself European, "myriadislanded";[5] yet he returns obsessively in his art to that earlier heritage—he even writes home to check out his facts. He encompasses as well the major intellectual currents of the century: Freud and Jung, Frazer and Marx, Bergson and the Existentialists—from folk tale to comparative myth, from the individual psyche to the history of the race—all these too find a place in his canon. He is influenced as well by traditional Romantic concerns: his life-long interest in demotic speech, resulting in the collecting and even in the coining of a few words, leads to puristic complaints that he is destroying the language for literature; his passion for freedom and the exotic leads him in his fiction to use the wandering Jews as a symbol of man's persistent alienation; in both his life and his work, he views himself as an exile, cut off from society because of his art. Above all, he dedicates himself like some hierophant to his art, putting behind him politics and family affairs, surrendering even his health—converting everything in life into matter for fiction: "brought to blood heat, gallic acid on iron ore, through the bowels of his misery, flashly, faithly, nastily, appropriately, . . . [he] wrote over every square inch of the only foolscap available, his own body."[6] He devotes more than a dozen years of his life to a single masterpiece.

Anyone familiar with Joyce will easily recognize him in this picture, but it is obvious by now that it applies equally to Kazantzakis. Still, such a comparison of two such different writers[7] must inevitably be a bit superficial—it may point up interesting connections between the sources of their art and their attitudes toward that art, but it tells us little about the art itself or about its relationship to the times in which it developed. For these we must look not to the lives of the artists or to their canons in general, but more specifically to their two Odysseys, the *Modern Sequel* of Kazantzakis and Joyce's *Ulysses*, which stand together as the greatest of modern epics—rivals as well, in their vastly different ways, of the greatest of ancient epics.

Ulysses at heart is a comic epic, an ironic inversion of Homeric myth that details the collapsing position of modern man. The representative hero of our myth-less time, Joyce repeatedly suggests, is inherently an outsider, an alien in the city of his birth, a failure as father, as husband, as man of affairs. As Joyce's hero Leopold Bloom spills his seed on the beach at Sandymount, we realize how far we have lapsed from the fertility of Homer's representative hero. But there is nothing comic about Kazantzakis' epic: in its diction, its hero, its handling of myth—in the philosophical premises upon which it is based—it strives for the grandeur of Homer and not for the humor of Joyce. His is not the small world of Dublin in 1904, or even of the Bronze Age Mediterranean; the mind and the travels of his Odysseus encompass all the known world and even beyond. Even in asceticism Kazantzakis' hero has a force and vigor unknown to Bloom, a sense that he controls not only his own destiny but the entire world, an awareness that he has mastered the world—that he can contend with the gods as an equal—because he has come to know himself fully. Wherever he goes, fertility follows; when he lies with the young girl on the way to Helen in Sparta and "flowers sprang up from sterile sands wherever she passed" (III, 542), we know that we are a long way from Sandymount and Bloom's spilled seed.

T. S. Eliot said of *Ulysses* that it set the pattern for all subsequent Modernist works in its treatment of myth. "In using the myth [of Ulysses]," Eliot pronounced, "in manipulating a continuous parallel between contemporaneity and antiquity, Mr. Joyce is pursuing a method which others must pursue after him. . . . It is simply a way of controlling, of ordering, of giving a shape and a significance to the immense panorama of futility and anarchy which is contemporary history." The mythic method, Eliot went on, is "a step toward making the modern world possible for art," toward developing "that order and form" which, in the years after the First World War, seemed to be lacking in life itself.[8] As Eliot saw it in 1923, then—just one year after the novel's appearance—Joyce used myth in *Ulysses* as a means of giving order and meaning to art and thereby perhaps to life as well. Eliot, of course, did not know Kazantzakis' *Odyssey*, which would not appear in English translation for some thirty-five more years. But it is likely that he would have disapproved of it had he known it, for its conception of myth—and of life—is diametrically opposed to his own. To Kazantzakis, the function of myth is not simply to provide an orderly structure from which art can view life: myth, to Kazantzakis, is the very matter of life; it is myth that enables man to comprehend and to master his life, to rise above the circumstances of his time, and to achieve harmony with the experiences of other men in other times. For every generation, as Kazantzakis perceives it—even one as chaotic and self-destructive as his own—is capable of creating its own significant body of myth. And so he gives us a sequel to Homer and not a parody, a work that attempts to recreate the spirit and tone of the original and not simply to invert it ironically.

If myth, as Joseph Campbell suggests, "is the secret opening through which the inexhaustible energies of the cosmos pour into human cultural manifestation," if a society reveals itself—its deepest concerns, its fears and desires—in its handling of myth, then it is apparent that we moderns reveal ourselves too in the uses to which we put the ancient mythologies. "It has always been the prime function of mythology and rite to supply the symbols that carry the human spirit forward, in counteraction to those other constant human fantasies that tend to tie it back."[9] We are surprised perhaps to discover that Joyce too perceived this function of ritual and myth, to find that beneath the comic surface of his novel there emerges a genuine hero, of sorts. Half a century ago, Bloom seemed little more than a schlemiel, the first in a long line of negative heroes, an inescapable sign of the decay of our age. Today, from the perspective of Dachau, Hiroshima, and My Lai, the little man who retained his dignity and sense of humanity under inhumane circumstances may appear to us as genuinely heroic, worthy at least of respect if not quite of emulation—little enough perhaps, but better than no myth at all. Kazantzakis' hero, however, arising out of the same defeated generation, needs no such rationalization.

In the fertility of his myth-laden life, in the harmony that he achieves with the natural order, in his effort to reach out at his death somewhere beyond mortality, the Odysseus of Kazantzakis—indeed, all the heroes of his major fictions—serves not simply as a symbol of one generation but as archetype of man's perpetual search. "The hero," Campbell concludes, speaking of the archetype of our innermost dreams, "is the man ... who has been able to battle past his personal and local historical limitations. . . . [His] visions . . . are eloquent, not of the present, disintegrating society and psyche, but of the unquenched source through which society is reborn. The hero has died as a modern man; but as eternal man—perfected, unspecific, universal man—he has been reborn."[10] So Odysseus does more than carry forward the spirit of man in difficult times—a significant feat in itself as Bloom manages it; far more than the humanity of Bloom, more even than the persistence and cunning of Homer's protagonist, he offers in his myth a way for us all to surpass our times, to overcome our mortality. It is this vision of man's mythic potential—this sense of his enduring humanity—that ties Kazantzakis to Joyce and the other Modernists and at the same time distinguishes him from them: it is not alienation he gives us, but the possibility of reconciliation through myth—a vision derived, of course, from the experience of Crete.

We find in Kazantzakis' novels little of the narrative innovation that characterizes most Modernist fiction, little interest in the new Bergsonian flow of time (one aspect of Bergson's teaching that his student somehow ignored), little awareness of current reflexive techniques or modes of irony. The occasional exceptions to each of these points merely prove his fundamental indifference to them: he was evidently aware of their significance to the other novelists of his time yet found little use for them in his own work. Only through his handling of myth, that other major Modernist concern,[11] can Kazantzakis be convincingly linked with his Modernist contemporaries, and even here his attitudes and approach are strikingly different from theirs. Where the function of myth to such writers as Eliot, Joyce, and Mann is in large part structural, to Kazantzakis it is a way of dealing with life itself—a matter of theme, that is, and not one of form, a quality inherent within life and not one to be imposed upon it. And when these other writers do deal with thematic overtones arising from myth—as Joyce does, as Lawrence does—they invariably do so as a means of expressing their alienation from a worthless society, convinced that we live in a new Iron Age, existing—to paraphrase Achilles in Hades—on iron rations and iron values. Something greater is at stake for Kazantzakis, however, some more compelling sense of what myth is and what we are, a far different perception both of the spirit and meaning of myth and of the possibilities still open to man even in a diminished age. Fully aware of the attitudes of his contemporaries, Kazantzakis continues to believe that man can find meaning and coherence in life, that through closeness to myth—to old myth and to new myth, to new myth sprung from the old—man can control and order his life as well as his art.

To Lawrence, who could never quite escape the spectre of the coalfields of the north of England, this would have seemed sheer sentimentality, a foolish unwillingness to accept the indisputably negative facts of existence; to Joyce, the bourgeois Dubliner who could perhaps overcome his provincial background by means of his art but who could likewise never escape it, it would have provided an occasion for irony. But viewed against the background of Cretan history and culture, there can have been for Kazantzakis no other way: it was a necessity perhaps, but one that he chose. Immersed as he was in the civilization of the West, appalled as he must have been at certain aspects of his Cretan inheritance, he could not deny its central theme: even in the most despairing of times, in the most destructive of circumstances, man can survive; by his struggle he can be ennobled. This vision goes directly against the past century and a half of Western literary experience—of the long, strait line that begins with the malaise of Stendhal's *The Red and the Black* in 1830, that continues with the total responsibility expressed in Gide's *The Immoralist* in 1921 and the total acceptance of Camus' *The Stranger* in 1942, and that appears to conclude with the dead-end denial of meaning and relevance in *In The Labyrinth* of Robbe-Grillet in 1959. As different as they may have been in all other respects, Lawrence and Joyce represent new way stations along this line; as like as he may have been to both of them in certain respects, as much as he may have been part of this intellectual tradition, Kazantzakis denies its terminal vision. Despite the evidence around him of man's degradation, despite the wisdom that insists that only nihilism is possible in such a world, that modern man is incapable of creating new and viable bodies of myth, Kazantzakis persists in affirming our value as humans, insists on our mythic potential. His reading of the Cretan experience, his use of the metaphor and myth emerging from Crete, lead almost inevitably to this choice. Modernist he may be, European he may have become, but in the end—as at the start—it is Crete he affirms. Like El Greco, his ancestor and townsman, Kazantzakis "inscribed [his] name wide and broad on [his] paintings, and below it, with magisterial pride, the title CRETAN."[12] It is a legacy we might all do well to partake of.

1. Kimon Friar, *Modern Greek Poetry*, p. 32.

2. D. H. Lawrence, *The Plumed Serpent*, originally published in 1926. References here are to the Penguin edition of 1968; p. 434.

3. "Admitting his blood-unison, Ramón at the same time claimed a supremacy, even a godliness. He was a man, as the lowest of his peons was a man. At the same time . . . he was still something more. Not in the blood nor in the spirit lay his individuality and his supremacy, his godhead. But in a star within him . . . the mysterious star which unites the vast universal blood with the universal breath of the spirit, and shines between them both. . . . The star which is a man's innermost clue, which rules the power of the blood on the one hand, and the power of the spirit on the other. . . . The strange star between the sky and the waters of the first cosmos: this is man's divinity. And some men are not divine at all. They have only faculties. They are slaves, or they should be slaves. But many a man has his own spark of divinity, and has it quenched, blown out by the winds of force or ground out of him by machines. . . . Only the man of a great star, a great divinity, can bring the opposites together again, in a new unison. And this was Ramón. . . . And this is the god-power in man." *The Plumed Serpent*, pp. 434–35. It is impossible to imagine Kazantzakis writing such a passage.

4. James Joyce, *Finnegans Wake*, Compass Books edition (New York, 1959), p. 184.6.

5. James Joyce, *Ulysses*, Modern Library edition (New York, 1946), p. 48.

6. *Finnegans Wake*, p. 185.32.

7. There are many other points of comparison as well, some of them no more than circumstance, others suggesting useful analogies between their respective views of the world and of their art. On the simplest biographical level, for instance, Kazantzakis' almost legendary confrontation with Nietzsche—the alleged story of the alleged resemblance between him and the famed philosopher—takes place in the Bibliothèque Sainte-Geneviève in Paris; in *Ulysses*, Stephen Dedalus, who serves in this case at least as Joyce's ironic surrogate, similarly remembers "the studious silence of the library of Saint Genevieve where he had read, sheltered from the sin of Paris, night by night" (p. 26). The serious young exiles gravitated naturally enough to the same great library at about the same time. More significant are their views of themselves as Romantic artists (Matthew in *The Last Temptation*, ostracized by his fellows yet capable of moving them and necessary to them for their place in eternity, is very much like Joyce's Shem the Penman) and the attraction that each felt toward the Jews, who appear regularly as friends in their lives and as metaphors in their fiction. Both Kazantzakis and Joyce saw in the Jewish experience an analogy of sorts to the beleaguered histories of their own countrymen, Cretans or Irishmen, who had similarly suffered and survived their suffering, offering in the process varying metaphors of the possibilities of heroism and degradation open to all men.

8. T. S. Eliot, "Ulysses, Order, and Myth," in Seon Givens, ed., *James Joyce: Two Decades of Criticism* (New York, 1963), pp. 201–2.

9. Joseph Campbell, *The Hero with a Thousand Faces* (New York, 1956), pp. 3,

10. Campbell, pp. 19–20.

11. Perhaps the best of the several attempts to define the Modernist move-

ment in terms of its primary concerns is Maurice Beebe's "*Ulysses* and the Age of Modernism," *James Joyce Quarterly*, 10 (1972), pp. 172–88. The four major characteristics of Modernism, as Beebe sees it, are (1) a formalistic insistence on "the importance of structure and design" (the most important aspects of which, I would add, are point of view and the handling of time); (2) an attitude of ironic "detachment and non-commitment"; (3) the use of myth "as an arbitrary means of ordering art"; and (4) a reflexive concern with the theme and process of "its own creation and composition" (p. 175)—works, that is, which are ultimately about themselves.

12. *Report to Greco*, p. 500.

INDEX

Achilléid, 163
Akritic Songs, 163
Alexander, Ian W., 96
Augustine, St., 129

Balzac, Honoré, 64
Barth, John, 140 n
Bergson, Henri, xiv, 12, 13, 15, 29, 88, 89, 91, 95–98, 103, 106, 108 n, 136, 177, 181
Bien, Peter A., 87 n, 108 n, 113, 139 n
Borges, Jorge Luis, 86 n
Buddha, 88, 90, 91, 99, 101, 103, 105, 167

Cacoyánnis, Michael, 88–89, 107 n
Campbell, Joseph, 84 n, 180–81
Camus, Albert, 182
Caváfis, Constantine, 3
Chevalier, Jacques, 97
Cornaro, Vincenzo, xv, 9–10, 11, 17 n, 163
Crete: art of, 9, 21–22; history and culture of, 3–8, 11, 20, 22–25, 27–28, 31–33, 34; Minoan civilization in, 4, 7–8; connections of, to the West, 3, 4, 9, 11, 25

Dante, 10, 15, 91, 98–99, 100, 110, 135, 136, 142 n, 152, 158 n
Dhamaskinós, Mihális, 9
Dhaskaloyánnis, Song of, 11, 21–22, 31

Don Quixote, 15, 143, 148, 149, 157 n
Durrell, Lawrence, 177

Eliot, T. S., 112, 122, 179–80, 181
Elýtis, Odysseus, 3
Evans, Sir Arthur, 7, 122, 127

Fiedler, Leslie A., 139 n
Frazer, Sir James G., 86 n, 127, 136, 140 n, 178
Freud, Sigmund, 26, 39, 136, 141 n, 178
Friar, Kimon, xv, xvi, 10, 12, 16 n, 18 n, 19 n, 58 n, 110, 111, 114, 115, 129, 138 n, 140 n, 141 n, 176

Geanakoplos, Deno John, 9
Gide, André, 142 n, 182
Goethe, Johann Wolfgang von, 16, 64
Greco, El, xv, 3, 7, 8, 9, 15, 17 n, 141 n, 154, 159 n, 174 n
Gunn, Thom, 85 n

H. D. [Hilda Doolittle], 140 n
Homer, 60, 88, 111, 115–17, 135, 170

Istrati, Panaït, 90, 168, 174 n

Joergensen, Johannes, 156 n
Joyce, James, 3, 4, 32, 56, 80, 89, 104, 112, 136, 166, 176, 178–81, 182, 183 n
Jung, Carl Gustav, 26, 31, 136, 141 n, 152–53, 155, 178

Kafka, Franz, 3, 4, 32, 166
Kalomíris, Manólis, 110
Kazantzakis, Ghalátea, 18 n, 56, 59 n
Kazantzakis, Helen, xvi, 16 n, 33, 107 n, 109 n, 139 n, 163, 173 n, 174 n
Kazantzakis, Nikos: critical reputation of, in Greece, 56, 61, 111, 166; Jewish connections of, 21, 28, 54, 58, 68, 174–75, 178, 183 n; concern of, for language, 10–11, 61, 111, 113–14; life of, used in his art, 21, 34–35, 38–39, 75, 89–91, 104, 167; and the Modernists, xiii, 3, 4, 5, 12, 16, 25, 32, 60, 61, 62, 79, 84, 111, 112, 113, 136, 166, 168, 172, 176–82, 184 n; and making of myths, 22, 44, 45, 47, 58, 62–71, 74, 78, 82, 118–24, 127, 135–38, 144, 151, 179, 181; narrative technique of, 56–57, 66–67, 78, 79–83, 131–34, 147, 148, 166, 168–71, 181; philosophical background of, 91–98; political thought of, 29, 48–49, 52–55, 57, 115, 117, 127–31, 160, 167–68, 172; spiritual impulse of, 12–14, 39, 45, 51–55, 77, 118, 122, 125, 128–30, 133–35, 143–45, 148–52, 153–55, 165, 167, 177; attitudes of, toward women, 145–48; works by (*Christos*, 49; *The Fratricides*, xv, 15, *160–75*; *Freedom or Death*, xiv, xv, 5, 11, 15, *20–33*, 78, 102, 114, 163, 165, 169, 174 n; *The Greek Passion*, xiv, xv, 15, *34–59*, 60, 77, 78, 80, 83, 114, 138 n, 147, 161, 162, 165; *The Last Temptation of Christ*, xiv, *60–87*, 94, 113, 114, 124, 134, 143, 144, 147, 178, 183 n; *The Odyssey: A Modern Sequel*, xiv, 5, 11, 12, 93, *111–42*, 163, 170, 174 n, 179, 180; *Report to Greco*, 8, 91, 113, 174 n; *The Rock Garden*, 165, *166–67*, 169; *Saint Francis*, xiv, 113, *143–59*, 160, 165; *The Saviors of God: Spiritual Exercises*, *12–14*, 31, 48, 50, 61, 78, 79, 93, 110, 128, 160, 162, 166, 167, 170, 173 n; *Toda Raba*, 162, 165, 166, *167–68*, 169, 172, 173 n, 174 n; travel books, 166, 167, 174; *Zorba the Greek*, xiv, xv, 6, 15, 62, 77, *88–110*, 113, 114)
Klephtic Ballads, 106

Lawrence, D. H., xiii, xiv, 64, 176–78, 181, 182, 183 n
Lenin, Nikolai, 15
Lepídis, Clement, 51

Mallarmé, Stéphane, 91, 98, 100
Malraux, André, 59 n, 166
Mann, Thomas, 3, 4, 32, 166, 181
Martinu, Bohuslav, 138 n
Marx, Karl, 29, 136, 178
Miller, William, 6
Moore, George, 64
More, Sir Thomas, 129

Nietzsche, Friedrich, xiv, xv, 12, 13, 15, 29, 61, 88, 89, 91, 92–95, 96, 101, 106, 108 n, 136, 144, 177, 183 n

Pascoli, Giovanni, 142 n
Plato, 129
Poe, Edgar Allan, 142 n
Prevelákis, Pandhelís, 16 n, 17 n, 18 n, 93, 107 n, 110, 173 n
Proust, Marcel, 3, 4, 56, 80, 166
Psiharís, Yánnis, 10
Psihoundákis, George, 17 n, 23, 24

Rítsos, Yánnis, 3
Robbe-Grillet, Alain, 182 n

Sabatier, Paul, 144, 145, 156 n, 157 n
Schliemann, Heinrich, 119
Schonfield, Hugh J., 63, 69, 84 n, 85 n
Seféris, George, 3, 17 n, 60–61, 83–84, 112, 140 n
Sikelianós, Angelos, 3, 18 n
Solomós, Dionýsios, 170
Stanford, W. B., 135
Stavridhákis, Yánnis, 90
Stekel, Wilhelm, 39
Stendhal, 182

Tennyson, Alfred, Lord, 136
Tolstoy, Leo, 92
Twain, Mark, 126

Vassilikós, Vassílis, 56, 139 n, 163
Venézis, Élias, 51

Venizélos, Eleuthérios, xv, 7, 34–35
Voltaire, 61

Wiesel, Elie, 85 n
Williamson, G. A., 68
Woolf, Virginia, 80

Zefferelli, Franco, 154, 157 n
Zográfou, Lilí, 56
Zola, Émile, 61
Zorbas, George, 88–90